Administrative Aspects
of Investment-Based
Social Security Reform

A National Bureau
of Economic Research
Conference Report

Administrative Aspects of Investment-Based Social Security Reform

WITHDRAWN

Edited by   **John B. Shoven**

The University of Chicago Press

Chicago and London

JOHN B. SHOVEN is the Charles R. Schwab Professor of Economics at
Stanford University and a research associate of the National Bureau
of Economic Research.

The University of Chicago Press, Chicago 60637
The University of Chicago Press, Ltd., London
© 2000 by the National Bureau of Economic Research
All rights reserved. Published 2000
Printed in the United States of America
09 08 07 06 05 04 03 02 01 00   1 2 3 4 5
ISBN: 0-226-75485-5 (cloth)

The contribution by Shaun Mathews in chapter 6 is used with
permission from Aetna Retirement Services, Inc.

Library of Congress Cataloging-in-Publication Data

Administrative aspects of investment-based social security reform /
    edited by John B. Shoven.
        p.   cm.—(National Bureau of Economic Research conference
    report)
    Includes bibliographical references and index.
    ISBN 0-226-75485-5 (cloth : alk. paper)
        1. Social security—United States—Finance—Congresses.
    2. Social security—United States—Congresses. 3. Privatization—
    United States—Congresses. I. Shoven, John B. II. Conference
    report (National Bureau of Economic Research)

    HD7125 .S59929 2000
    368.4'3'00973—dc21

                                                            00-036883

Contents

Acknowledgments

This volume consists of papers presented at a conference held on 4 December 1998 in Cambridge, Massachusetts. The papers are part of an ongoing NBER project on social security. We thank the Ford Foundation for financial support. Any opinions expressed are those of the authors and not those of the National Bureau of Economic Research.

Introduction

John B. Shoven

This volume contains five research papers presented at a National Bureau of Economic Research (NBER) conference on the administrative costs of individual accounts as part of social security reform held on 4 December 1998 in Cambridge, Massachusetts. The conference also featured a panel of financial industry representatives commenting on the costs and feasibility of a mandatory individual account component of a reformed social security system. The remarks of the panelists are included in this volume. Also included are the remarks of the conference participants in the general discussion sessions.

There are many potential advantages of individual accounts as part of social security reform. First and foremost is that it is easier to generate and protect a real and significant accumulation of assets in individual accounts with accompanying property rights than in the central trust fund of social security. The additional personal and national saving facilitated by the individual accounts structure translates in the long run into a higher standard of living for workers. The additional saving potentially generated by a reformed social security system would earn a substantial real rate of return for the economy as a whole unlike the pay-as-you-go system, which merely transfers resources from workers to retirees. A second advantage of the individual accounts is that they provide a direct link between the contributions of workers and the benefits that they receive in retirement. This transforms what is now a distortionary tax and transfer system into a true pension system. Under many of the partial privatization plans, some of the current payroll tax would be converted into deferred compensation.

John B. Shoven is the Charles R. Schwab Professor of Economics at Stanford University and a research associate of the National Bureau of Economic Research.

This means that social security reform can amount to tax reduction and reform with the accompanying improvements in the efficiency of the economy. At the very least, the partial privatization plans avoid the major increases in the payroll tax that would be necessary to restore the solvency of the existing social security system.

Still, despite these and other advantages, the advocates of individual accounts must answer one major criticism. Critics of this approach argue that a system of approximately 140 million small individual accounts will be extremely expensive to run. The present social security system has relatively low administrative costs. Adding an expensive set of individual accounts could potentially wipe out all the alleged advantages of this type of reform. There are many types of expenses to consider. These include the costs of communicating with participants, the record-keeping costs borne by individual workers, their employers, the investment managers, and the government, and the investment-management fees of the money managers. Depending on how the system is set up, the various investment managers may spend vast amounts marketing their services. If the administrative costs are large relative to the earnings of the assets in the individual accounts, then the whole advantage of the approach will have been lost. The purpose of this conference and volume is to explore the costs of various ways of setting up individual accounts as part of a reformed social security system.

This volume is different from many NBER books that feature papers on an assortment of related topics. Four of the six chapters in this volume deal with precisely the same topic. The issue is how a system of individual social security accounts can be set up in a cost-effective way. Goldberg and Graetz, Schieber and Shoven, James et al., and Diamond all independently tackle this issue. Fortunately, there is more agreement than disagreement among their findings. All of them find that administrative costs are an important issue. They also all find that implementing a prudently designed system can dramatically reduce these costs. Several of the cost elements (particularly those related to record keeping) are essentially fixed charges per account. If costs are to be allocated in proportion to assets in the accounts, this implies that there will be a cross-subsidization from large accounts to small ones. The important element of fixed costs also means that costs as a percentage of assets should fall as the accounts become larger through time.

Goldberg and Graetz concentrate on two important sources of cost saving. First, they suggest that the existing program of wage reporting and payroll-tax collecting and crediting be used to collect and credit contributions to the new individual accounts. They assert that piggybacking on the existing payroll-deduction system would mean that there would be very little incremental cost in collecting the contributions. Second, they suggest that the government organize a simple "bare-bones" investment program with a limited number of funds managed by private companies. They estimate that the total administrative costs of this "no-frills" option could range between 0.3 and 0.5 percent of assets within three to four years of the start of the program. In addition to this basic service, Goldberg and Graetz suggest that privately sponsored funds with additional investment options and services could compete for the individual account assets. The presence of and competition from the cost-efficient bare-bones government-sponsored plan would discipline the private-sector offerings. Nonetheless, the private-sector plans would face some government regulation.

Goldberg and Graetz suggest that a symmetrical two-part program could be designed for the distribution phase of the individual account program. Social security could offer to annuitize the individual account accumulation at the time of retirement by simply supplementing the regular defined-benefit pension annuity. Private insurance companies could compete with this government program by selling inflation-indexed life annuities directly to retirees. Once again, competition between the two programs would discipline the terms of the private-sector plans. Still, there would be government regulation to assure the financial soundness of the private market products.

Schieber and Shoven analyze very similar cost-efficient ways of organizing individual accounts. They survey the experience with privatized and partially privatized social security programs in other countries (Chile, Australia, the United Kingdom, and Sweden). They note that Australia has a relatively new program, begun in 1973 and still in its start-up phase. Nonetheless, the average administrative costs for the private accounts was 0.835 percent of assets in 1997. As one would expect, the average cost is going down fairly rapidly as the average account size is growing. This again reflects the fact that administrative costs have a large fixed-cost element to them. In general, U.S. financial markets are far more efficient and competitive than Australian markets. Therefore, we should be able to administer a program of individual accounts for less than the Australians do.

Schieber and Shoven also examine the administrative cost experience of U.S. 401(k) accounts. In 1997, the average total administrative cost for 401(k) plans was 0.77 percent of assets. There are reasons why social security individual accounts should be less expensive to administer (e.g., the disallowance of loans and early withdrawals), and there are other reasons that would tend to make them more expensive (lower average earnings of participants). Schieber and Shoven report that some large mutual fund companies currently manage IRA accounts (with minimum balances as low as $500) for total administrative fees ranging from 0.19 to 0.77 percent of assets.

In evaluating cost-efficient structures for social security individual accounts, Schieber and Shoven offer ideas that are similar to those of Goldberg and Graetz. They argue that cost efficiency suggests that there be only one central record keeper, which they call PSA (personal security account) Central. This central record keeper could be operated by social security itself, or it could be run by a private firm operating under contract with the federal government. Like Goldberg and Graetz, Schieber and Shoven suggest that a government-sponsored bare-bones program be offered in addition to a wide variety of individual private offerings. Again like Goldberg and Graetz, Schieber and Shoven propose piggybacking on the existing payroll-tax deduction system. In their plan, private investment managers chosen through a request-for-proposals (RFP) procedure would run the basic program. The higher-service, higher-cost program offered directly by private asset managers could accept direct deposits (like the existing 401[k] plans), keeping the central record keeper informed of all transactions. Interestingly, both Goldberg and Graetz and Schieber and Shoven (and discussant Olivia Mitchell) argue that a case can be made for the use of general federal government revenues in building the administrative infrastructure during the start-up phase of an individual accounts program.

The paper by James et al. investigates the cost effectiveness of three alternative ways of constructing a funded portion of social security. The three ways are (1) individual accounts invested in the retail market with relatively open choice (as with 401[k] accounts), (2) individual accounts invested in the institutional market with constrained choice among investment companies, and (3) a centralized fund without individual accounts or differentiated investments across individuals. The authors estimate the cost of each approach. In particular, they ask whether the cost differentials are large enough to outweigh other important considerations.

James et al. gather data regarding the costs of mutual funds and institutional funds in the United States and evaluate those data econometrically. Their findings based on this empirical evidence are that the retail market (alternative 1) approach allows individual investors to benefit from scale economies in asset management, but at the cost of high marketing expenses, which are needed to attract and aggregate small sums of money into large pools. In contrast, a centralized fund (alternative 3) can be much cheaper because it achieves scale economies without marketing costs but gives workers no choice and hence is subject to political manipulation and misallocation of capital. The system of constrained choice described by James et al. is much cheaper than the retail market and only slightly more expensive than a single centralized fund. It obtains scale economies in asset management and record keeping while incurring low marketing costs and allowing significant worker choice. It is much more effectively insulated from political interference than a single centralized fund. The authors estimate that a system of constrained choices and institutional investments can be offered at an annual cost of 0.14–0.18 percent of assets. The large administrative cost saving over a retail market approach can be close to a pure efficiency gain as long as choice is not constrained "too much."

In his paper on the administrative costs of individual social security accounts, Diamond differentiates between government-organized accounts and privately organized ones. By *government-organized accounts,* Diamond means an individual accounts system in which the government arranges for both the record keeping and the investment management for the funds in the account. These actual functions might be conducted by the government itself or contracted out to private firms. An example of this approach is the current Thrift Savings Plan (TSP) offered to federal government employees. Under Diamond's privately organized accounts, individuals directly select private firms to handle both record keeping and investment management. An example of this sort of arrangement is the IRA structure in the United States.

Diamond discusses several alternative ways of measuring and imposing the administrative costs of individual accounts. Chile imposes administrative costs as a front-load fee. That is, a fraction of each contribution is set aside for administrative costs. All costs are imposed on contributions— the return on assets in the account is not reduced by these costs. This amounts to a prepayment of all administrative costs over the life of the assets in the fund. Of course, the more common alternative is to allocate administrative costs to assets in the accounts.

Diamond describes a low-cost government-sponsored program. In estimating the costs of the program, he uses the costs of the TSP program as a starting point. His best estimate is that the administrative costs for such accounts would be $40.00–$50.00 per year. This translates to an average of 0.40–0.50 percent of assets per year over a forty-year career for 2 percent accounts. Given the economies of scale, the costs for accounts with higher contribution rates would be correspondingly lower. Five percent accounts would cost 0.16–0.20 percent of assets per year.

Diamond estimates that the costs of privately organized accounts would be much higher than those of government-organized ones—at least twice as high. He bases this on the experience in Chile and the average costs of U.S. mutual funds. Further, he expresses skepticism about the feasibility of capping administrative costs at any particular level (such as the 1 percent of assets suggested by Schieber and Shoven). Diamond argues that measuring administrative costs on such diverse things as certificates of deposit, equity mutual funds, guaranteed-investment contracts, and the like would be somewhere between very difficult and impossible. In Diamond's opinion, government-organized accounts dominate privately organized ones. His discussant, Martin Feldstein, disagrees with his cost estimates for privately organized accounts (he thinks that they are too high for a number of reasons) and disagrees with Diamond about the relative desirability of government-organized individual accounts.

The first four papers all illustrate that there is a continuum between full privatization and a purely public social security program. None of the papers evaluates a completely unregulated, fully private system for cost and, presumably, other reasons. All of them suggest that there is a role for the government in structuring individual accounts programs in a cost-effective manner. On the other hand, the types of institutions described in these papers still give individuals considerable choice and control over how their individual account assets are invested. It is my opinion that the papers correctly balance the advantages of a privatized or partially privatized social security program with the cost efficiency of centralized record keeping and regulation.

The fifth paper in this volume is on a distinctly different topic. Poterba and Warshawsky present evidence relevant to the administrative costs of the payout phase of individual accounts. They examine new data regarding the costs of purchasing private annuity contracts in order to spread a given stock of assets over an uncertain future lifetime. Their paper reports three types of evidence and describes the operation of individual annuity arrangements within two large group retirement-saving plans. First, it presents current information on life-annuity contracts that are currently available in the individual single-premium immediate-annuity market-place. For a sixty-five-year-old male annuity buyer, the expected present discounted value of the payouts offered by the average policy that was available in June 1998 was approximately 85 percent of the purchase price of such a policy. This assumes that the individual faces the mortality risks of the average individual in the population. However, the expected present value of payouts is much higher, 97 percent of the purchase price, and the "cost of annuitization" dramatically lower if the buyer faces the mortality rates of the typical annuitant. People who buy annuities have significantly lower mortality risks than average individuals. This adverse-selection problem would disappear if annuitization of individual accounts were mandatory.

The second part of the Poterba-Warshawsky paper considers individual annuity policies that are available to participants in the federal government's Thrift Savings Plan. Because these annuities are purchased through a large group retirement-saving program, some of the administrative costs are lower than those in the national individual annuity market. Correspondingly, the expected present value of payouts is higher than that in the individual annuity marketplace. Finally, the paper describes the individual annuity products offered by TIAA-CREF, the retirement system for college and university employees. TIAA offers participating annuities, which have among the highest payouts in the individual annuity market. The ability to offer these payout levels owes mainly to superior investment returns and low expenses.

The bottom-line interpretation of the Poterba and Warshawsky paper in terms of including individual accounts in social security reform is that private annuity markets function more efficiently than had been previously thought. If the adverse-selection problem can be mitigated (by, e.g., requiring everyone to buy annuities), the market promises to be quite efficient. Poterba and Warshawsky do not convince David Cutler, their discussant, that private annuity markets are highly efficient.

Perhaps the most important conclusion from the panel of investment-industry representatives presented in chapter 6 is that all of them believe that a program of cost-efficient individual accounts can be designed and operated. That is not to say that administrative costs can be ignored. Far from it—all the panelists think that the details on how the plan is designed can affect costs dramatically. Still, statements from executives or former executives from Fidelity Investments, the Vanguard Group, State Street Bank, Barclays Global Investors, and Aetna Retirement Services that an individual account system can be made to work in a cost-efficient manner are extremely encouraging for advocates of partially privatizing social security.

There are some themes that come out of the panelist remarks and out of the research papers. First, central record keeping rather than record keeping by each plan sponsor or money manager offers considerable cost efficiencies. Second, the program of individual accounts should piggyback on existing structures where possible. In particular, the collection of contributions and the crediting of accounts should take advantage of the existing payroll-tax program and/or existing private-sector defined-contribution pension plans. Of course, some proposals for individual accounts do not depend on contributions per se but rather are funded from the federal government budget surplus. Third, there are important advantages to having a strong low-cost default option for small accounts or for participants who are willing to sacrifice some level of choice and service for low cost. The low-cost nature of the default option is feasible but may require periodic valuation (monthly or quarterly) rather than daily valuation, limited asset choices, restricted withdrawals (no early withdrawals or loans), and infrequent deposits (e.g., once per year). Fourth, costs could be reduced if employees or employers were involved in the record keeping, but not both.

After attending the conference and assembling these papers, my own conclusion is that there is a general consensus on both the feasibility of cost-efficient individual accounts and the design features necessary to achieve low administrative expenses. That is not to say that there still is not a lot of work to be done before we choose how to reform social security. One issue that is briefly discussed in this volume that needs more examination (and is getting it in an NBER volume edited by John Campbell and Martin Feldstein, tentatively entitled *Risk Aspects of Investment-Based Social Security Reform*) is the risks borne by individual participants in the alternative social security reform proposals. The issue is how to preserve the social safety net in a program with individual choice with respect to asset allocation and risk taking. A second issue (briefly discussed by Robert Pozen in this volume) is the effect that individual account investments could potentially have on asset prices. Would this effect be particularly severe if most of the money were placed in passively managed index funds? This is an important topic for future research. My own prior is that even the largest of the partial privatization plans being discussed (those with 5 percent of covered payroll being invested) could be absorbed by U.S. and global financial markets with only a slight effect on prices. Nonetheless, additional attention to this issue is warranted. While this volume cannot possibly address all the issues surrounding individual accounts, it does make a significant contribution toward social security reform—it offers clear guidance on how to organize a cost-efficient program of personal accounts.

Reforming Social Security
A Practical and Workable System of Personal Retirement Accounts

Fred T. Goldberg Jr. and Michael J. Graetz

1.1 Background

Since it was first enacted in 1935, social security has been enormously successful in improving the financial condition of the disabled and the elderly. Despite this success, however, demographic trends make change inevitable. As the baby boom generation approaches retirement and longevity increases, social security faces a funding shortfall. The accumulation of surplus, now being built up, is currently projected to be exhausted by the year 2032, and social security actuaries project that, during the seventy-five-year period used to project revenues and benefits, a deficit equal to 2.19 percent of taxable earnings will occur.

Reflecting social security's extraordinary success and universal acceptance, most reform proposals start from the same fundamental premise: the system must maintain disability and survivor benefits and continue to provide a guaranteed benefit that keeps both the disabled and the elderly out of poverty. Consistent with these goals, and in order to achieve a broader participation in capital markets, especially by low- and moderate-wage workers, many recent proposals also embrace the idea of adding a defined-contribution feature in the form of personal retirement accounts (PRAs) that would be owned and controlled by individual workers.[1] Polling data also suggest strong public support for making individual accounts

Fred T. Goldberg Jr. is a partner with the law firm Skadden, Arps, Slate, Meagher, and Flom. Michael J. Graetz is the Justus S. Hotchkiss Professor of Law at Yale University.

Financial and technical support was provided by Merrill Lynch & Co. The authors thank Armando Gomez of Skadden Arps for his assistance in the preparation of this paper. The views expressed in this paper are the authors' and should not be attributed to any other person or organization.

1. See, e.g., National Commission on Retirement Policy (1998); *Report of 1994–1996 Advisory Council on Social Security* (1997); and legislation introduced in the 105th Congress by

a part of social security.[2] There are many variations on this theme, and PRA proponents justify their support on a wide variety of grounds: Over extended periods, PRAs should generate higher returns than the Social Security Trust Fund, thereby helping maintain adequate retirement income. PRAs will provide a source of financial wealth (and stock market returns) to the roughly half of Americans who have none aside from the promised benefits of social security. Unlike the Social Security Trust Fund, the money in PRAs is "walled off" and cannot be used to fund other government expenditures; unlike social security benefits, PRAs are owned by individual participants and represent vested property rights. Social security is a pure defined-benefit program that is of most value to those who live the longest, while PRAs represent assets that are owned by participants; PRAs could be of particular benefit to the families of those who die early and groups with short life expectancies (e.g., minorities and low-income workers). Because single individuals, single parents, and two-income married couples are relatively disadvantaged by the way in which social security benefits are computed, PRAs may be of particular benefit to those groups. PRAs will provide a universal infrastructure to promote savings and help create wealth for all Americans.

To date, the PRA discussion has focused principally on policies and politics; not much has been written on ways in which to implement and administer such a program. The purpose of this paper is to address this latter question. While not a glamorous topic, the mechanics of PRAs will have a major effect on whether they become a part of this nation's national retirement policy. PRAs may be good policy and good politics, but, if they cannot work, they will not happen.

In addition, the ability to implement PRAs at a reasonable administrative cost is critical to their ultimate success. Large administrative expenses have the potential to erode the earnings of PRAs substantially, particularly for the large number of relatively small accounts that will exist.[3] Thus, a workable low-cost system is widely accepted as a prerequisite for the successful implementation of PRAs.

Senators Moynihan and Kerrey (S. 1792), Gregg and Breaux (S. 2313), Roth (S. 2369), and Grams (S. 2552) and Representatives Porter (H.R. 2929), N. Smith (H.R. 3082), and Kolbe and Stenholm (H.R. 4824). Other countries have already reformed their national retirement policies to implement PRAs (see app. A).

2. For example, 67 percent of the respondents to a poll conducted on behalf of the Democratic Leadership Council in August 1998 would prefer setting up PRAs. When asked about the risk of stock market downturns, which could diminish the value of PRAs, 55 percent of the respondents to the same poll still would prefer PRAs. Similarly, results from an August 1998 poll conducted on behalf of Americans Discuss Social Security indicate that approximately 58 percent of respondents with an opinion on proposals to reform social security by creating PRAs reacted favorably to such proposals.

3. Some have proposed direct investment of Social Security Trust Funds in stocks and bonds. While this change would achieve some of the advantages of PRAs, it would fail to achieve others and raises important additional questions. A discussion of this alternative is beyond the scope of this paper. We do recognize, however, that the cost of administering such investments would be less than the cost of administering PRAs.

While the PRA policy options are legion, our approach has been designed to satisfy three basic administrative criteria: (1) to minimize administrative costs and distribute those costs in a fair and reasonable way; (2) to minimize the burden on employers, especially small employers who do not now maintain a qualified retirement plan; and (3) to meet the expectations of everyday Americans for simplicity, security, control, and independence in ways that are easy to explain and easy to understand. While PRAs raise difficult administrative issues, this paper demonstrates that they can work. It describes a practical system for implementing and administering PRAs—a system that fulfills the three criteria listed above.

While these three criteria are generally accepted, there is a fourth requirement that has not been considered by other commentators but has influenced the design that we describe. Because the policy and political debate over PRAs is just getting started in earnest, there is a premium on flexibility—the capacity to accommodate a wide range of funding options and policy objectives. The system that we describe here will work whether PRAs are mandatory or voluntary; whether PRAs are funded by allocating an existing portion of the payroll tax to PRAs (a so-called carve-out), funded by collecting an additional amount from workers and/or employers (a so-called add-on), or funded from general revenues; whether or not PRAs are partially integrated with social security to help cover the funding shortfall when baby boomers begin to retire; regardless of how administrative costs are funded (in particular, regardless of what costs are funded from general revenues); regardless of the rights that spouses and ex-spouses have with respect to PRAs (e.g., some suggest that PRAs should be divided from the outset between the worker and his or her spouse); whether or not workers are allowed to make additional, voluntary contributions to their PRAs; and whatever investment and distribution options are available to participants and however those options are regulated. The system that we describe would accommodate a wide range of potential answers to these policy issues. Of equal importance, the system would be flexible enough to accommodate *changes* in the ways in which these questions are answered over time, after the PRA program is put in place.

1.2 Overview

The most important point to keep in mind is size—both big and little. The PRA system will involve an enormous number of accounts, and, in many of those accounts, the dollar amounts will be quite small. For example, approximately 137 million workers would have been covered during 1996.[4] Table 1.1 presents the number of those covered workers at vari-

---

4. The term *covered workers* refers to workers who participate in the social security system

Table 1.1   Covered Workers

| | Workers | |
Annual Covered Wages	Number (in millions)	As % of Total
$5,000	29,554	22
$10,000	46,438	35
$15,000	61,816	46
$20,000	76,178	58
$25,000	88,900	67
$30,000	99,458	73
$40,000	114,629	85
$50,000	123,641	91
$60,000	128,591	95
$63,000	129,578	96
All covered workers	136,689	100

ous levels of covered wages (National Academy of Social Insurance 1998).

Assuming that the amount going to PRAs each year equaled 2 percent of wages covered by social security, accounts for nearly 62 million workers would have been credited $300 or less for 1996; accounts for the approximately 9 million part-time and seasonal workers making less than $3,000 would have been credited with less than $60. At 3 percent of covered wages, nearly 47 million workers would have been credited with $300 or less. The average amount of covered wages for 1996 was nearly $25,000. Thus, at 2 percent of covered wages, the *average* amount credited to accounts for 1996 would have been $500, and the aggregate amount of contributions for 1996 would have been approximately $68.5 billion.

This paper focuses on the three fundamental administrative functions that are common to all systems of PRAs: (1) collecting PRA funds and crediting funds to each participant's retirement account; (2) investing funds on behalf of individual participants; and (3) distributing funds from PRA accounts to participants and beneficiaries.

1.3   The PRA Program

1.3.1   Summary

Any system of PRAs will provide for the funding of accounts, the management and investment of funds, the maintenance and dissemination of

---

and are liable for payroll taxes that fund social security and medicare. While most workers are covered, there are exceptions—notably, approximately 3.7 million workers employed by state and local governments. The term *covered wages* refers to wages subject to the payroll tax—in general, wages of covered workers up to a cap of approximately $68,400 in 1998. Except as otherwise noted, data are from SSA (1997).

account information, and the distribution of funds on retirement, disability, or death. A brief summary of procedures follows, illustrating how to minimize administrative costs and the burden on employers at the same time as providing participants with an understandable and workable system that will meet their needs for simplicity, security, independence, and control.

Funding PRAs. The current wage-reporting, payroll-tax, and income-tax systems provide an in-place vehicle for collecting PRA funds and crediting PRA accounts. Because these systems are already up and running, this aspect of the program will cost little to administer, will impose no additional burden on employers, and should be relatively easy to explain to participating workers.

Investing PRAs. From the standpoint of investment options, a two-tiered approach responds to the need for a simple and inexpensive system and meets the desire to provide individuals with control over their PRAs and a wide range of investment options. First, all workers could elect to invest their PRAs in a limited number of funds sponsored by the Social Security Administration (SSA) under a "no-frills" system managed by the private sector (simple personal investment funds [SPIFs]). Alternatively, workers could direct that their funds be invested in one or more privately sponsored qualified private funds (Q-funds). Some regulation of Q-funds will be necessary to limit investment options (as is now done with IRAs and 401[k] plans), to provide for times and methods for shifting investments, to ensure the solvency of fund managers, to provide for methods and times of disclosures to investors, and to regulate the allocation of administrative costs. The Treasury Department and the Labor Department, along with the Federal Reserve and the SEC, have long been performing these functions for private investments and therefore have the expertise and experience to implement any necessary regulation of Q-funds.

Distributing Funds from PRAs. Workers could not gain access to their PRAs prior to disability, retirement, or death—at which point it may be required that some or all of the PRA funds would have to be annuitized. As with the investment options, annuity alternatives should operate under a two-tiered approach. Either workers could elect to have their PRA balances transferred to the SSA in exchange for an appropriate increase in their monthly social security benefits, or, alternatively, workers could use their PRA balances to purchase qualified annuities from the private sector. Private companies that offer annuities should be required to provide all-comers annuities at the same age-based price to reduce costs and limit adverse-selection problems.

1.3.2   Funding PRAs

In General

An efficient and flexible mechanism for funding PRAs can be built off of the existing wage-reporting, payroll-tax, and income-tax systems. As explained below, this approach would involve four basic steps to direct funds into a PRA for the benefit of an individual worker. These steps are summarized below as they apply to employees (comparable procedures would apply with respect to self-employed workers).

Step 1. Employers withhold payroll taxes from wages and deposit those taxes (together with the employer's share) with the IRS, as required under current law. If PRAs are funded through a carve-out of existing payroll taxes or from general revenues, no additional collection mechanism would be necessary. If, on the other hand, PRAs are funded through an add-on in the form of additional withholding, the additional funds would be collected through the existing payroll-tax system in the same manner as payroll taxes, but PRA amounts would be designated as such in employers' deposits of withheld taxes and PRA contributions. If PRAs are financed from general revenues, the government would simply transfer the appropriate amounts into individuals' PRAs.

Step 2. Employers provide employees with W-2 forms at the close of the calendar year and file those forms with the IRS, as required under current law. If PRAs are funded through a carve-out from existing payroll taxes or from general revenues, no additional information would be required from employers. If PRAs are funded through an add-on, employers' W-2 forms would include both payroll-tax and PRA information for each employee.

Step 3. Employees file 1040 forms with the IRS, attaching copies of W-2 forms, as required under current law. The employee would also indicate how to invest amounts to be deposited in the PRA, using a form filed with his or her tax return. The IRS would collect the information necessary to set up and fund PRAs. (Most of this information, other than workers' investment choices, is already collected by the IRS under current law in the processing of tax returns.)

Step 4. On the basis of information collected in step 3, the employee's PRA would be funded as directed or funded as required by statute if the employee does not specify an investment option (presumably, into a specified SPIF).[5]

---

5. If a worker's account is divided from the outset between the worker and his or her spouse, then the worker and the worker's spouse would designate their respective investment choices on their joint or separate tax returns.

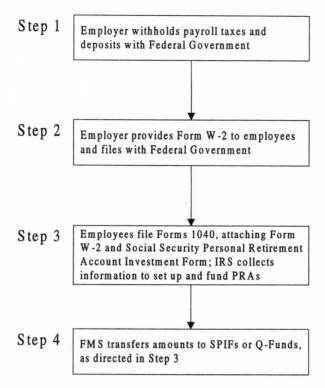

Step 1 | Employer withholds payroll taxes and deposits with Federal Government

Step 2 | Employer provides Form W-2 to employees and files with Federal Government

Step 3 | Employees file Forms 1040, attaching Form W-2 and Social Security Personal Retirement Account Investment Form; IRS collects information to set up and fund PRAs

Step 4 | FMS transfers amounts to SPIFs or Q-Funds, as directed in Step 3

Fig. 1.1   Funding PRAs

The flow of information and funds reflected in these four steps is summarized in figures 1.1 and 1.2.

Structuring PRAs around the existing system minimizes administrative costs and would impose no significant incremental burden on employers.[6] As under present law, employers would withhold payroll taxes from wages paid and would deposit those funds with the IRS according to the applicable deposit schedule. Similarly, self-employed individuals would continue to make payments of the self-employment tax to the IRS according to the applicable payment schedule. Because workers select their investment options when they file their tax returns, no additional burden is imposed on employers, and the additional burden on workers is minimized. This approach for collecting funds and crediting accounts would minimize the costs of initiating a system of PRAs.

6. As noted below, the task of informing workers regarding the operation and administration of PRAs (including information and education regarding investment options) should be the responsibility of the SSA and other federal agencies.

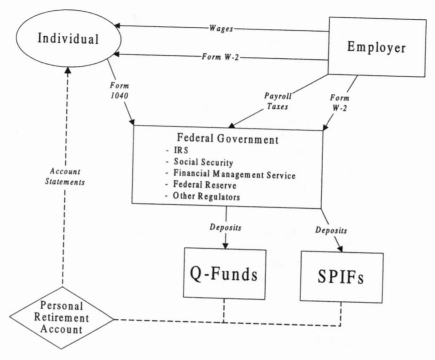

Fig. 1.2   Flow of funds and information

Establishing PRAs and Funding Investment Options

Most of the information necessary to establish and fund each worker's PRA—worker identifying information (name, social security number, and address) and amount of covered wages—is already provided to the IRS through employers' W-2 forms and by workers filing their tax returns. The only additional step would be for each worker to select a particular investment option by completing a form that could be filed along with the worker's tax return. Some proponents of PRAs have expressed concerns that workers not have to deal with the IRS in connection with their PRAs. To address this concern, the form could be designed and labeled to make clear that this is a social security PRA investment form. (Of course, investment elections could be required to be made directly with the SSA on a separate form apart from tax-return filing, but we believe that the additional burden and administrative costs of separate filings are unwarranted.)

The IRS would gather all the necessary information relevant to PRAs as part of its routine processing of tax returns. Because the IRS already gathers most of this information, the additional costs of processing the social security PRA investment form would not be significant. As now occurs with respect to tax refunds, the IRS would provide each worker's PRA information to the Treasury Department's Financial Management Service (FMS). In much the same way in which it handles other funding activities on behalf of the federal government, the FMS would then wire transfer the appropriate amount to each worker's designated investment fund. Once again, because the funding mechanism builds on existing systems, this approach should minimize the government's additional cost and facilitate the implementation of PRAs.[7]

Funding accounts in connection with the processing of tax returns, and having participants designate their investment choices with those returns, accomplishes several objectives: (1) Because substantially all workers already file income-tax returns, it minimizes the burden on participants and the government's processing costs (as, e.g., compared to a requirement that workers make a separate filing with the SSA). It also minimizes the start-up costs that would be associated with other systems of crediting accounts. (2) It avoids imposing any additional burden on employers. (3) The fact that most employers still file their W-2s with the IRS on paper is irrelevant. Paper filing causes no delay, and a very small number of corrections will have to be made.[8] (4) It protects workers' privacy. (5) Since wage reports filed by employers throughout the year do not identify wages allocable to each employee, the filing of the worker's tax return is the first occasion when the government has the information necessary to fund each participant's account. (6) Taking the information from the participant's tax return minimizes the lag in funding.[9] This greatly simplifies crediting funds to workers' accounts because funding takes place once annually, rather than at each pay period. It also eliminates any need to "credit" PRAs for earnings prior to the time at which individual accounts are cred-

7. The relative ease of this system is illustrated by the following: More than 80 percent of all taxpayers already file refund returns, and the IRS and the FMS are generally able to issue those refunds within two to four weeks after returns are filed. Moreover, under current law, taxpayers may instruct the IRS to issue refunds through direct deposit to a bank account owned by the taxpayer by including such instructions on the 1040 form. The information required from the taxpayer for this purpose, and the administrative burden on the IRS and the FMS, is similar to that which would be required in the context of PRAs. During the 1998 individual income-tax filing season, approximately 19.1 million individuals—more than 20 percent of all those receiving refunds—used this direct deposit system. Similarly, the increasing reliance on electronic-funds transfers in other contexts, e.g., the payment of welfare benefits, also suggests that the system described above can be implemented with relative ease.

8. Of the more than 1.1 billion information returns filed each year with the IRS, approximately 5 million, or less than 0.5 percent, are subsequently corrected. Applying this ratio to the more than 223 million W-2 forms actually filed in 1997, all of which were required to be filed in magnetic media, in electronic format, or on scannable paper, we expect that only 1 million W-2 forms would need correction.

9. For example, in 1998, approximately 32 percent of all individual returns were filed within two months after the end of the year, and approximately 90 percent of all returns were filed by 1 May, only four months after the end of the year. It now takes the SSA approximately nine months after the end of the year to process most W-2s, and it generally takes the IRS and the SSA up to eighteen months to complete reconciliation of W-2s.

ited.[10] (7) Any discrepancies between amounts reported on individual tax returns and amounts reflected through the reconciliation of W-2s by the SSA can be readily rectified through direct adjustments to PRAs. The only difficulty that can arise is when a downward adjustment is required to a PRA that has been defunded before the discrepancy is discovered. (Even in these rare cases, "transferee liability" similar to that now provided under the tax code could recapture erroneous amounts in virtually all circumstances.) (8) The IRS and the FMS experience with refunds generally, and with the electronic deposit of tax refunds in particular, demonstrates that the funding technology is already in place and can be implemented easily. (9) This approach provides maximum flexibility. For example, it is well suited to any financing approach (whether through carve-out of payroll taxes, through additional mandatory contributions, or from general revenues) because each funding method requires the same information from participants (worker identification, covered wages, and investment choices). Likewise, using the tax return as an information source has substantial advantages in accommodating voluntary additional contributions, particularly if those contributions are encouraged by tax incentives.

We considered, but rejected, implementing PRAs by requiring employers to deposit withheld funds directly into their employees' investment accounts. Such an approach would substantially increase the burdens on employers, particularly small employers. Not only would they be responsible for monthly reporting and funding, but they would also be responsible for providing information, selecting among funds, and correcting errors. We do not believe that those additional burdens would produce adequate additional value.

Currently, 401(k) plans are offered to only 7 percent of workers in firms with fewer than twenty-five employees. Workers earning less than $15,000 a year account for just 8.3 percent of workers who participate in any 401(k)-type retirement plan and only 16 percent of participants in any type of employer-based defined-contribution retirement plan (Olsen and Salisbury 1998). In contrast, the 62 million workers with $15,000 or less of wages will constitute 46 percent of participants in PRAs. For those workers, the lag between the time when they earn wages and the funding of their PRAs will cost at most about $20 a year (the income lost from a

---

10. We recognize that there is still some lag in funding (whether measured from the time taxes are withheld or from the end of the year). Nonetheless, on an account-by-account basis, there is no feasible or practical alternative to the approach that we recommend. Two other approaches have been suggested to minimize the effect of this lag: credit all accounts with some kind of imputed earnings (e.g., the short-term Treasury rate, using a six-month convention) or have the government invest funds on an aggregate basis during the year in SPIFs, using estimated investment choices. The former would be workable (the contribution to each account would be "grossed up" by the same percentage). The latter would likely impose substantial additional administrative burdens.

twelve-month delay at a 7 percent return following year-end is at most $20, or less than $2,100 over a lifetime).[11] To compensate for this loss of income, the government might credit individual PRAs with the return on Treasury borrowing for the period between earning the wages and funding the PRA. Alternatively, the government could remit an appropriate amount of aggregate PRA funds to a default SPIF with the income subsequently paid out to individual PRAs on the basis of wage reports. We regard the first alternative, which is simpler, as adequate, but either of these options is preferable to requiring employers to deposit funds directly into their employees' PRAs.

*Workers Not Required to File; Error Correction; Workers Who
Do Not Make an Investment Election; Noncompliance*

It is also necessary to provide for workers who choose not to file tax returns because their incomes are below the applicable filing thresholds.[12] The easiest way to address this issue is to permit these workers to file their social security PRA investment election form, along with copies of their W-2s, with an IRS service center.[13]

At present, the IRS and the SSA are able to "perfect" the information regarding each worker's covered wages within approximately eighteen months after the end of the calendar year. While the information on most workers' covered wages is accurate (and most of it is now filed electronically), there are a significant number of errors that must be corrected each year.

While the error numbers are large in absolute terms, they are small as a percentage of the entire program (see n. 9 above). Moreover, because a system of PRAs would place a greater premium on timely and accurate information, it is possible that there would be fewer errors over time. What is important to note is that these errors occur—and have to be corrected—under current law. As a result, under the implementation scheme described above, no new information processing is required. The only additional step is that some adjustment in the funded accounts will be required (subject to *de minimis* tolerances). Because the PRAs that must be adjusted will virtually always exist, any over- or underfunding can be remedied with

11. Olsen and Salisbury (1998) show that, after forty years, a once-per-year deposit of $1,200 would yield $8,315 less than a once-per-month deposit of $100 at a 7 percent rate ($254,166 rather than $262,481). For a $300 annual deposit, the lifetime loss would be only about $2,080.

12. While several million individuals file returns each year showing income below the applicable filing thresholds and almost 1 million individuals file returns each year showing no adjusted gross income, several million individuals do not file returns at all because their income falls below the applicable filing thresholds.

13. While the SSA does not process W-2s below a certain threshold, this procedure would enable all workers to get PRA credit for their earnings.

relative ease.[14] With respect to both over- and underfunding situations, it would be necessary to provide rules regarding actual or imputed earnings (or loss) prior to the correction date. Thus, for example, where accounts are overfunded, the withdrawal could reflect actual gains or losses, and, where accounts are underfunded, earnings could be credited at a specified rate, for example, the Treasury rate applicable to the correction period.[15]

For any worker who does not designate an investment option, his or her PRA would be invested in the manner specified by statute. In the case of workers filing tax returns, the IRS would gather the necessary information (e.g., covered wages) from the 1040 form. In the case of workers not filing tax returns, the information would be gathered from W-2 forms filed by employers. Because there could be a substantial lag in this latter context, it raises the issue of whether these accounts should be credited with imputed earnings (see nn. 4, 10, and 11 above).

A more difficult issue arises where no information returns are filed with respect to a worker, there is no withholding with respect to that worker's earnings, and the worker fails to file income-tax returns. Under these circumstances, crediting any amount to the worker's PRA will be virtually impossible without direct contact with the worker and/or the worker's employer. These cases will be quite rare and serve to show only that no law is 100 percent enforceable.

1.3.3   Investment Options

As noted above, a two-tiered system of investment options seems most appropriate.

SSA-Sponsored Options

Workers could elect to invest their PRAs in a limited number of funds sponsored by the SSA, with the management and administration of the funds contracted out to the private sector (SPIFs). From an investment and management standpoint, the SSA-sponsored funds would operate similarly to the federal employees' Thrift Savings Plan (TSP).[16] This alter-

14. As a practical matter, this would avoid many of the compliance problems encountered in other contexts (e.g., the earned income-tax credit).

15. Presumably, the SSA (rather than the IRS) should have responsibility for these error-correction activities, and the costs of this activity should be funded from general revenues.

16. The TSP, which is a retirement savings and investment plan for federal employees that was established by Congress in the Federal Employees' Retirement System Act of 1986, is a defined-contribution plan that provides federal employees with a choice of three investment options. First, employees can allocate all or a portion of their accounts to the "G Fund," which consists exclusively of investments in short-term nonmarketable U.S. Treasury securities issued directly to the TSP by the U.S. Treasury. Second, employees can allocate all or a portion of their accounts to the "C Fund," which is invested in a Standard and Poor's 500 stock index fund. Third, employees can allocate all or a portion of their accounts to the "F Fund," which is invested in a Lehman Brothers Aggregate bond index fund. Presently, the

native would be administered on a no-frills basis. Obviously, there is a trade-off between offering a variety of choices and keeping costs low. For example, SPIF investments could be limited to so-called lifestyle funds—a mix of debt and equity index fund investments with the proportion of equity adjusted to provide a level of risk appropriate to the participant's age. Alternatively, participants' investment options could be limited to the following: (1) one or two equity index funds, for example, one based on the Standard and Poor's 500 and one based on the Russell 2000 or Wilshire 5000,[17] and (2) one or two bond funds, one limited to U.S. Treasuries and the other based on corporate debt. (Two default funds might be provided for people who fail to elect any investment option. The first—a 60 percent equity, 40 percent debt fund—would apply to all individuals under age fifty-five. The second—an 80 percent debt, 20 percent equity fund—would apply to all individuals age fifty-five or over.) Participants would receive their account statements once (or perhaps twice) each year (additional statements could be made available for a fee). Automated account information would be available at any time. Participants could reallocate funds twice (or perhaps four times) a year without any additional charge (additional changes could be permitted for a fee).

This configuration represents a reasonable balance among competing objectives: it keeps administrative costs low while providing reasonable investment choices and market-comparable services to the millions of workers likely to participate in the SPIFs. It would, of course, be possible to increase or decrease investment options and services in ways that would increase or decrease costs of administering the program. Given the large number of relatively small SPIF accounts, however, keeping costs low is important so that investment returns will not be eroded.

After a phase-in period (which we estimate to be up to five years), the annual costs of administering SPIFs in the configuration described above are expected to be in the range of thirty to fifty basis points.[18] By way of comparison, appendix B provides more detailed information regarding current costs of a variety of investment funds.

Federal Retirement Thrift Investment Board, which is responsible for the oversight and management of the TSP, contracts with Barclays Global Investors to manage and invest the amounts allocated to the C and F Funds by participants in the TSP. The TSP also plans to add two additional investment options (a Russell 2000 index and a foreign stock index) in the near future.

17. By law, the TSP may make equity investments only in a "commonly recognized index" that is a "reasonably complete representation of United States equity markets."

18. Although we have seen cost estimates ranging from five to more than one hundred basis points, this is similar to the range of costs estimated in National Academy of Social Insurance (1998). It is also similar to the range of costs estimated by representatives from State Street Bank and Fidelity at a conference on the feasibility of PRAs ("Beyond Ideology" 1998).

Regardless of the specific configuration of investment options and account services, the SPIF approach raises a number of policy and administrative issues. Some examples follow:

What portion of the administrative costs should be financed from direct charges to accounts? How should such amounts be allocated? Allocating such amounts on the basis of the amount of assets in accounts, rather than on a fixed-dollar-per-account basis, seems most consistent with the goal of broadening capital market participation by low- and moderate-income workers.

What portion, if any, of the administrative costs should be financed from general revenues? In considering this question, two points are worth noting: (1) To deal with transition costs, it may be useful to cap administrative costs charged to PRAs at some level (e.g., thirty to fifty basis points) and fund any excess from general revenues. (2) It has been suggested that some or all administrative costs should be funded from general revenues on one or more of the following grounds: it would increase the net return on PRAs; from a "fairness" standpoint, it would be progressive; PRAs are a "public good" (everyone benefits from increased savings and the creation of wealth for all workers); general revenues cover the administrative costs of similar government functions (e.g., medicare, social security, and the IRS). On the other hand, fully funding administrative expenses from general revenues may remove any incentive for individual investors to see that such costs are minimized.

By requiring that the SPIF investments be contracted out, we have sought to minimize the risks that the government will use these funds to interfere in the capital markets (e.g., by rewarding or punishing certain industries or companies, by competing with the private sector, or by making investment decisions to address fiscal, social, or foreign policy issues).

We have illustrated rules governing the choice of SPIF funds for workers who do not elect any investment option, but there are obviously other alternatives. Presumably, as we have noted, funds would be allocated on the basis of an age-adjusted formula. Should the default formulas be specified in legislation or left to the discretion of one or more regulatory bodies?

Should anything be done to address concerns over stock market volatility, especially as workers approach retirement age? For example, in the context of the SPIF, should there be rules mandating more conservative investment allocations as workers approach retirement age? Should the SPIF offer some kind of "risk insurance" or investment guarantee?

What kind of information should be provided to workers regarding their investment options, who should provide that information, and how should the costs of providing that information be allocated? Consistent with our basic goal of minimizing burdens on employers, especially small employers, placing responsibility for education with the SSA seems an appropriate first step. As all workers become investors through their PRAs, it seems likely that other avenues of education, including by nonprofit organizations, will emerge.

As a practical matter, answers to some of these questions may vary depending on whether the accounts are funded through a carve-out, through an add-on mechanism, or from general revenues. We want to emphasize that the implementation system outlined here can accommodate a wide range of answers to these and other policy issues.

Private Fund Options

In addition to SSA-sponsored SPIFs, the PRA program could permit individuals to invest their funds with one or more privately sponsored qualified private funds (Q-funds). There are several reasons for making such an option available to workers: It allows individual workers to avail themselves of the wide range of investment alternatives and investment services offered by the private sector.[19] Because workers can take advantage of private-sector options, it will be easier to maintain the SPIF as a low cost, easy-to-understand, limited-choice alternative. It will reduce the risk that the federal government will "compete" with the private sector through manipulating the SPIF. Finally, it will reduce the risk that politicians and interest groups will seek to use the SPIF to pursue unrelated political, social, economic, or foreign policy objectives.

As we have said, the financial institution offering Q-funds, and the Q-funds themselves, will need to be regulated regarding permitted investments, financial solvency, and disclosure requirements. We expect existing regulatory mechanisms to be adequate for this purpose.[20] For example: As with qualified retirement plans and IRAs under current law, Q-funds should be segregated from other investment funds (i.e., there should be no commingling of assets). The diversification requirements applicable to mutual funds (regulated investment companies) and the fiduciary obligations under the Employee Retirement Income Security Act (ERISA) provide a starting point for addressing various risk-related issues; Q-fund sponsors could be required to offer a minimum range of investments (e.g., index equity funds and short- and long-term bond alternatives).[21] While any Q-fund sponsors could offer a wide range of investment alternatives, limiting individuals to one PRA account may be appropriate to avoid the excessive administrative costs that multiple accounts would entail; this would mean that an individual's account would be invested through either an SPIF or the Q-funds of a single financial institution. The system could build on current reporting requirements to assure that the government

---

19. For the reasons noted above (e.g., the wire-transfer of almost 20 million refunds), this alternative could be implemented at little incremental cost to the federal government.

20. We also think that it is preferable to rely on that structure to the maximum extent possible, rather than create yet another regulatory regime.

21. These alternatives are currently required by sec. 404(c) of ERISA.

receives the information necessary to monitor the Q-funds and the status of individual workers' accounts.[22]

There are two ways in which to determine which institutions would be permitted to offer Q-funds and the conditions under which those Q-funds could be offered. One approach would be to impose a uniform set of licensing criteria that would be centrally administered by a single regulatory agency. Alternatively, those same criteria could be administered separately by the agency now responsible for regulating the sponsoring financial institution. In either event, because the federal government, rather than individual workers, would provide original transfers of funds to Q-funds, workers would be protected from fraud by unauthorized promoters. As for the licensing requirements themselves, one approach would be to integrate them with existing regulatory standards regarding permitted investments, safety and soundness, and disclosure. In this context, the legislation could impose additional requirements that were deemed appropriate (e.g., bonding or insurance requirements, net-worth requirements, etc.).

From the standpoint of ongoing compliance, financial institutions and Q-funds could be monitored by existing regulatory authorities as part of their overall responsibilities (e.g., the Department of Treasury and Labor, the Federal Reserve Board, and the SEC; table 1C.1 in app. C summarizes the current regulatory structure of financial institutions likely to offer Q-funds). This structure would also permit rules limiting and allocating the administrative costs of Q-funds. We believe that, in the light of the SPIF alternative, these rules could be limited and should focus on disclosure requirements. Nonetheless, in the light of concerns about the potential for marketing costs to increase administrative costs and reduce investment returns, financial institutions offering Q-funds might be limited in allocating marketing costs to Q-funds or offering "bonuses" for individuals to shift funds to a different offeror. In addition, as with SPIFs, Q-fund sponsors could be required to allocate all costs within each fund on an asset rather than a fixed-dollar-per-account basis.

Some commentators have expressed the concern that Q-funds might attract a disproportionate share of PRAs with relatively high dollar account balances, increasing the per account cost of SPIFs. One response might be to levy an asset-based charge on Q-funds and/or their sponsors to defray the cost of administering SPIFs. Likewise, to limit skimming of large accounts by Q-funds, it may be appropriate to require Q-funds to accept PRAs above some asset value.

Once again, we want to emphasize that this administrative structure

---

22. This latter requirement would be particularly important if PRAs are funded from general revenues and those accounts are integrated in some manner with social security to address social security's funding shortfall.

provides Congress substantial flexibility in addressing numerous policy issues (e.g., bonding, insurance, and/or net-worth requirements applicable to the Q-fund and the sponsoring institution; limitations, if any, on permitted investments; age-based portfolio requirements; rules governing spousal rights; the protection of workers' assets from creditors' claims; and disclosure requirements). Thus, while we believe that it is possible to keep any such regulation to a minimum and that, to the extent possible, such regulation should be integrated with existing rules, the legislation authorizing Q-funds could impose whatever regulatory requirements Congress deems appropriate.

On the basis of industry experience with 401(k) and IRA accounts, Q-fund accounts should cost about $15–$25 annually, depending on the amount and kind of service provided (e.g., frequency of statements, frequency of free telephone inquiries, etc.). In the system that we describe here, such costs would be allocated on the basis of assets, not on a per account basis. We have suggested that each individual have only one account, but, if people are permitted to elect to have multiple Q-fund accounts with different financial institutions, they should bear the costs of such choices.

SPIFs and Q-Funds Together

Most of the commentators who have considered PRAs have proposed that all investments be made either through a simple investment vehicle (resembling our SPIF) or through privately run accounts (resembling our Q-fund). This naturally raises the question why *both* the SPIF and the Q-fund options are desirable. In our judgment, the SPIF and Q-fund investment choices work together in important ways. Standing alone, each has the potential for problems that will be policed by the other if both options are made available. For example, the existence of the Q-fund alternative makes it more likely that the SPIF can be preserved as a simple, low-cost system with a limited selection of investment alternatives. It also reduces the risk—which a government-contracted fund standing alone entails— that the SPIF will be used for political, social, or foreign policy purposes. At the same time, having the SPIF in place will keep pressure on Q-fund sponsors to minimize costs and marketing abuses of the sort that have plagued some PRA systems abroad while allowing Americans great independence and flexibility in their investment choices.[23] Likewise, having the SPIF in place will reduce pressure to impose detailed regulations on Q-funds (e.g., a requirement that all Q-fund sponsors offer SPIF-type funds; restrictions on fees). The balance provided by SPIFs and Q-funds together

---

23. For example, the SPIF alternative may be the most effective deterrent to the marketing-cost concerns under the Chilean and U.K. systems.

makes the approach that we are suggesting preferable to a PRA system limited to either alternative standing alone.

Education and Error Correction

As we have suggested, giving the federal government primary responsibility for educating workers regarding all aspects of the PRA program, including basic information regarding eligible Q-funds, accomplishes a number of objectives. Most notably, it minimizes the burden on employers and helps assure uniformity and quality control. One approach would be to give primary responsibility to the SSA. The SSA would work with other federal agencies (e.g., the Departments of the Treasury and of Labor, the SEC, and the Federal Reserve) and have substantial latitude to contract out various activities to the private sector. Funding these efforts with general revenues seems appropriate. The nature of the program also makes it likely that a great deal of education would be provided at no cost to the program or the federal government and that a number of private nonprofit organizations will participate in educating the public (e.g., popular and specialized media; educational institutions; employers [on a volunteer basis]; sponsors of Q-funds).

As noted, there is a high level of accuracy associated with wage reporting and the issuance of tax refunds under current law. Nonetheless, in absolute terms, there are certain to be a sizable number of errors in the crediting of accounts and a significant number of inquiries regarding SPIF account-related matters.[24] One approach would be to give the SSA primary responsibility for handling these questions and resolving any account discrepancies. The SSA would work with other federal agencies (primarily, the IRS) and have substantial latitude to contract out various activities to the private sector. While both the IRS and the SSA have substantial call-site operations, the SSA may be better equipped to handle the likely range of inquiries (perhaps subcontracting with the IRS to handle certain calls). This approach also avoids concerns over the appearance of telling participants that they must resolve account issues with the IRS.

1.3.4   Distributions from PRAs

Policy Issues

As a preliminary matter, it is important to note that the rules governing distributions from PRAs pose difficult policy issues. For example, to what extent, if any, should beneficiaries be required to annuitize their PRAs on retirement? Among the options are that all PRA funds must be annuitized, that there be no mandatory annuitization requirements, that PRA funds must be annuitized to the extent necessary to provide some minimum in-

---

24. Account-related inquiries regarding Q-funds would be handled directly by those funds.

come level (when combined with other social security benefits), and that there be limited annuitization alternatives (e.g., for funding of joint-and-survivor long-term-care coverage).

If some type of annuitization is required, what form must those annuities take? Among the options are that annuities should provide benefits parallel to existing social security benefits (e.g., inflation adjusted; joint-and-survivor annuities, with reduced payments to the survivor); that benefits should parallel the qualified plan/IRA rules (account balance divided by life expectancy); and that there be a limited number of acceptable annuity alternatives (e.g., the ability to include other beneficiaries under joint-and-survivor annuities; no reduction in payments to survivor; varied payment streams; term certain, on early retirement).

When can workers first gain access to their PRAs? Among the options are the following: at the normal social security retirement age (or when they qualify for social security disability payments); whenever they first begin collecting social security benefits; at their election, any time after they first begin collecting social security benefits (i.e., permit continued accumulation); and before they begin collecting social security benefits if their PRA funds are sufficient to provide some minimum monthly payment (taking into account anticipated future social security benefits) (i.e., use PRAs to facilitate early retirement).

What will happen to PRA contributions on behalf of the several million individuals who continue working, and continue paying payroll taxes, after they begin collecting social security? If the worker continues to maintain a PRA, then his or her contributions would simply continue. If, however, the entire balance of the worker's PRA has already gone to purchase some form of annuity, his or her withholding could be reduced by an amount that would otherwise go to fund the worker's PRA (e.g., if PRAs are funded by an add-on or a carve-out), funding could stop for the worker's PRA (if PRAs are funded from general revenues), or the worker could be given a refundable tax credit equal to the amount added to his or her PRA (if PRAs are funded by a carve-out or from general revenues).

If PRAs are funded in whole or in part from general revenues and/or integrated in some way with social security, how should that integration be structured? Among the options are the mandatory annuitization of PRAs, with a partial offset against payments otherwise due under social security, or the lump-sum transfer of a specified portion of PRA balances to social security on the death, disability, or retirement of the worker.

To some degree, the answers to these questions will depend on how PRAs are funded. As before, however, the goals of implementing any of these policy decisions will be to promote fairness, to keep administrative costs to a minimum, and to devise a system that the American people can easily understand. We discuss the options below.

SSA-Sponsored Annuity Option

Under this alternative, a worker's PRA funds would be transferred to social security when the worker first begins receiving social security benefits. The amount of the worker's and survivor's social security benefits would be increased on the basis of the value of the worker's PRA. In other words, the government would decide what amount of annuity to pay for a given PRA accumulation. The primary virtue of this alternative is its simplicity. From the worker's perspective, it requires no choices or decisions. The worker will receive only one monthly payment and will deal with only one party making payments (the SSA). From the government's perspective, the only additional administrative costs occur at the outset: collecting the PRA funds and making the appropriate adjustment to social security payments.

Social security could implement this alternative by contracting out all aspects of the program (other than processing beneficiary payments) to the private sector, with the private sector setting the annuity amount (with indexing for inflation) and thereby bearing investment and mortality risks. We believe that contracting out is a better alternative than social security directly administering PRA-funded annuities. For example, what return would the government assume on the funds that it received from the worker's PRA—and would the government be permitted to invest those funds in the same way that private insurers invest premiums? Given the relatively long period of retirement that workers can now be expected to enjoy, depriving them of equity market returns during this entire period seems inconsistent with one key purpose of enacting PRAs in the first place: expanding low- and moderate-income workers' access to capital markets. Who would bear the risks if the government underprices its annuity (taxpayers or beneficiaries?), and what mechanism would be used to implement the allocation of risks? What effect, if any, would this role for the government have on the private annuities market?

Contracting out to the private sector under rules that protect against companies segmenting longevity risks permits the market to resolve the pricing issues and avoids any potential adverse effect of a government-run system on the private annuities market. The government's role would be limited to setting appropriate annuity specifications, processing payments, and regulating and supervising the private-sector financial institutions responsible for the program.

In this regard, it is important to note that a market structure is already in place to implement this system. Thus, for example, most defined-contribution plans offer annuity options that are provided by insurance carriers (rather than the plan itself).[25]

---

25. For more extensive discussion, see Poterba and Warshawsky (chap. 5 in this volume).

Private Market Annuity Options

Workers and their beneficiaries could also be permitted to purchase private annuity options so long as problems of adverse selection and risk segmentation are addressed. Permitting individual workers and their beneficiaries to avail themselves of the wider range of annuity alternatives available from the private sector offers several advantages. For example, a family may prefer a joint-and-survivor annuity with a pattern of payments that differs from the SSA-sponsored model, a family may prefer annuity payments that cover a disabled child or elderly parents, or a worker may want to retire early with a "retirement-gap" annuity that runs for a term of years, until social security benefits begin. By allowing workers to take advantage of private-sector options, it will be possible to maintain an SSA-sponsored annuity option as a simple, low-cost, easy-to-understand alternative.

It would be necessary to regulate the institutions offering private market annuities in exchange for PRA balances with regard to segmentation of longevity risks, safety and soundness, and disclosure.[26] Because insurance has been regulated historically at the state level, there is no existing federal regime to regulate annuities. For this reason, a threshold decision is whether to rely on the existing state-based structure, create a new federal structure, or create a hybrid system of federal standards for qualifying annuities, enforced by the states.

It is also important that administrative costs of private annuities be kept to a minimum and allocated fairly. As with the PRAs themselves, we believe that this means that the costs of the SSA-sponsored annuities should be allocated on the basis of asset size rather than on a per account basis. Because the administrative costs of individual annuities may be as much as 5–10 percent of the purchase price (even without premiums for adverse selection), we believe that it is appropriate for retirees who choose to purchase such annuities to bear these costs themselves.

1.4   Conclusion

Two conclusions emerge from the foregoing. First, any system of PRAs will have to resolve many difficult policy questions. The most fundamental are, Should federal retirement policy move in the direction of universal PRAs? How should personal retirement accounts be funded (as a carve-out from payroll taxes, from mandatory additional contributions, or from general revenues)? What rules should govern distributions from PRAs?

26. Likewise, as noted above, policy considerations may place constraints on the types of annuities that can be offered. It may be appropriate to impose some kind of minimum guarantee requirement on participating carriers to deal with credit and performance risks.

Second, regardless of how these *policy* questions are answered, institutions and mechanisms already exist that make it feasible to introduce PRAs in a way that minimizes administrative costs, distributes those costs fairly and reasonably, imposes little or no incremental burden on employers, is easy to explain and easy to understand, and meets the expectations of everyday Americans for simplicity, security, independence, and control.

We believe that the system that we have outlined above meets these criteria. There are no doubt other ways in which a system of PRAs might be implemented. However, most of the alternatives suggested to date impose greater burdens on employers than does the system that we have outlined here because they give employers responsibility for transferring their employees' funds directly into investment funds and require employers to provide information about investment choices to their employees. These are burdens that we have endeavored to avoid. There are also many possible variations on the themes that we have outlined here. For example, some have suggested that—rather than permitting direct transfers of funds into Q-funds, as we have suggested here—all funds should move directly into SPIFs, with rollovers permitted only after some period of time or after the individual's PRA balance has reached some threshold amount. We do not view such a limitation as necessary, but, to be sure, this is the kind of issue over which reasonable people may differ.

The plan for implementing PRAs that we have offered here will work no matter how various policy questions are decided. It will work however PRAs are financed, whether from existing payroll taxes, from general revenues, or through new mandated savings; whether PRAs are mandatory or voluntary; whether PRAs are integrated with social security benefits or not; whatever the regime of spousal rights; and whether or not distributions are required to be annuitized. And it will work at reasonable administrative costs with those costs allocated fairly among beneficiaries.

Building on existing public and private systems and existing regulatory structures—as the approach that we have described here does—minimizes start-up costs and makes it more likely that the program can be implemented relatively quickly and smoothly. This approach also takes advantage of the fact that administrative, market, and regulatory systems are dynamic; they tend to change in response to changed incentives. The system that we have described creates incentives that are likely to improve current practices in a variety of areas. For example, all the affected participants (workers, employers, the IRS, the FMS, and the SSA) will be motivated to improve the timeliness and accuracy of W-2 reporting and the filing and processing of income-tax returns. In turn, these improvements will benefit workers, employers, and the government in ways that go well beyond PRAs. Other areas where improvements are likely include increased financial literacy among workers and beneficiaries, growth and flexibility in the annuities markets, and, perhaps, unification and simplification of the regime for regulating financial intermediaries. Moreover, while the PRA program would encourage additional investment in technology and improving a variety of administrative operations, those additional investments are not a prerequisite for the effective implementation of PRAs.

Our key point is simply this: if PRAs are wise public policy, they can be implemented at a reasonable cost in a manner that imposes relatively little stress on existing public and private institutions.

To put the administrative challenge of PRAs in context, it is worth recalling what the world was like when social security itself was introduced in 1935. There were no social security numbers. Many Americans did not have a telephone. There were no computers—all records were maintained on paper; all information was entered by hand; all correspondence was sent and delivered by mail; there was no computer-based financial infrastructure. Implementing social security under these conditions was hard; by comparison, implementing PRAs today would be easy. While there are difficult administrative issues regarding PRAs, they are not insurmountable. Administrative concerns should not become an excuse for not implementing PRAs—the only question is whether PRAs are good policy.

Appendix A

Background on PRAs in Foreign Countries

Australia

The Australian retirement-income system is a two-pillar model. The first pillar provides a flat-rate, means-tested pension known as the *age pension*. The second pillar is the private retirement provision and mandates compulsory concessionally taxed saving for retirement through an employment-based system known as the *superannuation guarantee* (SG). The SG is a compulsory, occupation-based, defined-contribution superannuation system. Under the SG, employers are required to make on behalf of their employees prescribed minimum contributions to complying superannuation funds, or PRAs. By 2002, this minimum contribution will be 9 percent of employee earnings. Employees also contribute 3 percent of their earnings to the superannuation funds, and the government can make contributions of as much as 3 percent of pay for lower-paid employees.

Unlike the Chilean or the Latin American model, the key feature of the Australian model is the fact that, rather than having individual accounts with individual choice, the employer and/or union trustees choose the investment manager for the company or the occupation group as a whole. Superannuation funds are managed by professionals in the financial service industry. The superannuation system has only one fund per employer, but workers still have a choice of investment because each fund offers several investment options. Superannuation funds operate as trusts, with the trustees being solely responsible for the prudential operation of their funds and for formulating and implementing an investment strategy. Superannuation funds face few investment restrictions; there are no asset requirements or floors, no minimum rate-of-return requirements, and no government guarantee of benefits. The prudential regulation of the superannuation system is currently the responsibility of the Insurance and Superannuation Commission.

Chile

Chile replaced social insurance with individual funded pensions in the early 1980s. Under Chile's pension savings account (PSA) system, neither the worker nor the employer pays a social security tax to the state. Nor does the worker collect a government-funded pension. Instead, during his working life, he automatically has 10 percent of his wages deposited by his employer each month in his own, individual PSA. This percentage applies only to the first $22,000 of annual income. A worker may also voluntarily make additional tax-deductible contributions of up to 10 percent of wages.

A worker chooses one of the twenty-one private pension fund administration companies (*administradoras de fondos de pensiones,* or AFPs) to manage his PSA. The companies were specifically created for this purpose and are not allowed to engage in other business or financial activities. They are also subject to government regulation intended to guarantee a diversified and low-risk portfolio and to prevent theft or fraud. A separate government entity, a highly technical "AFP Superintendency," provides oversight of these companies.

Each AFP operates the equivalent of a mutual fund that invests in stocks and bonds. Investment decisions are made by the AFP. Government regulation sets only maximum percentage limits both for specific types of instruments and for the overall mix of the portfolio, and the spirit of the reform is that those regulations should be reduced constantly with the passage of time and as the AFP companies gain experience. The AFPs are under no obligation to invest in government or any other type of bond. Legally, the AFP company and the mutual fund that it administers are two separate entities. Thus, should an AFP go under, the assets of the mutual fund—that is, the workers' investments—should not be affected.

Workers are free to change from one AFP company to another on short notice. Each worker is given a PSA passbook and every three months receives a regular statement informing him how much money has been accumulated in his retirement account and how well his investment fund has performed.

The Chilean PSA system includes both private- and public-sector employees. All employed workers, with the exception of members of the police and armed forces, must have a PSA. Self-employed workers may enter the system at their option.

A worker who has contributed for at least twenty years but whose pension fund, on his reaching retirement age, is below the legally defined minimum pension receives benefits from the state once his PSA has been depleted. The PSA system also includes insurance against premature death and disability. Each AFP provides this service to its clients by purchasing group life and disability coverage from private life insurance companies.

Sweden

Sweden's social security system, known as a "notional account" system, is a pay-as-you-go, defined-contribution system. Workers have individual accounts and passbooks that show accumulations and interest on accumulations, but, in reality, there is no money in the accounts; it is notional. The defined-contribution scheme has a rate of 18.5 percent shared equally between employees and employers.

A small funded component to the system allows employees to allocate 2.5 percent of their pension contributions to either a new pension fund, a new state-owned investment company, or an approved private investment fund. Collection and record keeping for the funded component will be centralized, and workers will choose the investment manager from a list of mutual funds. A guaranteed pension acts as a safety net at the bottom of the income scale.

United Kingdom

The U.K. model is similar to the Australian model. It is a two-tiered pension system that is funded on a pay-as-you-go basis. The first component of the system is a flat-rate pension whereby both employees and employers contribute a fraction of the employees' earnings to the system. Employees receive the full flat-rate benefit under the first tier of the system if they contribute to the system for the required number of qualifying years. The second tier of the system is the supplemental earnings-related pension scheme (SERPS), which provides benefits on a supplemental basis.

In the 1980s, employees were given the option of contracting out of the SERPS and taking a cut in their payroll tax of approximately 4.6 percent of their earnings and investing it in a private retirement account. In general, in order to opt out, employees must receive a private, earnings-related pension at least as high as the pension that they would have received had they fully participated in SERPS. Those who exercise the personal pension account option forgo their SERPS benefits. Britain allows only qualified institutions to accept and manage deposits made to personal pension accounts. At present, at least seventeen hundred mutual funds and investment funds can accept deposits. The system also places restrictions on the riskiness of investments, limiting the funds from investing more than 15 percent of their assets in commodities, futures, or options.

Appendix B

Table 1B.1   Sample Average Total Expenses from Selected Types of Mutual Funds

Fund Category	Average Total Expenses	Fund Category	Average Total Expenses
Growth	1.055	Capital appreciation	1.103
Growth and income	0.832	High current yield	1.119
International	1.197	Municipal debt	0.742
Balanced	0.869	Investment grade debt	0.748
Equity income	0.803	Flexible portfolio	1.213
Small cap	1.309	GNMA	0.699
Mid cap	1.174	A-rated	0.797
Global	1.243	California municipal debt	0.702
S&P 500	0.229	U.S. government	1.131

Source: Authors' calculations from Lipper Analytical Services (1997).
Note: GNMA = Government Natural Mortgage Association.

Appendix C
Regulation of Financial Institutions

The banking, securities, and insurance companies that could offer Q-funds presently are subject to extensive regulation and oversight by federal and/ or state regulators as well as self-regulatory organizations. The comparison shown in table 1C.1 and the brief discussions that follow provide an overview of the breadth and depth of the supervisory and regulatory framework governing insurance, banking, and securities businesses.

Banking

All depository institutions insured by the FDIC, including national banks, state-chartered banks, federally and state-chartered thrift institutions, and credit unions, are subject to comprehensive federal regulation, supervision, and examination by their appropriate regulators. The appro-

Table 1C.1   **Financial Institution Regulation**

Regulation	Banking	Insurance	Securities
Capital adequacy	✓	✓	✓
Transactions with affiliates	✓	✓	✓
Safety and soundness	✓	✓	✓
Examination	✓	✓	✓
Record keeping	✓	✓	✓
Nondiscrimination and fair dealing	✓	✓	✓

priate regulators include the Office of the Comptroller of the Currency in the case of national banks; the FDIC and the Board of Governors of the Federal Reserve System in the case of state nonmember and member banks, respectively; the Office of Thrift Supervision for federal and state thrift institutions; the National Credit Union Administration for credit unions; and various state regulators in the case of state-chartered institutions. The operations and financial condition of these institutions are subject to extensive regulation and supervision and to various requirements and restrictions under federal law, including requirements governing capital adequacy (tier 1 and total risk-based capital requirements as well as a "leverage" capital requirement based on the ratio of tier 1 capital to total assets), activities and investments, bank transactions with affiliates, dividends, management practices, record keeping, and "year 2000" compliance. Insured depository institutions file annual, quarterly, monthly, and other reports with their regulators, which also perform on-site examinations. Federal and state regulators have broad enforcement authority over insured depository institutions, including the power to impose substantial fines and other civil penalties.

Securities

Broker-Dealers and Investment-Management Companies

These companies are regulated, supervised, and examined by the SEC, the Commodities Futures Trading Commission, and/or self-regulatory organizations, including the National Association of Securities Dealers (NASD), a registered securities association, and various national securities exchanges. In accordance with section 15(b) of the Securities Exchange Act of 1934, broker-dealers are members of the NASD and of various securities exchanges. Pursuant to delegated authority from the SEC, the NASD and the exchanges enforce the substantive Securities Exchange Act rules and provide compliance oversight of the broker-dealer's activities.

Mutual Funds

Mutual funds are regulated, supervised, and examined by the SEC under the Investment Company Act of 1940, as amended, and other federal securities laws. In addition, their major service providers are regulated, supervised, and examined by the SEC, the Commodities Futures Trading Commission, and/or self-regulatory organizations such as the NASD and various national securities exchanges. The 1940 act regulates, among other things, the amount of financial leverage that mutual funds may use, portfolio liquidity, investor redemption rights, record keeping, mutual fund disclosure and advertising practices, fees, and transactions among a mutual fund and its affiliates. Mutual funds file reports with the SEC semi-annually and maintain continuously updated registrations for the sale of shares under the Securities Act of 1933, as amended. The SEC has extensive enforcement authority over mutual funds and their major service providers, including the power to impose substantial fines and other civil penalties, prohibiting violators from continued activities in the securities industry, and referral to the Justice Department for criminal proceedings.

Insurance

Insurance companies are regulated, supervised, and examined by state insurance regulators. The primary regulator for a company is generally the state in which it is domiciled, although there is an element of extraterritorial application of investment and other insurance laws to companies not domiciled in a state. The National Association of Insurance Commissioners (NAIC) promulgates model laws and regulations that are generally followed by the state insurance departments. These include a formula and a model law to implement risk-based capital requirements for life insurance companies and property and casualty insurance companies that are used as early warning tools by the NAIC and state regulatory agencies to identify insurance companies that merit further regulatory action. Insurance companies are also subject to various state statutory and regulatory restrictions on the amount of dividends or distributions that they can make to their stockholders as well as an extensive legislative and regulatory regime with respect to investment practices, strategies, and procedures. The state insurance regulatory system incorporates tools to audit each insurance company domiciled within that state to determine that the insurance company is observing regulations regarding solvency, risk-based capital requirements, and dividend and investment restrictions. In addition, individual products are reviewed by state regulators as to both forms and rates, and market-conduct examinations are utilized by state regulators to ensure that all the consumer-protection regulations governing products, prices, sales, advertising, agent licensing, claim handling, and fraud detection are strictly observed by any insurance company selling life or property-casualty insurance products in the state.

References

Beyond ideology: Are individual social security accounts feasible? 1998. Employee Benefits Research Institute–Education and Research Fund policy forum, 2 December, Washington, D.C.

Individual Social Security Retirement Accounts Act. 1997. H. R. 2929, 105th Cong.

Lipper Analytical Services. 1997. *The third white paper: Are mutual fund fees reasonable?* Summit, N.J., September.

National Academy of Social Insurance. 1998. *Report of the panel on privatization of social security.* Washington, D.C., November.

National Commission on Retirement Policy. 1998. *The 21st century retirement security plan.* Washington, D.C., 19 May.

Olsen, Kelly A., and Dallas L. Salisbury. 1998. *Individual social security accounts: Issues in assessing administration, feasibility, and costs.* Washington, D.C.: Employee Benefits Research Institute, November.

Personal Retirement Act. 1998. S. 2369, 105th Cong.

Personal Security and Wealth in Retirement Act of 1998. 1997. S. 2552, 105th Cong.

Report of 1994–1996 Advisory Council on Social Security. 1997. Washington, D.C., 6 January.

Social Security Administration (SSA). 1997. *Annual statistical supplement, 1997.* Washington, D.C.

Social Security Solvency Act (or Voluntary Investment Contribution Act). 1998. S. 1792, 105th Cong.

Twenty-first Century Retirement Act. 1998. H. R. 4824, 105th Cong.

Twenty-first Century Retirement Act. 1998. S. 2313, 105th Cong.

Comment   Gloria M. Grandolini

The experience of the countries that have moved to some version of personal retirement accounts (PRAs) shows that, as noted by Fred Goldberg and Michael Graetz, during the design phase most of the effort is focused on policies and politics. The mechanics and administration of the reformed system are dealt with during the implementation phase. Often, this approach has led to delays in the implementation of or to extensive fine-

Gloria M. Grandolini is special assistant to the senior vice president and chief financial officer at the World Bank.

tuning of the initial design. Detailing as they do the mechanics of implementing and administering PRAs as part of social security reform in the United States, Goldberg and Graetz provide an important contribution to the debate.

The authors focus on three fundamental administrative functions: collecting and crediting funds to individual accounts; investing funds on behalf of individual participants; and distributing funds. As noted by the authors, the most important feature of the proposed scheme is size—a very large number of accounts, the majority of them with very small amounts. These characteristics are shared by the PRA systems implemented in several Latin American countries. Establishing the mechanisms for funding the PRAs and for distributing funds from the PRAs would appear to be a less daunting task in the United States than it has been in Latin America. In the funding phase, the United States already has in place a system for wage reporting as well as payroll-tax and income-tax systems. For the distribution phase, the United States has a developed private insurance industry to provide the annuity alternatives.

This commentary focuses on the investment-management phase. It summarizes the key lessons learned and challenges ahead deriving from the practical experiences of those Latin American countries that have implemented a pension scheme based on privately managed individual accounts (see Grandolini and Cerda 1998; and "Latin American Pension Systems" 1998).

Any PRA system must be practical and workable, but its ultimate objective is to maximize returns. To achieve this objective, four general themes are highlighted by the Latin American experience. First is the *critical importance of good governance* to establish the proper balance of accountabilities and ensure the most appropriate overall investment strategy. The importance of educating the members of the oversight committee, given their key role in setting investment policy, must also be emphasized. In fact, finance theory, historical data, and empirical studies stress the critical importance of the investment-policy-setting process, particularly the asset-allocation decision. Approximately 90 percent of investment performance appears to result from the asset-class decision and the policy weights assigned to each eligible asset class. In U.S. plans, the trend is toward increasing allocation to riskier assets (i.e., equities) and toward more sophisticated choices for individual investors within 401(k)s.

Second, on the theory and practice of *strategic asset allocation and risk management,* one critical—and often overlooked—fact is that the investment- and funding-policy process for defined-benefit (DB) and defined-contribution (DC) plans is the same. DC plans also have a target replacement rate—albeit implicit and intermediate. This remains true even if the ownership of the liability is different—the sponsor in DB plans and the individual in DC schemes. In terms of risk management, the focus should be on the liability structure. The probability of not achieving the desired ratio of assets to liabilities is the most important risk for both schemes. Hence, even within a DC environment—which is the overall direction of the Latin American pension reforms—the risk of the plan should not be analyzed only in terms of the volatility of asset returns.

Third, in terms of *performance management,* two areas are key. The importance of setting appropriate benchmarks for asset and risk management and the need to focus on after-fee returns and increase the use of decision-based performance-attribution analysis. Finally, regarding the *optimal degree of flexibility of investment guidelines,* in the Latin American context there appears to be a consensus that, in the initial stages of a pension reform shifting to private management of mandatory social security contributions, it is appropriate to implement limited portfolio choices— particularly in terms of exposure to equities and foreign securities. However, there also seems to be agreement that these constraints should be relaxed and investment choices expanded as participants' financial education increases.

The main challenges in the investment-management area currently faced by PRAs in the Latin American context include the following seven policy themes, several of which appear to be relevant for the design of a practical and workable system of PRAs in the United States as well, a system that can also deliver appropriate after-fee returns: strengthening of the governance structure of the reformed systems; bringing to the forefront of the debate the most appropriate division of labor in setting the strategic asset allocation among the regulators, the investment-management industry, and the affiliates; ensuring the continued flexibility of the regulatory system to ensure timely response to changing market conditions, particularly, deemphasizing maximum and minimum investment limits, expanding eligible asset classes, and allowing/increasing diversification in foreign securities; developing performance-presentation standards (incorporating risk and not focusing only on return); reducing the administrative costs of the system; continuing efforts at enhancing disclosure; and focusing on the education of the participants in the system (both those in charge of oversight and the individual affiliates), particularly in the areas of risk and the need for a longer-term horizon in decision making and in judging performance.

References

Grandolini, G., and L. Cerda. 1998. *The 1997 pension reform in Mexico.* Policy Research Working Paper no. 1933. Washington, D.C.: World Bank, June.
Latin American pension systems: Investing for the 21st century. 1998. Seminar organized by the Investment Management Department and the Economic Development Institute, World Bank, Washington, D.C.

2

Administering a Cost-Effective National Program of Personal Security Accounts

Sylvester J. Schieber and John B. Shoven

In the debate about social security reform, many people today are either advocating or considering options that would have individuals accumulate some of their retirement savings through personal accounts. Among the issues that repeatedly arise in the discussion of these reform options are the administrative feasibility and the cost of such an approach to social security reform. For example, the recently released report of the National Academy of Social Insurance on privatizing social security raises the issue directly. It notes that "Dallas Salisbury does not think than [*sic*] an individual account system for over 140 million workers, with less than an 18 to 24 month lag in account recording, is feasible at acceptable administrative costs in the absence of new technological developments, including moving 5.5 million small employers from paper filing to automated filing" (NASI 1998, n. 21). In an analysis of the Chilean retirement system, Peter Diamond (1996, 217) raises the question of whether an individual account system "is desirable, because compulsory savings are less attractive when costs are eating up a large fraction" of the savings.

In this paper, we investigate these issues. In section 2.1, we look at how various defined-contribution plans are administered around the world. In section 2.2, we focus on the cost of administering these plans. In section 2.3, we lay out a possible administrative structure for implementing an efficient individual accounts program in the United States and make some

Sylvester J. Schieber is vice president of Watson Wyatt Worldwide. John B. Shoven is the Charles R. Schwab Professor of Economics at Stanford University and a research associate of the National Bureau of Economic Research.

The authors thank Michael Maxwell, Lisa Steinberg, Michael Weddell, and Louis Valentino, all of Watson Wyatt Worldwide, for their help and comments. The analysis and conclusions presented here are the authors'.

ballpark estimates for the cost of such a system. Finally, we address the issue of whether the administrative-structure and cost issues are sufficiently daunting to preclude further consideration of partial privatization of social security in the United States.

2.1 Administering Individual Account Plans

Defined-contribution (DC) plans have been popular as employer-sponsored plans in the United States for years. They have become increasingly prevalent here and elsewhere around the world over the last few decades. In recent years, DC plans have also become a popular vehicle for reforming national retirement systems. We first look at how DC plans have been organized in three countries as part of their nationally mandated retirement-income-security systems. Then we look at how DC plans are organized in the United States as part of our employer-based retirement system. The purpose of this survey is to explore what is feasible by examining what is already in place in various countries, including our own.

Chile is often considered to be the preeminent example of a country that moved from a defined-benefit (DB) retirement system to a mandated retirement-saving program. Since 1981, all covered Chilean workers have been required to contribute 10 percent of their monthly earnings to a savings account for retirement purposes. These contributions must be invested through a highly regulated set of intermediaries known as *administradoras de fondos de pensiones* (AFPs). Workers can choose which of the AFPs they want to use for investments, but they can invest through only one at a time. Each of the AFPs can manage only one retirement portfolio, and there is a strict separation required between that fund and others offered by the management firm. The AFP allocates the returns on the investment funds to the individual accounts. At retirement, workers can choose either to buy an annuity or to take periodic distributions designed to last a lifetime. In addition to the retirement benefits, the AFPs also provide a system of survivors and disability benefits. These latter benefits and the administrative costs of the system are financed by an additional contribution of 3 percent of pay (Edwards 1998).

Australia has traditionally had a means-tested old-age pension system that provides a flat benefit to the elderly. The level of benefits is approximately 25 percent of average weekly wages. During the 1980s, concerns arose about the cost of Australia's old-age pension system owing to the high rate of qualification for benefits. Fully 81 percent of the elderly were qualifying for some benefits under the program, and two-thirds qualified for full benefits. Australia has a baby boom generation similar in relative size to that in the United States. The prospect of Australia's baby boomers approaching retirement age sparked an interest in finding an alternative means of providing retirement-income security in the future. Today, approximately 15 percent of the population of Australia is over age sixty-five, and this segment of the population is expected to grow to 23 percent by 2030. While the evolving demographics of the society posed a problem for the finances of the old-age pension system, at the same time there was a concern that only 40 percent of the workforce were covered by voluntary employer-sponsored superannuation systems.

The government had stuck its toe in the water of a mandated savings plan in the mid-1980s as part of a mandatory wage-negotiation process between employers and the Australian Council of Trade Unions (ACTU). The ACTU was negotiating for a 6 percent general wage increase in 1986. The government was concerned about the potential inflationary consequences of such a wage increase and managed to strike a compromise with the ACTU. It granted a 3 percent wage increase but prevailed on the unions to accept the remaining 3 percent as a contribution to retirement funds for workers. As a result of this agreement, contributions to individual accounts were gradually introduced into wage contracts as they were renegotiated. The payments went into existing superannuation funds or into newly created union funds that were managed by private asset-management firms.

In 1991, the Australian government announced that it intended to expand this initial program of mandated retirement saving. The Superannuation Guarantee Charge Act of 1992 was adopted and implemented in July 1992. The act required employers to contribute to complying superannuation funds a specified percentage of earnings on behalf of employees. The initial contribution rate was 3 percent of pay. In 1997 and 1998, the required contribution was 6 percent of pay and, in 1999, 7 percent. In 2001, it will be set at 8 percent and, in 2003 and after, at 9 percent of pay. One of the intended benefits of the new system has already begun to materialize. Workers' reliance on the state for retirement security appears to have declined sharply as the system has been implemented. The Research Unit of the Association of Superannuation Funds of Australia estimates that voluntary contributions made on top of mandated contributions equal an average of 4 percent for all employees covered by compulsory superannuation. This second pillar of the retirement system (the mandated pensions) will not eliminate the first pillar of the system (the old-age pension program) for workers who fare badly in the labor market throughout much of their career but should eliminate the dependence on it over time for the majority of workers.

There are several types of superannuation funds offered through the second pillar of Australia's retirement system. They include corporate or enterprise funds provided by single employers or groups of firms that band together for efficiency purposes. There has been a decline in such employer-based plans in recent years with a growth in industry funds or retail master trusts. The industry funds are often sponsored by employer and employee organizations. These were developed primarily in response to the establishment of the original 3 percent contribution agreements that got the whole ball rolling in the mid-1980s. From the outset, the industry funds followed a policy of contracting out all services—that is, administration, provision of death and disability coverage, and, most important, investment services. The trusteeship of the industry funds was from an early stage shared between equal numbers of employee (union) and employer representatives, with an independent chairman. Some plans for individuals and small firms are invested through retail funds offered principally by the large financial institutions. These accounts can come in the form of master trusts, personal superannuation products, rollover products, and allocated pension and annuity products. Another class of funds, known as *excluded* funds, is used mainly by individuals or family groups of one to four members. Recently, these funds have witnessed rapid growth because of tax incentives favoring their establishment. Finally, this line of funds includes superannuation products offered directly by life insurance companies and banks. For workers in the public sector, public plans established by federal, state, and local governments provide coverage. Like many similar plans worldwide, these are largely unfunded. The distribution of assets and the number of plans within each specific category are shown in table 2.1.

The whole mandated second-tier retirement system in Australia has been organized to take advantage of the structure of financial institutions and retirement systems already in place. Other than the funds that are offered to individuals, virtually all the investment of the superannuation accounts now takes place in an environment of pooled funds. The Australian Prudential Regulatory Authority (APRA) estimated that, in June 1998, the asset allocation in superannuation funds was 7 percent in cash and deposits, 28 percent in fixed-income holdings, 37 percent in equities, 8 percent in direct properties, and 16 percent in international funds.

The United Kingdom has a two-tier public retirement system with voluntary employer-sponsored pensions as the third tier. The first tier of the U.K. system is the basic state pension, a floor old-age benefit that retirees qualify to receive on the basis of the length of their career. The second tier of the U.K. system is called the supplemental earnings-related pension scheme (SERPS). The government allows workers to opt out of this second tier of the system, and about 83 percent do so. Workers are required to use employer-based pensions or personal pensions if they opt out of the state-provided system. The SERPS program establishes the minimum benefits or contributions that must be provided for/by workers who opt out of the state program. For the most part, workers who contract out of SERPS are required to annuitize their accumulation at retirement (Budd and Campbell 1998).

In the United Kingdom, about two-thirds of the workers who have

Table 2.1   **Profile of Australian Superannuation Funds as of 31 December 1997**

	Total Assets, December 1997		Total Number of Funds, June 1997		Number of Accounts, December 1997	
	$Billions (Australian)	Distribution (%)	Number	Distribution (%)	Millions	Distribution (%)
Corporate	64.7	20.5	4,277	3.38	1.4	8.0
Industry	21.5	6.7	116	0.08	5.5	30.9
Public sector	74.6	23.6	122	0.09	2.8	16.0
Retail	79.9	24.4	319	0.31	7.8	43.4
"Excluded"	38.4	11.7	157,084	96.14	0.3	1.7
Balance of statutory funds	46.6	13.1	N.A.		N.A.	
Total	325.7	100.0	161,918	100.00	17.7	100.0

Source: Insurance and Superannuation Commission Bulletin (Australian Insurance and Superannuation Commission), December 1998, 30.
Note: N.A. = not available.

contracted out of SERPS are covered by occupation pension programs run by employers, and the remainder are covered by personal pension plans. The personal plans are DC plans. All the employer-based plans had to be DB plans until legislation adopted in 1986 allowed those in occupation plans to be covered by a DC plan. Employer plans in the United Kingdom are going the same route today as their counterparts in the United States; namely, they are shifting to DC plans. Larger plans are typically self-administered, with the assets being managed by the plan itself or through insurance companies. Smaller plans are typically insured. Personal pension investment can be handled through a wide range of providers, including insurance companies, building societies, unit trusts, and other financial organizations. There are few restrictions on how the assets in the plans can be invested (Budd and Campbell 1998).

Sweden has recently adopted a set of sweeping reforms to its national retirement system that, when fully phased in, will provide retirement benefits purely from a DC environment. Their old plan was a pay-as-you-go DB plan. People born in 1937 and earlier will receive their pension under the old system. For those born between 1938 and 1953, part of the retirement benefit will be based on the old system and part on the new. Those born in 1954 and later will receive benefits purely under the new system.

Sweden's revised retirement system requires contributions of 18.5 percent of pay on earnings up to $37,000 per year. Of that, 16 percentage points are used to finance current benefit payments to retirees. The extra 2.5 percentage points are contributed to a "premium reserve account." Workers' contributions under the pay-as-you-go element of the new system are credited to individual accounts on the basis of each individual worker's earnings level and taxes paid. The account is also credited with an interest accrual each year that is equal to the rate of growth of incomes in the economy. Since the contribution is actually spent to finance current benefits, these accounts are phantom or "notional" accounts in that they do not hold real investments. At retirement, a worker's individual account will be converted to an indexed annuity. The index is the average income growth in the economy. The size of the initial annuity will be based on the life expectancy of the birth cohort to which the worker belongs and his or her age at retirement.[1]

Under the Swedish reforms, the worker can choose an investment manager for his or her premium reserve account. Under this system, capital management is to take place through independent fund managers. The Premium Pension Authority (PPA) is to be a unitholder in the funds where the assets are invested, but it is the individual worker who chooses the investment manager and how to invest the money. The assets can be in-

---

1. The Swedish reforms are described at http://www.pension.gov.se/in%20English/ summary.html.

vested in domestic securities funds or in foreign funds managed by fund managers with the right to do business in Sweden according to the Swedish Mutual Funds Act. A national fund company is also being set up to manage funds where the worker does not make an active choice of fund manager. This will be a special fund of the National Swedish Pension Fund and will be managed by a newly established fund board.

The PPA will approve the fund managers that can offer management services. Approval will require agreeing to cooperate with the PPA on setting up mechanisms for transmitting information and funds between the manager and the PPA. The PPA will also place a cap on the price of management services. The managers will be expected to adapt to the technical solutions adopted by the PPA regarding communications and the transmission of information on participants, funds, and so forth. The fund managers will be required to provide brochures explaining the funds to investors periodically and to make such information available to potential investors on request. There are to be no withdrawal charges for taking periodic distributions from the funds on retirement. Each year, the fund managers are to provide the PPA with a report on all costs associated with the fund's management. These reports from all the funds will be summarized by the PPA and made available to the public annually. It is anticipated that all the approved plans will be managed on an indexed basis.[2]

Until the early 1980s, the assets in employer-sponsored DC plans in the United States typically were held in pooled trusts, and each participant in the plan was credited with his or her vested pro rata share of the pool. During this era, the vesting periods could last as long as ten years. Because of this lengthy vesting period, significant amounts of the money in the plans at any point in time were not yet the property of the individuals to whom they had been credited. Today, employee contributions to 401(k) plans, according to law, vest immediately; 90 percent of the plans vest some part of the employer contribution within one year; and a significant majority have full vesting within five years of service. This change in "ownership" of the assets in the plan has been accompanied by a change in the management of the assets as well. With the evolution of 401(k) plans during the 1980s, sponsors of DC plans increasingly offered participants the opportunity to direct the investment of their retirement accounts. Today, virtually all participants in 401(k) plans have some discretion in the investment of the assets in their accounts.

The Employee Retirement Income Security Act (ERISA) is the major piece of legislation regulating employer-sponsored retirement plans in the United States. It requires that fiduciaries of benefit plans discharge their investment responsibilities prudently, including diversifying plan invest-

---

2. The operation of the PPA is described at http://www.pension.gov.se/in%20English/fundmana.html.

ments to minimize the risk of large losses. If these duties are breached, the fiduciary is liable to the plan for losses. ERISA, however, includes an exception to this provision in section 404(c), which states that, where participants can direct their own investments, the plan fiduciaries are not liable for any loss or breach that results from the participant's exercise of control. In the late summer of 1987, the Department of Labor released preliminary regulations under section 404(c) detailing rules under which employers could hand off some of the fiduciary obligations for managing DC-plan assets.

The precipitous decline in U.S. stock prices during October 1987 raised a number of fiduciary issues for plan sponsors still managing their DC-plan portfolios. For example, many plans at that time calculated the value of distributions on the basis of the last valuation date of assets in the plan prior to a worker's termination. Many valuations were done on a quarterly basis. Plans whose valuation dates coincided with the end of a calendar quarter were in the position of paying individuals who terminated prior to the end of 1987 considerably more than the value of their account at the date of termination. Paying someone terminating on 31 October 1987 the value of his or her account on the basis of a 30 September 1987 valuation would further drain the value of the remaining portfolio for those workers who remained in the plan. Thus, in addition to the restructuring of retirement plans and the changing perception about ownership of plan assets, there were practical developments that encouraged plan sponsors to allow participants to direct their own investments.

The section 404(c) regulations were finalized by the Department of Labor in September 1992 and were somewhat less onerous than the proposed regulations had been. Section 404(c) requires that a plan allow participants to "exercise independent control" over the assets in their individual accounts. This means that the participant must be able to give investment instructions to a plan fiduciary, who must generally comply with them. In addition, the regulations require that sufficient information to make informed investment decisions be made available to participants in these plans. The regulations allow plans to restrict the frequency with which investment changes may be made but require that participants be able to give investment instructions with a frequency that is appropriate for the expected market volatility of the investment. The regulations outline general rules requiring that the available investment alternatives be sufficient to give the participant a reasonable opportunity materially to affect both the potential return on assets in his or her account and the degree of risk of the portfolio. The regulations require that the participants be able to choose from at least three investment alternatives. This diversification requirement means that an employer's own securities cannot be one of the three investment options required to meet the minimum amount of choice, but, once a plan sponsor has provided three diversified options, the plan sponsor's own securities can be offered as an added option. Of the three required choices to meet the standard, each has to have materially different risk and return characteristics. Overall, the participant must be able to minimize risk through diversification across the investment choices offered. In return for setting up the 404(c) plan, the sponsor is not liable to participants for any loss or breach of fiduciary responsibility that results from the participant's exercise of control.

The evolution of this system in recent years has resulted in the typical plan participant being offered at least five to eight investment options into which savings can be directed. These would typically include a money market fund, a bond fund, a general equity index fund, and, possibly, a couple of more-segmented equity funds, often including an international equity fund. Most workers allocate their contributions and balances across more than one of the funds offered to them. Under most of these plans today, workers can check the balances and reallocate contributions and balances on a daily basis using automated voice-response systems. Those not offering such high-technology capabilities typically allow workers to reallocate balances either monthly or quarterly and give corresponding statements of accumulated funds.

2.2   The Cost of Administering Individual Account Systems

The prevalence of individual account retirement systems of various types around the world and in the United States makes it difficult to argue that we could not organize an individual accounts–based social security reform in this country. A second objection to this type of social security reform is that, even if we could devise a system to administer individual accounts, the costs associated with running such a system would absorb much of the added efficiency that would result from the reform itself.

Peter Diamond (1996, 215–16) estimates that, in 1991, Chile's per capita administrative costs for its national retirement system were 2.5–12.5 times those of the U.S. social security system. This follows from an estimate that the U.S. system costs were an average of $18.70 per person and that Chile's were $89.10. The 2.5–12.5 times ratios come from a rough estimate of the costs applied across contribution or account balances that would be held by workers with low versus high earnings rates. While the difference in costs in the two systems is notable, on its own Diamond's observation does not tell us much. Certainly, the inference with which he leaves us is that Chile's system is quite inefficient. On the other hand, he does not compare the rates of return in the two systems. Nor does he consider the possibility that social security in the United States is being administered at a level that is so inexpensive because people are not getting adequate levels of service from its administrators. Certainly, the latter is a prospect that Robert J. Myers (1992, 16), the former chief actuary of the system, has raised.

Sebastian Edwards (1998, 45) estimates that, in 1983, Chile's costs were about 15 percent of total accumulated balances at the time. But, by 1993, they had dropped to 1.8 percent of total assets. While the earlier figure is clearly not one that anyone would want to see sustained in a retirement system, it was drawn from the start-up period of Chile's individual accounts system. A system such as Chile's has a significant component of fixed costs. Such costs would generally be significantly higher relative to assets during the start-up phase than they would be once the system matured. Olivia Mitchell (1993, 409) observes that, by the early 1990s, the cost of the private account system in Chile on an active contributor basis was about the equivalent of the cost of its public social security system still in operation. On a total contributor basis, the private account system was only about two-thirds as expensive as the public system. So the private systems are not necessarily more expensive than public DB programs, even in Chile.

Even though Mitchell's observations about the relative costs of Chile's public social security system and its individual accounts system suggest that the latter is not necessarily less efficient, the prospect of a system costing 1.8 percent of total assets per year is not very reassuring. In his work on the cost of the Chilean system, Peter Diamond (1996, 216–17) points to the marketing costs associated with a system targeted at individual investors as possibly being responsible for the high administrative costs. He notes, for example, that, in the United States, the costs of mutual funds directed toward individuals are about three times those directed toward groups and those handling large accounts. Citing research on the relative costs of the Chilean and Australian systems, he notes that nearly 36 percent of the costs of the Chilean AFPs are attributed to marketing, compared to between 3.2 and 6.4 percent of the Australian funds' costs.

Other than the funds that are offered directly to individuals in Australia, virtually all the investment of the Australian superannuation accounts now takes place in an environment of pooled funds. Certainly, compared to Chile, Australia appears to have a cost-effective system of retirement funding based on the twin elements of mandating contributions and a large number of superannuation accounts being offered on a group basis through industry funds. The Association of Superannuation Funds of Australia ("Administration Costs $4.40" 1998) estimates that the average administrative costs of their system equal $4.40—that is, U.S. $2.85—per member per week. In U.S. currency terms, at this rate administrative costs for a system that held average balances of $1,000 would be nearly 15 percent of assets per year. For a system that held average balances of $5,000, the cost would drop to 3 percent per year. For one that held average bal-

Table 2.2   **Administrative Costs as a Percentage of Assets under Management in Australian Individual Account Superannuation Funds during 1996 and 1997**

Number of Members in the Plan	1996	1997
1–99	.689	.619
100–499	.849	.673
500–2,499	.803	.797
2,500–9,999	.854	.837
10,000 or more	.922	.846
Total	.900	.835

Source: Australian Bureau of Statistics, Belconnen, Australian Capital Territory, tabulations of a joint quarterly survey conducted by the Australian Bureau of Statistics and the Australian Prudential Regulation Authority.

ances of $10,000, administrative costs would be 1.5 percent per year. By the time average account balances got to be $30,000, administrative costs would be under 0.5 percent per year. This pattern is important because it reflects the pattern of accumulating balances in a retirement system like Australia's as it is being phased in, as Australia's is now.

The costs of the system as a percentage of accumulated funds should be falling with the growth in the funds over the implementation period, as they clearly did in Chile. The administrative costs stated as a percentage of funds under management in Australia's individual account system for 1996 and 1997 are shown in table 2.2. The expenses reported here include those associated with the administration of the accounts and the investment of the assets and other expenses related to running the system. It is somewhat surprising that smaller plans report lower expense rates than do larger plans. This may possibly reflect differences in communications or other services provided to participants in larger plans.

Two asides about the Australian system should be mentioned. First, there has been a growing interest in allowing workers somewhat more choice in the system than they have at the present time. So far, the discussion has focused more on choices of vendors than on choices of alternative segments of the financial market, similar to what American 401(k) participants typically enjoy. Second, the tax treatment of mandated superannuation savings in Australia is punitive. Contributions are made with posttax earnings. Earnings on the funds are taxed at the point at which they are earned. Finally, benefits are taxed when received. No plan for the U.S. pension or social security system of which we are aware involves such heavy taxation. There are no comparable cost data, at least any of which we are aware, on the administration of retirement plans in the United Kingdom. One of the problems with the U.K. system that has received widespread attention is the so-called misselling scandal. From the establishment of the SERPS program in the late 1970s, workers could contract out of the second tier of the national retirement program. Originally, however, the only way to contract out of the SERPS was to be an active participant in an "occupation" retirement plan—that is, an employer- or union-sponsored plan. In 1988, the government allowed contracting out into personal pension plans. A number of life insurance companies began selling what are called *rebate only* pensions and other insurance products to set these up. The rebate only plans accept only the government's national insurance rebates given to fund the benefits of those contracting out of the SERPS. They will not take any additional contributions.

Insurance agents began selling these products in the late 1980s and early 1990s as an attractive alternative to the SERPS and to occupation plans where workers had previously contracted out of SERPS. By 1994, there was a government investigation of these personal plans (Securities and Investment Board 1994), which concluded that as many as 300,000 workers had been bid out of their occupation plans and had suffered losses because of bad financial advice, advice that was not in compliance with the Financial Services Act regulatory standards. Claims in the billions of pounds were pressed against the companies providing the plans because of the poor advice that was provided to workers in making their decision as to whether to go with a personal pension (*Financial Times,* 6 January 1996).

More recent analysis of personal plans in the United Kingdom suggests that the costs associated with personal pensions are highly variable and can potentially erode the full value of returns on investments over time (Budden 1997). The United Kingdom has taken a somewhat more laissez-faire attitude about regulating the providers of benefits to those who have contracted out of the SERPS than Australia has regarding its mandated savings program. The introduction of mandated superannuation in Australia in 1992 has resulted in relatively few consumer-protection issues being raised by policyholders. Committed to minimizing fraudulent activity or inappropriate conduct relating to the growing superannuation savings pool, the Australian federal government in 1987 bolstered consumer protection associated with this form of long-term saving. The Insurance and Superannuation Commission (ISC) was created in 1987 specifically to address some of the government's concerns about associated sporadic inappropriate selling of superannuation policies. Proactive regulation increased after the passage of the legislation establishing the current superannuation framework in Australia. Two of the major consumer issues with which the Australian government dealt in the early 1990s were the disclosure of key features linked with superannuation policies and the regulation of the selling practices of intermediaries who distribute such policies. The future approach toward disclosure, linked with superannuation, is summarized in the Australian Treasury (1997) statement that "it is highly desirable that a consistent and comparable disclosure regime for all financial instruments be developed. All financial instruments . . . will be subject to a requirement to disclose all relevant information to permit investors to make informed investment decisions" (p. 4).

The individual account system in Sweden is just getting organized, and no data are available at this time on the administrative costs that will be associated with it. Sweden has clearly opted for a system that is more regulated than that in the United Kingdom. Given that investments must be through index funds provided through licensed managers who must post their fees with the regulatory agency, the Swedish system is also going to be more regulated than either Australia's or Chile's.

Because the 401(k) system is voluntary in the United States, the regulatory authorities have not paid as much attention to administrative-cost reporting as have the corresponding authorities in Australia, which has a mandatory system. However, there are cost estimates for U.S. 401(k) plans. Access Research estimates that, in mid-1997, asset levels in 401(k) plans stood at approximately $865 billion and that the annual administrative fees for both record keeping and asset management for the year were $6.7 billion, or seventy-seven basis points—that is, 0.77 percent (Wuelfing 1997). This is similar to the charges levied against the Australian funds, which are also organized at the employer level.

The disclosure of tax-qualified plan operations that the government requires of plan sponsors requires reporting a range of plan costs, including the administrative costs charged to the plan. These do not include the asset-management charges. However, pure asset-management charges can be extraordinarily low (on the order of 0.01 percent) for indexed investment strategies. We have tabulated the administrative costs reported on the form 5500 tapes for 401(k) plans during 1995. Those results are shown in table 2.3. The table shows the mean and median administrative cost as a percentage of the average of beginning- and ending-year balances in the plans. We eliminated all plans that reported costs in excess of 200 percent of plan assets because we believed that there must be some reporting errors. We also eliminated all plans reporting zero administrative costs. In some cases, plan sponsors may be picking up the full cost of administering these plans, and it made little sense to include these plans in our tabulations. Finally, we included only plans that were at least three years old because we did not want to include plans that were still incurring substantial start-up costs. Including those plans did not radically change the results, but we were interested in seeing what plan costs would be in an ongoing environment.

From table 2.3, it is clear that there are substantial economies of scale related to various aspects of the administration of 401(k) plans. One should be careful in interpreting the costs among smaller plans because there were very few of them in the tabulation. In each of the two smallest size classes, there were twenty or fewer plans. And, in the size class twenty-

Table 2.3   Administration Fees in 401(k) Plans by Plan Size in 1995 Stated as a Percentage of the Total Assets in the Plan

Active Participants	Employer Subsidizes Administration		Plan Pays All Administration	
	Average	Median	Average	Median
1–10	0.701	0.223	1.852	0.445
11–25	1.100	0.780	1.372	0.982
26–50	2.840	0.471	1.360	0.863
51–100	0.529	0.296	0.907	0.682
101–250	0.436	0.201	0.763	0.557
251–500	0.422	0.202	0.716	0.487
501–750	0.332	0.161	0.613	0.405
751–1,000	0.375	0.180	0.462	0.314
1,001–5,000	0.302	0.145	0.343	0.176
5,001–10,000	0.276	0.106	0.291	0.148
10,001 or more	0.198	0.100	0.226	0.118

Source: Tabulations of the Department of Labor's form 5500 files.

six to fifty participants, there were fewer than forty in both cases. In addition to demonstrating economies of scale in plan administration, the table also suggests that there is considerable employer subsidization of the cost of running these plans. There are approximately three times as many plans where the employer is subsidizing some costs as where all costs are paid out of the plan.

There are some costs embedded in table 2.3 that would not likely occur in an individual account program created as an element of social security reform. First, we would not anticipate that the costs associated with processing loans under 401(k) plans would be relevant in a mandatory-savings program. The loan provisions in 401(k)s arise because of the voluntary nature of the plans. If people did not have a way to get access to their money in time of hardship, many would not participate voluntarily. Given that we are talking about a mandatory supplement to social security, this issue goes away. The second thing is that the trustee's fees and the record-keeping fees show tremendous economies of scale in other analyses of administrative costs associated with 401(k) plans. For example, record-keeping costs have been shown to drop below ten basis points per year, and trustees' fees have been shown to drop below one basis point for plans with as few as two thousand participants (HR Investment Consultants 1997). If we can devise a relatively efficient way in which to group workers into large systems, the costs of these functions can be even lower. Finally, the actual fees associated with money management in a national mandatory-savings program could be driven almost to zero. If we assume that they might be as high as fifteen basis points—that is, 0.15 percent of assets under management—the total cost of administering the system could be under twenty-five basis points. While this might seem optimistic to some, we note that it is possible to buy retail funds with annual costs at or below this level. We certainly believe that it is possible to devise a mass-scale system that would at least match what individual consumers can buy today.

One test regarding what fees might be for individual accounts is to look at the terms offered on retail products today. Table 2.4 shows six product offerings from three of the largest mutual fund companies in the United States. The table is not meant to be a comprehensive survey, but it does contain a selection of widely available, cost-effective ways in which to participate in financial markets. In all cases, the source of the information in the table is the 1998 prospectus of the fund. All the index fund products have total expenses under fifty basis points, and two have expenses under twenty basis points. Four of the funds charge small annual fees for accounts under $10,000. All have special low minimum initial investment amounts for IRAs, with four of them setting the amount at $500 and the other two at $1,000. One question that people who doubt the ability of the financial services sector to offer cost-effective social security individual accounts must answer is why offerings such as these are available in the IRA marketplace. All these products appear to offer inexpensive ways in which the holders of small accounts can participate in diversified portfolios. It is not clear why the costs of social security's individual accounts must be higher.

2.3 An Administrative Structure for Personal Security Accounts

In this section, we describe a cost-effective way of administering a system of individual accounts. This is meant, not as a proposal per se, but rather simply as a description of what elements are required to achieve cost effectiveness. The system is structured to give workers considerable control over the investment of their retirement funds. In that regard, it is different from legislative proposals that would create individual accounts but put government managers in charge of portfolio allocation. Giving workers some control over the investment of their assets may be important for at least three reasons. First, economic circumstances and tolerance for risk vary widely among American households. One size fits all never fits most people very well. Second, competitive markets tend to produce more efficient combinations of services and prices than do government programs. And, third, giving workers control or an active role in the investment of their retirement savings is likely to spur more retirement savings and more financial education, just as it has done in the 401(k) environment.

There are a number of issues that must be addressed in structuring a

Table 2.4   Sample of Cost-Effective Mutual Fund Products Available Today

	Description	Small Account Fee	Annual Total Expenses (%)	Minimum Initial Investment ($)	Minimum Initial IRA Investment ($)
Fidelity Spartan Market Index	S&P 500 Index Fund	$10 for assets < $10K	.19	10,000	500
Fidelity Asset Manager	Asset allocation with stocks and bonds	$12 for assets < $2,500	.77	2,500	500
Schwab 1000	1,000 largest market cap stocks	N.A.	.46	1,000	500
Schwab Total Bond Market Index Fund	Lehman Bros. Aggregate Bond Index	N.A.	.35	1,000	500
Vanguard Index Trust Small Cap	Russell 2000 Index Fund	$10 for assets < $10K	.23	3,000	1,000
Vanguard Index Trust 500	S&P 500 Index Fund	$10 for assets < $10K	.19	3,000	1,000

Source: The 1998 prospectus of the fund in question.
Note: N.A. = not applicable.

system of self-administered accounts at the national level. One overriding issue is whether the administrative system is appended to an existing government agency (i.e., the Social Security Administration [SSA]) or set up as a separate, quasi-government entity, such as the Federal Reserve Board. Another possibility would be to administer the program privately with government regulation in a manner similar to the way in which the Teachers Insurance and Annuity Association and College Retirement Equities Fund (TIAA/CREF) functions.

In the early part of the discussion about administrative approaches, we lay out the considerations, in very broad terms, for going one route or the other in resolving the issue of integrated or separate administration. Primary among these is the set of goals that should be met in structuring an administrative system for a national program of personal security accounts (PSAs). In addition, there are a number of practical issues that must be addressed in devising a system. These include such things as getting contributions from employers into individual accounts, record keeping, setting up a structure to allow workers to make investment choices and the choice of an investment manager, communicating the details of the program, controlling administrative costs, and the like. In the following discussion, we develop a step-by-step description of a system that would address most of these issues. After doing that, we return to the matter of whether the management of the system should be integrated with existing government agencies or set up independently.

2.3.1 Issues in Structuring an Administrative System for PSAs

Social security is a national program, and any program of mandatory PSAs would replace some part of the existing system on a national basis. To the extent that there would be some remaining element of social security, there would have to be coordination between the remaining system and any new mechanisms that would be put in place. Also, to the extent that there would continue to be payroll limits on contributions, there would have to be some centralized clearing of amounts earned and contributed across an extremely dynamic workforce and employer environment. This suggests that some sort of administrative entity would need to fill an oversight role. Some people conclude that the SSA should fill that role because it is already administering a national retirement system. While it is possible that the SSA could serve that role, its current activities and those for which it would be responsible in an individual account, retirement-wealth-accumulation system are significantly different.

One consideration in setting up the administrative structure for a PSA system is the extent to which the benefits provided by traditional social security and those provided by the PSA plan are directly intertwined. If the reform of social security includes benefit offsets under the current program that are based on benefit accumulations in the PSA accounts, it would likely make more sense to have the two systems fully integrated. If the reform of social security includes independent or supplementary PSA benefits, there is less reason for the administration of the two systems to be handled by the same agency. For now, we develop the concept of an administrative entity that we call *PSA Central.* The resolution of where it resides relative to government will be addressed later.

There are certain goals that can be stipulated regarding any administrative system. The first of these is that the system limit the burden on employers, especially small ones without sophisticated salary-administration systems and the staff to support cumbersome reporting requirements. Second, the system must meet the needs of a diversified public with regard to the security of the funds accumulated through the system, simplicity of operation, and ownership and control of accumulating wealth to the extent appropriate in the context of a nationally mandated retirement system. Third, the administrative structure should be reasonably easy to explain and navigate. Fourth, there should be limits on the concentration of wealth control in order to minimize the significant pressures to divert the system's assets to uses other than the efficient accumulation and securing of retirement income (see Jackson 1999; Romano 1993; Schieber and Shoven 1999; and World Bank 1994). Fifth, the system should be structured so as to keep administrative costs at reasonable levels and to distribute them fairly across the participant population.

The United States can learn from the Australian approach and design a system that takes advantage of the significant infrastructure that already exists for the collection of retirement contributions both through employers and through the SSA. The system could also take advantage of the infrastructure that already exists for the investment of retirement contributions in the financial markets. The system need not be organized to operate at the level of lowest efficiency of any participant in it. In fact, regulations could be implemented to require that the system be more cost effective than some of the more expensive 401(k) offerings in the marketplace. A reasonable goal would be to give workers control of their retirement accumulations in a regulated environment that aims for efficient management of the assets involved.

Regardless of whether PSA Central is organized within or outside government, it is possible to specify its administrative roles and functions in the operation of the PSA system. If it is organized within government, it might serve as a regulator as well as an administrator. If it is organized outside government, the regulatory function would continue to be fulfilled by a government agency. We are not addressing the role of the regulatory body in the development of the administrative system that is laid out here. Throughout the implementation of the system and its continuing operations, PSA Central would be responsible for all record keeping associated with the accumulation of individual accounts.

2.3.2 Depositing Contributions and Allocating
Them to Individual Accounts

Today, every employer required to withhold income tax from wages or liable for taxes under the Federal Insurance Contributions Act (FICA) must file a quarterly tax return using Form 941, unless the wages paid are for domestic service or agricultural labor. In the latter case, the tax return is filed annually on Schedule H with the employer's annual 1040 filing. Wage information is reported annually on W-2 forms. FICA returns and tax payments on form 941 are due on or before the last day of the month after the calendar quarter for which the return is filed. Deposits of accumulated taxes must be made more frequently. If an employer accumulates $100,000 or more of such taxes on wages paid, the taxes must be deposited the next banking day. Smaller employers are required to deposit either monthly or every two weeks. The actual requirement for a particular business depends on past tax liabilities. The determination is made by looking back over a twelve-month period each 30 June. Employers who reported a liability of $50,000 or less can deposit monthly. Those with a past liability of more than $50,000 report every two weeks.

Following the process that is now used in filing payroll taxes, the quarterly filing of form 941 occurs by 30 April, 31 July, and 31 October in the year in which a worker's earnings are paid and on 31 January in the year following wages paid up through 31 December. By mid-January, the SSA begins receiving W-2 and W-3 statements from employers. In mid-February, it begins processing paper reports. In mid-March, it begins processing magnetic reports. In April of the year after wages are earned, the SSA begins mailing notices back to employers about unverified social security numbers and names. In mid-April, most of the self-employed file their individual tax returns with the IRS. In the May–June time frame, the SSA receives quarterly tax-return data from the IRS and simultaneously sends W-2 data to the IRS. The two agencies compare data and begin a reconciliation process. By 1 July of the year following the year in which wages were earned, 98 percent of magnetic reports are fully processed, and workers are credited with their past year's earnings. In the July–August time frame, the IRS sends SSA tapes for posting of self-employment earnings and earnings for domestic workers. By the end of September, 98.5 percent of both paper and magnetic reports are fully processed, and most workers are credited with their earnings from the past year. At this juncture, a reconciliation process of the remaining open cases begins. This process stretches out until April of the third year after the year in which an affected worker's wages were earned.

In the start-up phase of a PSA system, payroll contributions would continue to be collected the same way they have been in the past. As workers' earnings records are posted electronically at the SSA, they would be transmitted to PSA Central. Once PSA Central has the earnings records, it would allocate contributions to workers' accounts. The allocation process is described in the next section. Before turning to that, however, it is important to note that, during the initial phase of the system, actual allocation of roughly 98 percent of all workers' contributions could take place within nine months after the close of a calendar year. For some workers, that means that, if contributions made in January of one year are not posted until nine months after the close of that year, some contributions will not be posted for twenty or more months after they are made. In the electronic age in which we live, that will be unacceptable to many workers.

After getting initial operations up and running, PSA Central could develop an alternative mechanism for reporting workers' earnings. Essentially, any employer willing to file monthly wage-earnings records electronically would be allowed to do so. Virtually all employers who have DC systems are already compiling and filing this information with administrators of their plans. Many other employers using widely available salary-administration systems could also provide this information with little effort and small marginal costs. PSA Central would reconcile monthly filings after the end of the year with the complete electronic filings that it receives from the SSA as it goes through its normal wage posting. For those workers who have their monthly earnings reported, PSA Central would allocate contributions to their individual accounts on a monthly basis. This policy would undoubtedly arouse employee pressure on those employers not reporting wages on a monthly basis to do so. Such market-based pressure for improved efficiency on the part of employers could be beneficial for the economy as a whole.

For workers with multiple jobs over a year whose covered earnings reach the maximum level of taxable earnings, their additional contributions would be held in a suspense account invested in government bonds. As these workers file their annual tax returns for the year, their excess contributions would be returned to them as a tax refund, just as they are today. If a worker in this category earns a part of his or her annual wages through an employer reporting on a monthly basis and part through an employer reporting under current procedures through the SSA, the part reported on a monthly basis would be treated as first earnings for allocation purposes. The excess from the SSA allocation process would be the source of refund to the worker after the end of the tax year.

2.3.3 Investing the Funds in the Individual Accounts

At the outset of a PSA program, as payroll-tax contributions are deposited with the government, the share that would ultimately be invested in individual accounts could be segregated and invested in a government bond account and immediately begin to accrue interest. Allocation of PSA funds into individual accounts could be done at the same time that wage records are posted with relatively low marginal administrative expense. The share of the fund representing records that have not been fully reconciled at any point could remain in the government bond fund as the remainder of the reconciliation process is completed. As outstanding cases are resolved, the fund could be allocated to the appropriate individual accounts.

This process does raise a slight equity issue in that someone who worked only in January of a year earning $10,000 would be credited exactly the same rate of interest on his or her contributions as someone who worked only in December of the year earning $10,000. The equity issues raised because of the inability actually to post wages on a month-to-month basis under current operating procedures are relatively trivial relative to a wide range of other equity issues that exist in the current system. While this situation is not optimal, it is the price to be paid for not imposing new administrative burdens on employers not willing to file wage records on a monthly basis.

It would facilitate the implementation of a PSA program and be more efficient if the administrative structure of the system was evolutionary. There could be two major phases to this evolution, with the second one proceeding for some substantial period of time. In other words, we do not see the evolution as being two discrete steps, with the full evolution of the system being completed at the time of the move to the second step. In the first phase of the evolution of the administrative system, PSA Central would create a limited set of funds that workers could designate for the investment of their contributions under the PSA system. These would be structured to encourage minimal administrative and investment costs. They would also be structured to facilitate workers' understanding and efficient utilization of the system. It would give those with considerable experience in self-directed investment the opportunity to choose among asset classes and diversify risk. But it would also offer a limited environment to navigate for those without investment experience.

Consider a system that initially offered six funds: a money market fund, a government bond fund, a corporate bond fund, a broad domestic large-cap equity index fund, a broad domestic small-cap equity fund, and an international equity fund. The Board of Governors of PSA Central would put out a request for proposals (RFP) to the investment-management community to manage funds in each of these asset classes. A group of managers will be chosen in each category on the basis of their proposed investment strategy in a given asset class and on the basis of their charges. Some minimum number of managers will be chosen to manage each class of assets. Having multiple managers in each area will, over time, encourage efficiencies that arise out of competition. Such a policy will also preclude the necessity of completely replacing the sole investment manager handling one particular class of investments with another. New investment managers could be added over time with the periodic solicitation of vendors that could replace existing vendors if they could offer more efficient investment services.

For the participant in the plan, this mode of operation would allow selection across a broad range of asset classes but would simplify the amount of information that would be required actually to direct the investment of PSAs. Having multiple vendors would minimize the concentration of assets in the hand of any individual investment manager or under the direct control of the managers of PSA Central. The investment fees under the system should be extremely low because the structure of the system would encourage broad ownership of a class of assets and minimal churning of particular assets within the class. Record keeping should be quite efficient because of the economies of scale that can be realized from a large system, as we have shown earlier.

In the second phase of evolution of PSA Central, individual fund managers would be able to offer a family of funds to individual workers. Their fund offerings would parallel those initially offered by PSA Central. Each fund manager in the system would have to offer a full range of funds. Although many managers would likely manage assets in the full range of asset classes included, some might offer several of the classes and contract with other managers to manage the others. Workers would be restricted in their ability to shift the management of their funds from the PSA Central group of funds to individual managers on the basis of their account balances. The limits on being able to move to individual managers might be set at $1,000, $5,000, $10,000, or some other reasonable level. No individual worker would be allowed to have his or her fund invested with more than one manager at a time. Fund managers would be chosen to enter the system on the basis of an RFP process that would focus on investment strategy within each class of funds, security, and fees for asset management.

It is possible that some entirely new groups of fund managers might arise under this approach, somewhat along the lines of the Australian experience. For example, it is likely that organizations like the AFL-CIO, or even one of its affiliate members, might organize a set of funds to offer to union members or contract with an existing fund-management company to do so. Such a fund might actually pursue investment policies that would serve its clientele's preferences—for example, avoiding investing in anti-union companies. The pursuit of such policies would be permitted as long as the equity fund offered under this manager was broadly diversified across the total range of assets in the economy and structured to operate efficiently. Over time, if it was deemed desirable, additional funds might be offered. The funds going to individual managers would still be flowing to those managers on a pooled basis. All record keeping would still be performed through PSA Central.

For the participant in the plan, this mode of operation would allow selection among a broad range of both asset classes and asset managers. Not implementing this phase until the system has been operating for a couple of years will give workers time to become familiar with the process of making their own investment choices. Requiring that workers have a minimum balance will also increase the likelihood that workers have had some time and experience dealing with choice in the base system. The investment fees under the system should remain low because the structure of the system would still encourage broad ownership of each class of assets and minimal churning of particular assets. Record keeping should continue to be efficient because it would still be centrally operated.

2.3.4   Worker Allocation of Funds

Initial allocation of workers' assets to particular funds could be accomplished in several ways. After wage records are posted and the initial allocation of funds to individual workers is accomplished, workers would make their individual investment choices. The three media that are used for doing this in 401(k) and similar plans are paper-based systems, voice-response systems, and Internet systems. It should be possible for the PSA plans to use all three of these media. Information relevant to workers' choices would be distributed through employers.

One of the questions that would have to be addressed at the outset is how frequently workers would be allowed to reallocate their assets in the system. The experience that Watson Wyatt Worldwide's consultants have had in the design, implementation, and administration of DC plans where workers direct the investment of the assets in them is that allowing workers the option of moving their money across funds on a daily basis actually results in fewer asset transfers than does allowing assets to be moved less frequently. Initially, the volume of work involved in start-up activities might preclude the option of allowing workers to move their assets daily. Ultimately, however, the value of giving workers true control of the investment of their assets and the fact that they exhibit more stable tendencies in the freer environment suggest that daily allocation is the best way to proceed.

Another question that must be addressed at the outset is how to invest the assets of workers who fail to allocate their own assets in the system. This is a policy question that may result in a wide range of answers. The point of this discussion is not to resolve all policy questions associated with a PSA system but to illustrate that such an administrative system can be developed that is both effective and cost efficient. The choices would seem to range from allocating nonresponsive workers' assets into one particular fund, probably the bond index fund, to allocating them on some pro rata basis across the range of funds. The latter approach might actually alter the pro rata distribution of assets on the basis of the age of the worker. This system would seem to accommodate the entire range of options or possibilities on an efficient basis.

2.3.5 Communicating about the System

During the start-up phase of the system, there would need to be a media campaign telling all workers about the implementation of the PSA system. Explanatory materials could be provided through all forms of news outlets, employers, the postal service, banks, churches, and other relevant community organizations. The asset-allocation materials would be distributed through employers. Presumably, the federal government has the names and addresses of all employers who are currently contributing payroll taxes for their workers, so this would seem to be the most direct way to get to workers. Indeed, going through employers was the mechanism used in 1936 to register workers for the assignment of the original set of social security numbers and resulted in significantly higher initial registration than had been anticipated (Schieber and Shoven 1999).

After the initial phase-in of the program, PSA Central would send workers periodic statements of their accounts. These statements would include information on contributions in the most recent period, including the allocation of contributions by asset class, returns earned in each case, total cumulative balances in each class of asset and in total, and rate-of-return information for relevant comparison periods. Participants could also gather such information through a voice-response system or the Internet.

As the second phase of the investment options open to workers is introduced, it is likely that some communications would come from fund managers offering investment services directly to individual workers. Under this phase of operations, when the worker calls with questions regarding his or her balances, the call would either go directly to the particular vendor—call it Investco—or be routed there through a call to PSA Central. Investco's service representatives would be plugged into the administrative-record database at PSA Central and would have access to all PSA records being managed by Investco.

At least once a year, PSA Central would mail participants in the PSA system a report on all the investment managers in the system. This report would break down the costs of administering the various elements of the system that were charged against the assets in the system. This would include specific charges related to administration and record keeping by PSA Central, communications costs, and asset-management fees charged by PSA Central for its fund offerings and those of each individual fund manager with individual accounts.

Under this structuring of the system, it is likely that asset-management fees will continue to be relatively low. Keep in mind that asset managers are not actually acquiring funds directly from individual workers. The money invested in their funds would flow to them on a pooled basis through PSA Central. If the individual managers' fees get to be too high, it is likely that workers would revert back to PSA Central. On the other hand, workers might be willing to pay somewhat higher management fees for using a particular investment manager because of the services provided. It would be possible to limit fund vendors' fees to such a level that the total administrative cost of the system, including all central administrative operations, is no more than one hundred basis points or some other reasonable level. Our expectation is that most vendors would offer services at cost rates well below such a ceiling. The fund manager would be required to report annually all costs associated with the operation of each of the funds offered and the returns on the fund. PSA Central would make this information available to the general public in a summary form through the news media and the Internet. Investco's call center would handle all queries about account balances, asset allocations, and the like for PSA balances being managed by Investco.

2.3.6   Paying Benefits to Participants

One of the other policy issues relative to the consideration of a PSA system is how benefits are to be distributed. In the case of retirement benefits, the issue is whether workers would be required to annuitize some or all of their PSA balance. Once again, the system can be structured to give policy makers maximum flexibility in choosing among the options available to them. Since PSA Central will have a full accounting of all account balances and where they are invested, it would be quite easy as a worker retires and begins to claim benefits to sequester a portion of the accumulation for the purchase of an annuity. Indeed, it is possible that PSA Central could provide participants in the system with a list of current annuity vendors and the pricing of their products on an easily comparable basis if annuities are to be offered through private markets. If they are offered through the government by the SSA, the necessary funds could be transferred from the PSA system into an indexed bond portfolio.

2.3.7   Start-Up Financing

Once a system similar to what we have described is up and running, its full costs of operations can be borne by the assets in the system. During the start-up phase, however, the government could appropriate the funds to put the system in place. The need for a system such as this is related to the goals of national government policies. The start-up phase of the system will create initial investment costs that can be thought of as national financial infrastructure.

2.3.8   The Location of PSA Central

Having outlined the functions of a central clearinghouse and record keeper for individual PSA accounts, it seems like a second-order matter whether PSA Central becomes an office within the SSA, another government office, or a private, regulated enterprise. Clearly, the details of any particular reform proposal might favor one location over another, but we can imagine the system working efficiently given any of the three arrangements.

2.3.9   Summary Comments

We have attempted to show that it is possible to design a system of individual accounts, or PSA accounts, that takes advantage of existing technology, systems, and approaches to providing retirement benefits. No employer would be forced to make payments through any new mechanisms or file any reports not already required by law. Employers could continue to file their tax payments and periodic reporting statements exactly as they do now. The SSA and the IRS can continue to conduct their processing exactly as they do now. The only point at which changes to the existing system would be required is that of allocating funds to specific accounts. But that is going to be required of any individual account system. The structure that we have outlined here should be highly efficient from an administrative point of view. In addition to individual account administration, sending money to trustees will require administrative and control mechanisms. But, if trustees can perform their functions for fractions of a basis point for a 401(k) with two thousand participants, PSA Central can certainly do the same for a system covering millions of workers.

The new internal record keeping of accounts at PSA Central would create some new activities for our national retirement system. But keeping the process essentially mechanical should minimize costs. PSA Central should be able to buy a record-keeping system almost virtually off the shelf to do the data processing required.

Under a system such as the one that we have described, employers, including small employers, would undoubtedly feel pressure from their workers to disclose workers' wages on a regular monthly basis. On the other hand, electronic reporting of payroll histories is highly desirable because it is the most efficient way to report such information. A by-product of partially privatizing social security could be a modernization of the way in which labor market information is communicated in this country. A system of the sort that we have described may require more communications than the system that we have now, at least to the extent that some workers today are not participating in voluntary contributory retirement plans. But the distribution of general materials required by the new system and the distribution costs should be relatively minuscule compared to the overall scope of matters under consideration. The government could develop financial education programs that it would run periodically on public broadcasting stations and encourage commercial stations to run those same programs as well.

2.4   How Important Are Administrative Costs?

To a certain extent, the opponents of individual account solutions to social security's financing problems have focused on administrative costs so intensively because this is an area where they perceive the current system has an advantage over the alternatives. The earlier observation (from Mitchell 1998) that this is not necessarily so notwithstanding, the current U.S. system is administered reasonably efficiently. But the administrative costs of a system are only one consideration in the discussion of the optimal means of providing retirement security to a broad cross section of the population.

Although the current social security system might be relatively efficient to administer, it has a number of other glaring inefficiencies. For example, Geanakoplos, Mitchell, and Zeldes (1998) estimate that at least a quarter of the current payroll tax is required essentially to pay interest on the unfunded liability of the system. The practical limits of a system financed on a pay-as-you-go basis cannot possibly provide workers a reasonable return given a relatively stable workforce and limited wage growth. There are those who are calling for the central funding of social security. But we have been unable to accomplish that for the last six decades. Even though Franklin Roosevelt was adamant that his social security be funded, repeated congressional action or inaction from the late 1930s through the mid-1950s disassembled his intentions. We slid into an unfunded pay-as-you-go system. Some people would have us believe that the accumulation of the trust funds since 1983 represents an increase in national saving, but that is highly questionable. At the same time as social security was raking up a surplus, the rest of the government was accumulating debt at an even faster pace.

The only way in which we can improve the lot of future workers under our current national retirement system is to raise national saving and begin to fund the system. We believe that a record of nearly sixty-five years of failing to do so under the current system suggests that there must be a better way. Central funding is not credible, and people are understandably reluctant to pay higher taxes with the promise of central fund saving. But individuals would be willing to contribute more to appropriately designed individual accounts. The administrative costs of such a system are probably higher than those of the current financially insolvent pay-as-you-go system, but the productivity benefits of a better-funded system outweigh the added costs. In this paper, we have tried to show that a cost-effective individual accounts system can be designed, particularly by piggybacking on systems already existing in our economy.

References

"Administration Costs $4.40." 1998. *Superfunds,* no. 218 (September): 16.

Australian Treasury. 1997. Financial markets and investment products—corporate law economic reform program proposals for reform. Paper no. 6. Canberra: Australian Government Printing Service.

Budd, Alan, and Nigel Campbell. 1998. The pension system in the United Kingdom. In *Privatizing social security,* ed. Martin Feldstein. Chicago: University of Chicago Press.

Budden, Robert. 1997. Rebate only pensions, money down the drain? *Money Management,* January, 46–53.

Diamond, Peter A. 1996. Social security reform in Chile: An economist's perspective. In *Social security: What role for the future?* ed. Peter A. Diamond, David C. Lindeman, and Howard Young. Washington, D.C.: National Academy of Social Insurance.

Edwards, Sebastian. 1998. The Chilean pension reform: A pioneering program. In *Privatizing social security,* ed. Martin Feldstein. Chicago: University of Chicago Press.

Geanakoplos, John, Olivia S. Mitchell, and Stephen P. Zeldes. 1998. Would a privatized social security system really pay a higher rate of return? In *Framing the social security debate,* ed. R. Douglas Arnold, Michael J. Graetz, and Alicia H. Munnell. Washington, D.C.: Brookings Institution Press.

HR Investment Consultants. 1997. *401(k) provider directory.* Baltimore.

Jackson, Jesse L., Sr. 1999. Oral statement before the Ways and Means Committee, House of Representatives, at a hearing on preserving and strengthening social security. 106th Cong., 1st sess., 21 January.

Mitchell, Olivia S. 1998. Administrative costs in public and private retirement systems. In *Privatizing social security,* ed. Martin Feldstein. Chicago: University of Chicago Press.

Myers, Robert J. 1992. Can the government operate programs efficiently and inexpensively? *Contingencies,* March/April, 15–17.

National Academy of Social Insurance (NASI). 1998. *Evaluating issues in privatizing social security.* Report of the Panel on Privatization of Social Security. Washington, D.C.

Romano, Roberta. 1993. Public pension fund activism in corporate governance reconsidered. *Columbia Law Review* 93, no. 4 (May): 795–853.

Schieber, Sylvester J., and John B. Shoven. 1999. *The real deal: The history and future of social security.* New Haven, Conn.: Yale University Press.

Securities and Investments Board (SIB). 1994. SIB announces programme to provide redress to people mis-sold personal pensions. Press release. London, October.

World Bank. 1994. *Averting the old age crisis.* New York: Oxford University Press.

Wuelfing, Robert G. 1997. Speech presented to the national conference of the Society of Professional Administrators and Recordkeepers, Washington, D.C., 23 June.

Comment   Olivia S. Mitchell

In policy matters, it is often said that the devil is in the details, and nowhere is this more true than in the current debate over how to reform the U.S. social security system. In their thought-provoking paper, Sylvester Schieber and John Shoven provide a substantial service by taking seriously some of the administrative details that need to be worked out in order to privatize part of the current social security system. They begin by showing how Chile and Australia worked to resolve structural design questions associated with individual accounts, and then they go on to show how a similar structure might function in the U.S. context. In this effort, they raise and address several questions that thoughtful observers recognize must be resolved before selecting a particular reform plan.

The four key tasks of a national old-age pension system are to collect taxes, to manage the money, to track participants, and to pay benefits.[1] Architects of a new system must therefore design mechanisms to handle each of these four tasks, and international experience shows that countries differ dramatically in how they have chosen to handle these tasks. Structure in turn affects the costs—and often the benefits—of the plan in question. On the tax-collection front, Schieber and Shoven indicate that it has proved fairly expensive to collect pension taxes using individual agents, as in Chile. By contrast, using a central collection authority (either a government or a union/employer model) can drive down collection costs, as in Australia and Mexico. On the money-management front, costs appear to decline with the size of the asset pool under management and tend to fall after a start-up period. Therefore, a low-cost design for an individual account plan would probably need to exploit scale economies and offer somewhat limited investment options, as in the U.S. Thrift Savings Plan.

Turning to record keeping, the third function of a pension plan, here, too, there are design choices. Tracking participants and their earnings appears to be less expensive when done centrally, as in Mexico's new individual accounts program, as compared to a system that relies on multiple

Olivia S. Mitchell is the International Foundation of Employee Benefit Plans Professor of Insurance and Risk Management and executive director of the Pension Research Council at the Wharton School of the University of Pennsylvania and a research associate of the National Bureau of Economic Research.

Opinions expressed in this comment are those of the author alone.

1. For further development of these themes, see Mitchell (1997, 1998a).

retirement-saving institutions.[2] Central record keeping is also appealing given the need to have regulatory oversight for individual account pensions. A national regulatory regime is now under construction in Britain that will stand in sharp contrast to the very complicated and (for many) confusing state of affairs in the United States. Mainly for historical reasons, the American approach to pension regulation is quite disperse: individual states regulate insurers, the U.S. Department of Labor oversees employer pension fiduciary responsibilities, the SEC supervises investment matters, and still other agencies (e.g., the IRS, the Pension Benefit Guaranty Corporation) have their own interests and exert additional sway over the pension environment. It would be inaccurate to levy on an individual accounts program all the costs of a much-needed pension regulatory reform, of course, but the need for systemic overhaul should be kept in mind when designing the new system.

The last and probably key function of an individual accounts pension system is the payment of benefits. It should be recognized that paying pension benefits is not a simple exercise since, in many reform proposals, individual account payouts must be integrated with a continuing pay-as-you-go old-age benefit guarantee. This has been true in Australia, as Schieber and Shoven note, and it is the case in virtually all the Latin American nations following the Chilean model for pension reform.[3] To the authors' credit, they devote serious attention to the underappreciated question of how the benefits are to be paid at retirement, whether they are to be accessible as a lump sum, how benefits will vary with years of service, benefit portability, and so forth.

On the payout front again, several choices need to be made, to many of which Schieber and Shoven correctly alert us. The annuity issue is, in my view, key. Some have argued that adverse selection in private insurance markets will rule out individual accounts since people might not be able to annuitize their accumulated funds. However, research shows that private insurance markets are likely to be able to meet the demand for individually purchased annuities and, indeed, even real (inflation-linked) annuities.[4] Additional evidence is available from the United Kingdom, where inflation-indexed annuities are required for a portion of old-age pension benefits. A related point—one not touched on by virtually any U.S. individual account reform plan—is how disability benefits are to be handled. For instance, if a worker is disabled, he will need to convert his individual account accumulations into a disability annuity, yet little discussion has

2. These comparisons are discussed in Mitchell (1998b).
3. For a review of the Latin American individual account plans, see Mitchell and Barreto (1997) and Barreto and Mitchell (1997).
4. Evidence that annuity markets in the United States could meet the demand for real annuities in an individual accounts system is offered in Brown, Mitchell, and Poterba (in press).

been conducted about how this is to take place. If disabled workers are left to decide whether they will annuitize their accounts, adverse selection might result when those facing shortened life spans take cash-outs and leave the remaining disabled group worse off. Examining the extent of this problem is an important area for future research that will have to be taken into account as reformers continue to shape specific proposals for individual accounts.

One subject that Schieber and Shoven mention but probably underemphasize is the fact that the current social security system needs to incur substantial modernization costs—even if an individual account system is not implemented. For instance, under the current OASDI program, earnings and contribution records take one to two years to be reconciled within the system, almost 15 percent of employers submit cumbersome paper rather than electronic records, and it is impossible to have earnings sharing between spouses since records are simply not kept this way. New institutions are needed to make it possible for employers and employees to benefit from the low-cost contribution, reporting, and disclosure mechanisms made possible by technological developments in the twentieth century. Once these new systems are built, the burden of adding investment options to social security would be relatively small and potentially dwarfed by the expected gains. Therefore, if the deferred-maintenance accounting were done properly, it is likely that the marginal cost of instituting individual accounts could be quite modest.

Meeting this modernization challenge will be expensive, and it is important to discuss how to spread the cost of modernizing social security across all the stakeholders—current retirees, current workers, and those in future generations. Most countries adopting individual accounts have forced a relatively short period for amortization of these costs, which in effect imposes modernization costs on workers at the time a new system is put in place. But other financing approaches could be compared, including one in which system-upgrade costs would be financed across cohorts other than current workers. To the extent that baby boomers already bear a substantial portion of the transition costs associated with the old pay-as-you-go system, there may be some support for spreading these costs more broadly.

Social security reform plans are debated by many who focus on the "big picture" with macroeconomic, generational, and political concerns. But, as noted at the outset, the details matter too, and they matter so much that Schieber and Shoven are absolutely correct to draw our attention to them. Indeed, it is not an exaggeration to say that design issues may be make-or-break propositions in the public arena. Most would agree that adding an individual account pillar to the U.S. old-age system will likely increase administrative costs, but it will also provide participants with a range of additional services, more opportunity to invest in diversified accounts, and a greater sense of ownership than under the current social security system, which confronts insolvency and uncertainty. And, as I have shown, the current system is in need of upgrading and will require a substantial investment to bring it in line with modern standards. Deferring the modernization of the social security system will inevitably raise the political—and probably the economic—costs of that modernization.

References

Barreto, Flavio A., and Olivia S. Mitchell. 1997. Privatizing Latin American retirement systems. *Benefits Quarterly* 13, no. 3:83–85.

Brown, Jeffrey, Olivia Mitchell, and James Poterba. In press. The role of real annuities and indexed bonds in an individual accounts retirement program. In *Risk aspects of investment-based social security reform,* ed. John Y. Campbell and Martin Feldstein. Chicago: University of Chicago Press.

Mitchell, Olivia S. 1997. Building an environment for pension reform in developing countries. Working paper. Wharton School, Pension Research Council, August.

———. 1998a. Administrative costs of public and private pension plans. In *Privatizing social security,* ed. Martin Feldstein. Chicago: University of Chicago Press.

———. 1998b. Evaluating administrative costs in Mexico's AFORES system. Working paper. Wharton School, Pension Research Council, November.

Mitchell, Olivia S., and Flavio Barreto. 1997. After Chile, what? Second-round social security reforms in Latin America. *Revista de Analisis Economico* 12, no. 2 (November): 3–36.

Discussion Summary for Chapters 1 and 2

Stephen Zeldes noted that the Schieber and Shoven paper seemed to indicate that administrative costs as a percentage of assets under management were increasing in the number of workers per plan for Australian individual account superannuation funds but were decreasing in the number of workers per plan for U.S. 401(k) plans. Zeldes suggested that perhaps the distinction between fixed cost *per plan* and fixed cost *per worker* needed to be fleshed out more precisely. That is, if much of the fixed cost is per worker cost, then it would not be surprising to find costs as a percentage of assets covarying positively with the number of workers per plan; but this result would be surprising if the fixed costs were mainly per plan. Zeldes suggested that, if most of the fixed costs are per worker costs, it is important to examine average balances in order to understand how the number of workers per plan will likely affect total plan costs as a percentage of assets. If, for example, average balances increase with plan size in Australia but decrease with plan size in the United States, and if most of the fixed costs were per worker fixed costs, this could explain the result implied by Schieber and Shoven's tables.

John Shoven agreed that these dynamics are important but also suggested that different levels of service in Australian as opposed to American plans could also be a driver of differential average costs. *Zeldes* commented that perhaps the most effective measure of average costs in general may be cost per worker.

Fred Grauer suggested that, in general, the number of investment choices available in Australia is much broader than it is in comparable plans in America. *Estelle James* disagreed, noting that, in the United States, employers have been increasing options, whereas, in Australia, there are perhaps only four or five options. *Grauer* replied that individuals in Australia have a significant amount of choice in selecting a plan vendor. But *Sylvester Schieber* supported James's observation, pointing out that individuals who are involved with superannuation plans through an employer are constrained in their choice by the options allowed by the employer, who sponsors the plan. Schieber noted that, although the issue of allowing multiple vendors to offer their portfolios to a given plan is currently under debate, there has been considerable resistance on the part of plan sponsors (e.g., employers) and therefore that choice for the individual employee in Australia remains quite limited.

Peter Diamond raised the point that, in addition to level of costs, one should also consider the significance of the way in which costs are charged to the individual: front load versus percentage of assets. Diamond noted the heavy reliance on front-load charges in the Chilean and Mexican pension schemes and cited evidence from a recent Investment Company Institute report indicating that a high percentage of U.S. equity mutual funds also used front-load fees. Diamond pointed out that Schieber and Shoven assumed no-load funds, and he questioned the appropriateness of this assumption given the evidence and the significant positive and normative implications of types of loads.

Estelle James offered an example of the normative implications of front-load charges. She noted that, in the Chilean system, the front loading of fees translates into very different effective annual charges and effective reduction of gross returns for individuals entering the system at different ages. Those entering the system at an earlier age experience lower effective annual charges and deduction from gross returns than do those entering the system at a later age.

James Poterba cautioned against using the assumption that 401(k) plans are breaking even when interpreting Schieber and Shoven's data detailing 1995 information on administrative fees of 401(k) accounts according to plan size. Poterba noted that 401(k) providers may undertake cross-subsidization within the mutual fund family. To investigate this possibility, he suggested comparing the Schieber and Shoven table to analogous data from before 1986. Poterba's recent research with David Wise indicates that this comparison might be of interest because, in the pre-1986 period, there were many fewer large 401(k) accounts than there are today—because, before 1986, 401(k)s in general had not been operating for very long. This suggests less opportunity for using revenues from the large accounts to subsidize.

John Shoven pointed out that a cross-subsidization type of effect may also arise if financial institutions presume that individuals depositing money in a 401(k) account may also open up additional accounts. This may affect fees on 401(k)s as the institutions attempt to attract and retain 401(k) money. *Poterba* suggested that some institutions, for example, banks offering CDs, actually may not want to accept retirement-plan money because the IRA and 401(k) rules give individuals significant freedom to move their money around within the account and banks may not want to deal with the transaction volume. *Shaun Mathews* of Aetna suggested that it would be fruitful to discuss this issue with "transfer agents," who provide services to 401(k) providers. Mathews suggested that transfer agents may have data that would allow one to back into fee and profit data for 401(k) providers.

Regarding churning costs, *Andrew Samwick* suggested that a small number of individuals would likely be responsible for most of the churning. *Michael Graetz* replied that the analysis of the Goldberg and Graetz paper assumed that individuals were limited as to the number of times they could reallocate their funds free of charge. He further noted that, although they had only explicitly assumed this for the "simple personal investment fund" (SPIF) accounts, it could also easily be built into the "qualified private fund" (Q-fund) accounts as well. *Martin Feldstein* argued that there is no particular reason why we would want to regulate how often individuals could reallocate funds if they paid the extra cost. *Graetz* agreed that a cap on the amount of churning is not necessarily needed, just a charge for churning after a certain point. Responding to this point, *Samwick* cautioned that this may lead to paternalistic policies on churning. Getting back to Samwick's original point, *Fred Goldberg* pointed out that the Goldberg and Graetz cost estimates did assume some level of churning. *Samwick* added that he was especially concerned about the different churning experience of different populations and that he was pleased to hear (from the Grandolini discussion) that Mexico had established a centralized clearinghouse for information, reconciliation, and reporting, which mitigates churning costs. He suggested that this was an encouraging precedent. *Graetz* responded on a related point, noting the crucial distinction between the institutions and costs associated with a reformed system on day 1 and the evolving characteristics of the system over time. He suggested that we need not consider the existence of such institutions as a clearinghouse for information and transactions (or, e.g., the consolidation of regulation of financial intermediaries) as a *precondition* for the establishment of a system of individual accounts. Rather, institutions such as these may well develop over time if the system is established with proper foresight.

Mark Warshawsky noted that Goldberg and Graetz assumed a prominent role for the IRS in their model of a system of individual accounts and questioned whether this would be politically viable given the recent expression of public dissatisfaction with the IRS. *Schieber* suggested that this should not be a problem, noting that, under the Goldberg and Graetz proposal, the IRS would not have access to any information to which it did not already have access. *Martin Feldstein* concurred, pointing out that many proposals currently circulating assume some processing role for the IRS. *Warshawsky* replied that he was referring mostly to public opinion/perception. *Michael Graetz* countered that he did not see this as an important issue and suggested that the Roth hearings investigating IRS misdeeds had been misleadingly inflammatory. *Fred Goldberg* noted that, despite the complaints about various aspects of the IRS, it performs its information-processing tasks remarkably well.

Picking up a point from the Grandolini presentation, *Leonard Glynn* posited that the World Bank staff retirement plan's experience suggests that it is difficult to achieve consistent overperformance from active management of pension assets. In particular, he suggested, it implies perhaps that any social security system with individual accounts ought to put every individual in a "default plan" that would be completely passively managed, with heavy restrictions on investor choice and ability to reallocate funds. (He conceded that perhaps individuals could eventually be allowed to opt out into a more flexible plan, but only after their account had reached a specified dollar amount.) He suggested that such a system would cut costs from churning and investor education while apparently not giving up much in terms of potential gains to active management.

Fred Goldberg replied that one could take that approach but that it is more a question of policy than of mechanics since the Goldberg and Graetz framework *does* allow for a more restrictive default option as well as a less restrictive opt-out option. *Olivia Mitchell* argued that the investor-education issues do not disappear altogether, as individuals would eventually be eligible to enter an opt-out plan and would need to understand the implications of doing so. *Leonard Glynn* agreed but noted that this option would not be available until the program had been in place for several years, during which time investors would have the opportunity to become educated about their options. Glynn further noted that annual statements could be a part of the education process by including information regarding the structure of the default plan's "life-cycle" investment allocations. This could also have the effect of convincing some individuals to stay with the default plan when they are presented with the option to switch.

Martin Feldstein argued that charging front-load fees was not a viable option because the individual would need to pay a new up-front fee every time he or she switched investment managers. Consequently, charging fees as a percentage of assets seemed the only viable option. Feldstein also commented that it was puzzling that there is not more of an attempt on the part of fund managers to offer quantity discounts to clients with larger funds. *Estelle James* replied that mutual fund managers are not allowed to offer different fees to different customers. But *John Shoven* pointed out that this occurs de facto when fund managers offer funds with high minimum investments and lower fees than similar funds without minimum investment requirements.

Kent Smetters noted that Goldberg and Graetz estimated the administrative costs of their default plan (the SPIF) as between thirty and sixty basis points and asked why that figure would not be closer to the eight- to nine-basis-point figure of the federal Thrift Savings Plan (TSP). *Estelle James* pointed out that the initial costs of the SPIF plan would be high because of the likely small size of the accounts. She noted that the same had been true of the TSP. *Fred Goldberg* concurred, noting that the thirty- to sixty-basis-point figure corresponded to a five-year time horizon, whereas, in the long run, the figure ought to be closer to the TSP figure. *James* suggested that, with passive management, it ought to be possible to get below the thirty- to sixty-basis-point figure within five years.

David Cutler noted that many individuals currently do not file tax returns and that it may be difficult to bring these individuals into an individual account system that relied on the existing IRS infrastructure. *Fred Goldberg* agreed that there are several million individuals who do not file tax returns and suggested that an additional form would be necessary for these individuals to receive credits to their individual accounts. He noted further that any future major tax reform would need to take special account of the implications of reform to the individual account system if that system relied on the IRS infrastructure. *Martin Feldstein* and *Daniel Feenberg* inquired about the size of the working, nonfiling population. *Goldberg* replied that, although it is difficult to determine an exact figure, there may be as many as several million such individuals. He cited as an example of the type of person falling into this category a young worker whose only annual income was a few hundred dollars from a summer job. Goldberg also noted that, even if an individual with official wage income does not file a tax return, he or she will still have a W-2 filed for his or her work. The system could still credit his or her individual account, although with a lag of approximately eighteen months.

3

Mutual Funds and Institutional Investments

What Is the Most Efficient Way to Set Up Individual Accounts in a Social Security System?

Estelle James, Gary Ferrier, James Smalhout, and
Dimitri Vittas

Prefunding is now seen as a desirable characteristic of old-age security systems because it helps increase national saving, makes the financial sustainability of the system less sensitive to demographic shocks, and reduces the need to increase taxes as populations age. With prefunding comes the need to determine how the funds will be managed. Those who fear political manipulation of publicly managed funds see defined-contribution (DC) individual accounts (IAs) as a way to decentralize control and thereby achieve a better allocation of the funds. But IAs have been criticized on other grounds, most important among them being high administrative costs. Costs are especially high relative to assets at the start of a new system because of start-up expenses and fixed costs associated with each account. To illustrate why administrative costs are important: an annual cost of 1 percent of assets (slightly more than the up-front fee now charged in Chile) can reduce a worker's retirement benefits by 20 percent. Moreover, costs are more predictable than returns and more amenable to policy choice.

This paper investigates the cost effectiveness of three options for constructing funded social security pillars: (1) IAs invested in the retail market with relatively open choice; (2) IAs invested in the institutional market

Estelle James is lead economist in the Development Economics Research Group of the World Bank. Gary Ferrier is associate professor at the University of Arkansas. James Smalhout is visiting fellow at the Hudson Institute and contributing editor of *Euromoney Magazine.* Dimitri Vittas is lead economist in the Development Economics Research Group of the World Bank.

The authors thank Deepthi Fernando and Marianne Leenaerts of the World Bank and Baglan Sultanbek of the University of Arkansas for their excellent research assistance on this project.

with constrained choice for workers among investment companies; and (3) a centralized fund invested in the institutional market without individual accounts or differentiated investments across individuals. Our questions are the following: What is the most cost-effective way to organize a mandatory IA system, how does the cost of an efficient IA system compare with that of a single centralized fund, and are the cost differentials great enough to outweigh the other important considerations?[1]

To answer these questions, we use data from pension funds in Chile (which was the first country to establish a decentralized IA system) and from mutual funds in the United States (because the best data are available here, the U.S. mutual fund industry is an example of a relatively well-run retail financial industry [which deals with numerous small investors], and the United States is currently considering how to reform its social security system). Observing that an institutional investment market (which deals with large investors) coexists with mutual funds in the United States, and at much lower cost, we also use these data to identify and quantify the sources of economies from operating in the wholesale money market. Costs in both the retail and the institutional markets would be higher in developing countries, but their relative positions should be similar to those described here. (For a discussion of applicability to developing countries, see James, Smalhout, and Vittas 1999.) We distinguish among asset-management, marketing, and record-keeping costs, showing how each varies with type and size of system.

Empirical evidence presented in this paper and elsewhere suggests the existence of large economies of scale and scope in asset management. All three options exploit these economies, but in different ways. The retail market (option 1) allows individual investors to benefit from scale economies in asset management, but at the cost of high marketing expenses (almost half of total costs), which are needed to attract and aggregate small sums of money into large pools. At the start-up of a new IA system, the fixed cost per account for record keeping and communications (R&C) is also high, relative to assets. In contrast, a centralized fund (option 3) can be much cheaper because it achieves scale economies without high marketing or R&C costs but gives workers no choice and hence is subject to political manipulation and misallocation of capital.

The system of constrained choice described in this paper (option 2) is

---

1. We concentrate on the asset-accumulation phase since annuities pose a host of other issues. We do not include the cost of pay-as-you-go schemes in this analysis since (unlike transfer systems) funded schemes represent either additional saving or diversions from other savings that would have incurred costs. Well-managed funded schemes cost more than well-managed pay-as-you-go schemes because they provide an additional service—the management of savings. Savings provide productive value to the economy that one does not get from pay-as-you-go schemes, and some of this value is passed on to workers in the form of higher retirement benefits than they could get from the same contribution to a pay-as-you-go scheme. This paper is about how to manage those savings, not about whether to save.

much cheaper than the retail market and only slightly more expensive than a single centralized fund. It obtains economies in asset management and record keeping while keeping marketing costs low and allowing significant worker choice, which helps insulate it from political interference. It accomplishes this by aggregating small compulsory contributions into a large pool, which is then allocated across a limited number of funds according to worker choice but with centrally negotiated rates (via competitive bidding with limited entry or open entry with price ceilings) that discourage high marketing expenses. In countries with well-developed financial markets, passive investment is likely to be emphasized if the object is low cost. If one values the cost saving as greater than the decreased marketing information and constraints on choice, this system will be more efficient than the retail approach, and, if one values improved political insulation and adaptability to individual preferences, it is more efficient than the centralized approach.

Section 3.1 sets up a hypothetical model that decomposes costs into asset-management, R&C, and marketing components. Section 3.2 provides an international perspective by examining costs in the mandatory AFP (*administradoras de fondos de pensiones*) system in Chile, which uses the most common method, the retail market. Section 3.3 draws on data from voluntary saving in mutual funds in the United States. Both in Chile and in the United States, individuals have diversified accounts that they can move from one company to another in a competitive retail investment market. Although the American mutual fund industry is vastly more developed than the Chilean AFP industry, we find strong similarities, in terms of annualized costs as a percentage of assets and the composition of these costs. Average annual administrative costs range between 1 and 1.5 percent of assets for most investors, and marketing is the largest cost component in both cases. In Chile, annual costs are less than 1 percent for those who start contributing early in their careers. In the United States, a low-cost niche of less than 1 percent has developed for passively managed funds indexed to various benchmarks. In both cases, costs were higher fifteen years ago and have declined slightly as a result of asset growth and competition. These two cases give us insights into how an IA system might develop in the retail market.

Section 3.4 explores costs in the institutional market, drawing on U.S. data once again. Administrative costs for pension funds and other large investors are estimated to be four to eight basis points (0.04–0.08 percent of assets) for passively managed portfolios and thirty-five to sixty-five basis points (0.35–0.65 percent of assets) for actively managed domestic portfolios—much less than the retail market. These large cost savings are due to economies of scale in the investment function, smaller costs in the marketing function, the virtual absence of record-keeping costs, and the greater bargaining power of large investors in an industry where average costs greatly exceed marginal cost. These would also be the costs in a well-run centralized funded pillar with no IAs and no choice.

Section 3.5 considers whether and how an IA system with constrained choice could be set up to benefit from these same economies. We outline the elements of such a system—which include worker choice among a limited number of money managers chosen through a competitive bidding process (or through fee ceilings that discourage marketing expenditures). We estimate that such a system could operate with approximately the same investment costs as the centralized fund. However, additional R&C costs will necessarily be incurred if workers have individual accounts with differing asset managers. Using data from the transfer-agent function of mutual funds and the experience of the federal employees' Thrift Savings Plan (TSP), we find a relatively fixed R&C dollar cost per account that falls rapidly as a percentage of assets as average account size grows.

Thus, the steady-state cost in a constrained IA system in countries with well-developed financial markets is likely to be 0.14–0.18 percent of assets annually for a passively managed investment strategy (or 0.49–0.79 percent if active management is chosen), including all money-management and record-keeping fees. For the system size that has been under consideration in the United States (average annual contributions of approximately $500), this amounts to $31–$39, or $106–$172, per account, respectively. This is only ten basis points, or $21, per account per year higher than the cost of a centralized scheme. It is much less than the expected return to saving or the cost of voluntary or mandatory individual accounts in retail markets. Constrained choice offers large administrative cost savings combined with political insulation and is likely to imply a Pareto improvement so long as choice is not constrained "too much."

3.1   How Administrative Costs Vary across Time and Systems

We start by setting forth a small model of the components of administrative costs that can be used to understand changes in costs across time and systems:

$$\text{TOTADMINCOST}_t^i = \text{STARTUPCOST} + \text{FCOST} + \text{R\&C} + \text{INV}$$
$$+ \text{MARKETING},$$

Where TOTADMINCOST_t^i = total administrative cost for pension fund or system i in year t, STARTUPCOST = capital costs incurred in the early years of a new system or fund, FCOST = fixed cost needed to operate in year t, R&C = record-keeping and communication (R&C) costs, INV = investment costs, and MARKETING = marketing cost.

Each of these cost components is determined quite differently. R&C costs tend to be technologically determined and standardized, depending on quality of service and number of accounts. Passive investment costs are also technologically determined, depending on volume and allocation of assets. Active investment costs are market determined, stemming from the premium that a manager who is deemed to be superior can command in a market for differentiated investment skills. Marketing expenses usually go together with active management since they are used to sell the skills of a particular asset-management company and they depend on profit-maximizing calculations about the costs versus the net returns of incremental marketing activities. Suppose that, in choosing an investment manager, all consumers have the same fallback option that is low in cost and returns (say, a savings bank account or money market fund). They will not choose an active manager unless they expect him to yield a higher net return, after subtracting all expenses, including his wages and marketing costs. Then the manager will be able to charge a larger dollar skill premium and to spend a larger amount on marketing while still staying above this threshold return, as total assets in the system grow. This scenario would lead active investment and marketing costs to rise with assets even though this relation is not technologically determined.

In comparing costs across funds or systems, it is necessary to take into account the total volume of assets and the number of accounts that determine costs and to ascertain how these are likely to change in the future.[2] Table 3.1 illustrates the total administrative cost and its breakdown between R&C and INV in three hypothetical systems as they evolve through time. Two cost measures are used—dollars per account and basis points per unit of assets (one basis point = 0.01 percent). The first measure is useful because it tells us how much it costs to operate an account for an average worker, while the second measure tells us how much gross returns are being whittled away by administrative costs. While economies of scale are probable (see James and Palacios 1995; Mitchell 1998; and sec. 3.3 below), in this section, for the purposes of exposition, we assume that R&C cost per account and INV cost per unit of assets are constant. Scale economies would slow down the growth and/or accelerate the decline in all these cost measures. We also abstract from annual fixed costs and high

2. Additionally, different countries face differing relative factor prices and productivities. If the relevant technologies tend to be capital intensive, then capital rich countries with relatively cheap capital will have lower costs per account and asset unit, while the opposite is true if the feasible technology set uses labor intensively, especially unskilled labor. Funds that operate in countries with a facilitating legal and physical infrastructure, such as enforceable contract rights and telephone lines that work, will be able to use their own labor and capital more productively. In international comparisons, costs are sometimes expressed as a percentage of the average wage, to normalize for differences in labor price and productivity across countries. Because of their relatively cheap costs of capital combined with the prevalence of capital intensive technologies as well as the availability of legal and capital infrastructure, we would expect industrial countries to have lower administrative costs than others (ceteris paribus) as a percentage of average wage and also in terms of dollars per account and basis points per unit of assets.

Table 3.1   Hypothetical Administrative Costs over Time as a Percentage of Assets and Dollars per Account

A. The Institutional Approach with Passive Management[a]

Year	Year-End Accumulation of Individual ($thousands)[b]	Average-Size Account in System ($thousands)[c]	R&C as % of Assets	R&C + Investment as % of Assets	Investment Expenses per Account ($)	R&C + Investment per Account ($)	R&C/Total Expenses per Account
1	0.5	0.5	4.00	4.10	0.5	20.5	0.98
2	1.0	1.0	2.20	2.30	1.0	21.0	0.96
3	1.6	1.6	1.28	1.38	1.6	21.6	0.93
4	2.2	2.1	0.95	1.05	2.1	22.1	0.90
5	2.8	2.7	0.76	0.86	2.7	22.7	0.88
10	6.4	5.6	0.36	0.46	5.6	25.6	0.78
15	10.9	8.8	0.23	0.33	8.8	28.8	0.71
20	16.7	12.1	0.17	0.27	12.1	32.1	0.63
25	24.1	15.4	0.13	0.23	15.4	35.4	0.57
30	33.6	18.5	0.11	0.21	18.5	38.5	0.52
35	45.6	20.8	0.10	0.20	20.8	40.8	0.50
40	61.0	22.0	0.09	0.19	22.0	42.0	0.47

B. The Institutional Approach with Active Management[d]

Year	Year-End Accumulation of Individual ($thousands)[b]	Average-Size Account in System ($thousands)[c]	R&C as % of Assets	R&C + Investment as % of Assets	Investment Expenses per Account ($)	R&C + Investment per Account ($)	R&C/Total Expenses per Account
1	0.5	0.5	4.00	4.60	3.0	23.0	0.87
2	1.0	1.0	2.03	2.63	5.9	25.9	0.77
3	1.6	1.6	1.28	1.88	9.3	29.3	0.68
4	2.1	2.0	0.99	1.59	12.1	32.1	0.62
5	2.7	2.6	0.78	1.38	15.4	35.4	0.57
10	6.1	5.4	0.37	0.97	32.2	52.2	0.38
15	10.4	8.4	0.24	0.84	50.2	70.2	0.29
20	15.7	11.4	0.18	0.78	68.4	88.4	0.23
25	22.3	14.4	0.14	0.74	86.1	106.1	0.19
30	30.5	17.0	0.12	0.72	102.0	122.0	0.17
35	40.7	19.0	0.11	0.71	114.2	134.2	0.15
40	53.5	20.0	0.10	0.70	119.8	139.8	0.14

(continued)

Table 3.1   (continued)

C. The Retail Approach[e]

Year	Year-End Accumulation of Individual ($thousands)[b]	Average-Size Account in System ($thousands)[c]	Costs as % of Assets			Costs in $ per Account		R&C/Total Expenses
			R&C	R&C + Investment	R&C + Investment + Marketing	Investment	R&C + Investment + Marketing	
1	2.0	2.0	1.50	2.10	2.60	12.0	52.0	0.58
2	4.1	4.1	0.74	1.34	1.84	24.3	74.5	0.40
3	6.2	6.0	0.50	1.10	1.60	36.3	96.5	0.31
4	8.5	8.2	0.37	0.97	1.57	49.0	119.9	0.25
5	10.8	10.2	0.29	0.89	1.39	61.4	142.6	0.21
10	23.9	21.0	0.14	0.74	1.24	126.1	261.2	0.11
15	39.8	32.1	0.09	0.69	1.19	192.7	383.3	0.08
20	59.3	43.3	0.07	0.67	1.17	259.8	506.2	0.06
25	82.9	53.9	0.06	0.66	1.16	323.2	622.5	0.05
30	111.6	63.1	0.05	0.65	1.15	378.8	724.5	0.04
35	146.6	70.1	0.04	0.64	1.14	420.4	800.8	0.04
40	189.1	73.2	0.04	0.64	1.14	439.0	834.9	0.04

[a]Assumptions: $520 is contributed each year. R&C costs are $20 per account, so net contribution (NCON) = $500. Gross rate of return = 5.1%, and investment costs are 0.1 percent of assets, so net return (NR) after subtracting investment costs = 5.0 percent.

[b]Individual's account accumulates at the following rate: $A_t = A_{t-1}(1 + NR) + NCON$, where NR = net return, and NCON = net contribution.

[c]Account size increases at above rate for individuals who stay in system. Withdrawals by high-account individuals who retire and their replacement by incoming workers with small new accounts decrease average account size in system. Workers are evenly distributed across forty age groups. Steady state is reached in year 40.

[d]Assumptions: $520 is contributed each year. R&C costs are $20 per account, so net contribution = $500. Gross rate of return = 5.1 percent, and investment costs are 0.6 percent of assets, so net return after subtracting investment costs = 4.5 percent.

[e]Assumptions: $2,020 is contributed each year. R&C costs are $30 per account, so net contribution = $1,990. Gross rate of return = 5.1 percent, investment costs are 0.6 percent of assets, and marketing costs are 0.5 percent, so net return after subtracting investment and marketing costs = 4 percent.

start-up costs at the beginning. While at this point these cost functions are hypothetical, we will see later that they are not implausible.

Panel A of table 3.1 illustrates a stylized cost profile for an IA system that uses the institutional approach, with passive investing that costs 0.01 percent of assets annually plus R&C costs of $20.00 per account. Panel B illustrates an institutional approach with active investing—INV cost rises to 0.6 percent. Panel C illustrates the retail approach, with marketing and investment expenses totaling 1.1 percent of assets plus R&C costs of $30.00 per account.[3] We see in table 3.1 the following: (1) Average (dollar) cost per account starts relatively low and rises through time as average account size grows, owing to increased investment costs. (2) In contrast, average cost as a percentage of assets starts high and falls as average account size grows, owing to constant R&C costs per account. (3) R&C costs dominate at the beginning, but their effect on net returns becomes much smaller in the long run, when investment and marketing costs dominate (particularly if a high contribution rate and expensive investment strategy are chosen [panels B and C]). (4) If an institutional approach with low investment costs is chosen, costs per account remain small, and costs as a percentage of assets become very small in the long run (panel A). (5) An expensive investment and marketing strategy increases dollar costs per account by a larger amount as time passes, although the negative effect on net returns is constant through time (panel C). And (6) a larger contribution amount leads to a more rapid increase in dollar cost per account, but it decreases cost per unit of assets at the same time (panel C).

While we have been defining costs to the fund and the system, costs (fees) to consumers may vary from this. In the short run, at the start-up of a new system, funds may run temporary losses in the expectation that they will increase their market share and recoup their capital expenses later on. In the medium term, they may earn profits that offset the earlier losses. We would expect that, in the long run, competition will eliminate pure profits so that fees to investors will just cover costs to the fund. But the existence of marketing competition, as well as potential skill and wage

---

3. For panel A, the annual contribution is assumed to be $520, the neighborhood of many IA systems in Latin America that feature decision making by the individual worker. The United States has been considering an IA contribution rate of about $500 per year. R&C cost is $20 per account, which might be the fee for a modest-quality system, and INV cost (including brokerage and custodian fees) is 0.1 percent per unit of assets, which is on the high side for a passive investment strategy. In panel B, INV cost rises to 0.6 percent, which might be charged by active asset managers in an institutional IA system. Panel C illustrates the retail approach. The annual contribution is $2,020 per year, the neighborhood of mandatory IA systems in several OECD countries. R&C cost is $30, INV cost is 0.6 percent, and MARKETING costs of 0.5 percent of assets are introduced. In all cases, a gross rate of return (before fees) of 5.1 percent is assumed. In order to abstract from the effect of a changing age distribution, we assume that participants are evenly distributed across forty age groups and take their money out of the system when they retire.

differentials across asset managers, makes it difficult to predict the cost and fee level at which this zero-profit equilibrium will occur. Moreover, price discrimination, used to recover fixed costs when heterogeneous consumers have different price elasticities, means that marginal cost and average cost may have different relations to price for different groups of investors. In this paper, we focus on fees that are paid by the average investor, we presume that, in the long run, these fees will bear a close relation to real costs, and costs depend on how the system is organized.

A well-run centralized fund without IAs has the cost advantage of lower R&C expenses since it features only one investment account (although additional records must be kept of the benefit entitlements of each worker) and potential use of bargaining power to secure low investment and marketing costs (as in panels A and B minus R&C costs). But it has the disadvantage of creating a principal-agent problem and lack of political insulation if it is managed by the government: for these reasons, it may not end up minimizing costs or maximizing returns or being run in the workers' best interests. In contrast, the retail market for IAs incurs R&C costs for many small accounts, expensive investment strategies may be chosen, and marketing costs are often high (as in panel C). We argue that, by operating in the institutional market, an IA system may achieve most of the cost advantages of centralized funds, but with greater political insulation and responsiveness to workers' preferences. The institutional approach to IA systems aggregates many small accounts into large blocs of money and negotiates fees on a centralized basis—via a competitive bidding process or open entry with price ceilings. This can keep costs and fees low by (1) constraining worker choice to low-INV-cost portfolios and strategies; (2) minimizing incentives for MARKETING cost by reducing allowable fees; (3) dampening R&C expenditures; (4) cutting STARTUPCOST and FCOST by avoiding excess capacity; and (5) increasing bargaining power, hence decreasing oligopoly profits. When these strategies are utilized, the cost of an IA system is only minimally higher than that of a well-run centralized fund without IAs.

3.2 How High Are Administrative Fees in Chile, and How Are They Spent?

In this section, we examine the administrative costs and fees of Chilean AFPs, which have been operating since 1981. These fees have been subject to great criticism by opponents of IA systems. In Chile, the worker pays a fee to the AFP, which is an administrator that sets up the fund and runs it. Practically all expenses are paid by the AFP, not the worker or the fund directly.[4] So fees do not necessarily represent real costs of operating the

---

4. An exception is the fees paid by AFPs to foreign mutual funds, which invest about 10 percent of the AFP assets abroad. These mutual fund fees are subtracted from the workers' accounts.

fund, especially in the short run, nor do they represent a long-term commitment. AFPs incurred losses in the early years of the new system when start-up costs exceeded revenues, but the industry as a whole is quite profitable and more concentrated at this stage (table 3.2). We might expect price competition to eliminate these profits, but price insensitivity among investors and entry barriers to new firms may prevent this from happening quickly. Deregulation and oligopoly may alter costs and their relation to fees in the future in ways that are difficult to predict. For example, in an industry characterized by differentiated competition, marketing costs play a large role, and we do not know whether they will increase or decrease as the industry grows more concentrated.[5] As regulations are liberalized, portfolio diversification increases, and managerial skill is deemed increasingly important, wages may rise for managers who are perceived as more skillful, costs to the AFPs that employ them may increase, expenditures to advertise their superior skills may become more costly, and fees to their members may rise. Despite this uncertainty about the future, the current fee structure poses costs to investors that reduce their net returns, so, in this section, we take them as given and examine their implications.

Chile adopted an unusual method of charging fees: the fee is imposed when the contribution first enters the system, and no management fees are charged on that contribution thereafter. The fee started at over 20 percent of contributions but has fallen to an average level of 15.6 percent. Anecdotal evidence indicates that many workers receive rebates on sales commissions, so, for them, the effective fee may be only 13 percent of contributions or less. (In other Latin American countries, such as Argentina and Mexico, where the contribution rate is smaller, fees are still over 20 percent of contributions, while, in Bolivia, which has experimented with a new administrative system, they are lower [see James, Smalhout, and Vittas 1999].) Charging fees that are based on new contributions is an extremely front-loaded method as compared with the customary practice in mutual funds of charging an annual fee that is based on assets, sometimes supplemented with a sales charge on purchases.

This fee structure means that, if a worker enters the system for a year but then drops out (e.g., to become self-employed or to withdraw from the labor market), he or she ceases to pay fees while keeping his or her assets in the system. For new systems (e.g., Poland, Uruguay), the number of contributors and affiliates is very close, but, for more mature IA systems (e.g., Chile, Singapore), the number of affiliates is roughly double the number of active contributors. (Inactive affiliates require the AFP to incur expenditures for annual statements and asset management, while active

---

5. The recent spate of mergers in Chile has decreased the number of AFPs from twenty-one in the early 1990s to eight currently. In Argentina, the number has decreased from twenty-five to sixteen and will probably decrease even more. This suggests that the market is gradually responding to economies of scale—as in the U.S. mutual fund industry.

Table 3.2   Assets, Fees, and Expenditures in Chile through Time

Year	No. of Affiliates (millions)	Contributors/ Affiliates	Assets (1998 U.S.$millions)	Total Assets/ Contributors (1998 U.S.$)	Total Assets/ Affiliates (1998 U.S.$)	Marketing Costs as % of Total Expenses
1982	1.44	.74	1,277.74	1,205	887	46
1983	1.62	.76	2,212.50	1,799	1,366	40
1984	1.93	.70	2,842.46	2,090	1,473	36
1985	2.28	.68	2,290.61	1,470	1,003	30
1986	2.59	.68	3,112.55	1,779	1,201	24
1987	2.89	.70	3,812.46	1,884	1,319	21
1988	3.18	.68	4,868.26	2,246	1,529	23
1989	3.47	.65	5,844.70	2,577	1,684	22
1990	3.74	.61	8,144.61	3,558	2,178	24
1991	4.11	.61	11,999.98	4,825	2,920	26
1992	4.43	.61	14,265.43	5,292	3,217	30
1993	4.71	.59	17,839.38	6,389	3,788	35
1994	5.01	.57	24,206.33	8,406	4,827	38
1995	5.32	.56	27,039.54	9,129	5,082	43
1996	5.57	.56	28,366.44	9,088	5,091	49
1997	5.78	.57	31,133.98	9,445	5,386	52
1998	5.97	.53	31,060.16	9,861	5,206	46

Year	Fee per Contributor (1998 U.S.$)	Expenses per Contributor (1998 U.S.$)	Fee per Affiliate (1998 U.S.$)	Expenses per Affiliate (1998 U.S.$)	Fee per Unit of Assets (%)	Expenses per Unit of Assets (%)
1982	113	145	83	106	9.39	12.00
1983	101	102	77	77	5.63	5.65
1984	102	97	72	68	4.90	4.65
1985	52	50	36	34	3.54	3.41
1986	52	46	35	31	2.93	2.57
1987	49	42	34	29	2.60	2.22
1988	58	50	39	34	2.57	2.23
1989	64	51	42	33	2.49	1.97
1990	71	63	43	39	2.00	1.77
1991	81	68	49	41	1.68	1.41
1992	95	74	58	45	1.79	1.39
1993	103	92	61	54	1.61	1.43
1994	123	114	71	65	1.47	1.35
1995	143	124	79	69	1.56	1.35
1996	145	128	81	72	1.59	1.41
1997	148	131	84	75	1.56	1.38
1998	134	112	71	59	1.36	1.13

Source: PrimeAmerica Consultores based on reports of *superintendencias;* authors' calculations.

contributors incur additional expenses for periodic contributions and fund switches.)

According to table 3.2, after the period of high start-up costs, cost and fee per account drop precipitously but then rise gradually as average account size grows, consistent with the hypothetical model presented in section 3.1. In 1998, average cost per contributor was $112 and per affiliate $71, and fees were slightly higher. As we shall see, these numbers are lower than in mutual funds in the United States, corresponding to the much higher average account size in the latter. Fees and costs as a percentage of assets have also been falling through time, but much more gradually, as predicted in the hypothetical retail model. They are now 1.36 percent (fees) and 1.13 percent (costs). We observe, too, that marketing costs are large.

Table 3.3 presents the results of a panel-data (fixed-effects) analysis that sums up this relation between assets, affiliates, costs, and fees over time and across AFPs. We see there that (1) start-up fees and, even more, start-up costs in the first three years of operations were high; (2) as number of affiliates grows, costs and fees relative to assets grow (because of R&C costs); and (3) as average account size increases, (investment) cost per account also increases but (because of scale economies) cost per dollar of assets (which ultimately determines the net return) decreases. This is consistent with the hypothetical retail market depicted in table 3.1 above. We infer from this that (1) it is misleading to extrapolate costs and fees from the first years of a new system, which unfortunately has often been done; (2) investment costs play an increasingly dominant role but scale economies stemming from large asset bases limit this increase; and (3) in comparing the administrative efficiency of systems across countries, it is essential to take into account whether they are in their start-up period and what their size is in terms of assets and affiliates since two systems that are equally efficient in the long run under similar conditions will differ at any point in time depending on their maturity and scale. Chile, and even more so other Latin American countries, will probably benefit further from maturation and scale economies in the future.

In any event, a 15.6 percent fee on contributions reduces the final capital accumulation and pension by 15.6 percent. Is this fee high or low? To answer this question, it is useful to compare the fee with other institutional arrangements for handling retirement savings, both in Chile and elsewhere. This paper concentrates on comparing it with fees in the retail and institutional market in the United States. For this purpose, we convert these front-loaded fees into their annual asset-based equivalents (which will yield the same final year accumulation). This tells us how much gross investment returns will be reduced to obtain net returns and enables a direct comparison with mutual funds and large institutional investors in the United States and elsewhere. This conversion depends on how long the worker will keep his or her money in the system, which in turn depends on his or her age and career pattern.

Table 3.3   Fixed-Effects Panel Regression Analysis: Determinants of Costs and Fees, Chile, Disaggregated by AFP and Year, 1982–98

	Dependent Variables					
Independent Variables	Total Administrative Cost	Total Cost/ Assets	Total Cost/ Affiliates	Total Fee Revenues	Total Fees/ Assets	Total Fees/ Affiliates
Assets/affiliates	.002	−.0003	.009	.002	−.0002	.01
	(10.42)*	(−3.83)*	(4.56)*	(10.56)*	(−5.82)*	(12.81)*
No. of affiliates	48.89	2.34	11.71	62.79	−.43	−3.72
	(21.96)**	(2.63)**	(.49)	(23.22)*	(−1.03)	(−.36)
Dummy, start-up year = 1982	11.28	14.02	96.33	10.72	5.20	32.77
	(6.12)*	(19.00)*	(4.89)*	(4.79)*	(15.23)*	(3.87)*
Dummy, start-up years = 1983–84	6.71	3.48	47.80	8.56	2.84	44.29
	(4.74)*	(6.13)*	(3.15)**	(4.98)*	(10.83)*	(6.81)*
Constant	−8.41	3.18	51.18	−12.5	3.34	33.24
	(−8.04)*	(7.61)*	(4.57)*	(−9.83)*	(17.21)*	(6.92)*
R^2:						
Within	.81	.68	.17	.82	.70	.50
Between	.56	.21	.04	.65	.74	.88
Overall	.78	.47	.21	.80	.69	.83
N	234	234	234	234	234	234

Note: *t*-statistics are given in parentheses. Units of measurement: costs, fees, and assets are 1998 U.S. dollars in millions; number of contributors and affiliates are in millions; cost/assets and fees/assets are in percentages; cost/affiliates, fees/affiliates, and assets/affiliates are in 1998 U.S. dollars.

*Significant at the 0.1 percent level.

**Significant at the 1 percent level.

Table 3.4   **Annual Asset-Based Fee Equivalent to 15.6 Percent Fee on New Contributions (as a percentage of assets)**

Starting Age	Contribution Made for 1 Year Only at Given Age (1)	Contributions Made for 20 Years Only, Starting at Given Age (2)	Contributions Made Every Year until Age 65, Starting at Given Age (3)
25	0.45	0.57	0.76
35	0.60	0.85	1.05
45	0.91	1.65	1.65
55	1.86	. . .	3.50
64	33.37	. . .	33.37

Note: This table shows the annual fee based on assets that will yield the same capital accumulation at age sixty-five as would a 15.6 percent front-loaded fee on incoming contributions. In col. 1 a single year of contributions is assumed at the starting age. The annual fee for age sixty-four is 33.37 percent because contributions and fees are assumed to be paid monthly, including the last month. In col. 2 the worker continues contributing a fixed percentage of wage for twenty years. In col. 3 the worker continues investing a fixed percentage of wage from starting age until age sixty-five. A rate of return of 5 percent is assumed. For cols. 2 and 3, annual wage growth of 2 percent is assumed. (Similar results were obtained for 3 percent rate of return and 1 percent rate of wage growth.) In U.S. dollars, the average contributor paid $134 in 1998 in Chile. The fee would increase 2 percent per year under these assumptions.

We have simulated the average annual fee on assets that is equivalent to the front-loaded 15.6 percent fee on contributions for workers of different ages at the point when the contribution was made (table 3.4). This simulation assumes that the same fee schedule remains in effect over the worker's lifetime, although of course there is no guarantee that this will be the case. For a twenty-five-year-old worker (who contributes for one year only but whose money stays in the system for another forty years), the 15.6 percent one-time fee is equivalent to 0.45 percent of assets annually; for a forty-five-year-old worker, it is 0.91 percent; and, for a worker who contributes monthly in his final year, it is 32.4 percent (col. 1). For a worker who contributes every year for forty years (e.g., from age twenty-five to age sixty-five), paying a fee on each new contribution, the annual equivalent of all these front-loaded fees is 0.76 percent of assets (col. 3).[6]

Many workers will contribute for twenty years only because this is the period that makes them eligible for the minimum pension guarantee. For these workers, the equivalent annual fee depends on whether the contributions were made early or late in their careers, which determines how many years their money will be under management. If a worker contributes only

6. These calculations assume a 5 percent gross rate of return and a 2 percent rate of wage growth. Calculations with 3 percent and 4 percent rates of return and/or a 1 percent rate of wage growth yield very similar results. These simulations show that workers with different employment histories will end up paying different annual equivalent fees as a subtraction from their gross returns even if they impose the same real cost on the fund—which may not be a desirable feature for a mandatory system to possess.

for his first twenty years of employment, the equivalent average annual fee for all his contributions is 0.57 percent, while, if contributions are made only in the last twenty years, the equivalent average annual fee is 1.65 percent (col. 2). (The latter is roughly consistent with the 1.4 percent of assets that is paid by the average worker today, eighteen years after the system got started.) Suppose that half of all workers contribute for forty years, one-quarter each for their first and last twenty years. The systemwide annual equivalent expense ratio would be 0.94 percent, almost 1 percent of assets per year.

These estimated lifetime fees are similar to but somewhat lower than average mutual fund fees in the United States (see sec. 3.3 below). American mutual funds, of course, provide greater diversification and service than Chilean AFPs, which would make their costs higher. But they also benefit from greater economies of scale and better infrastructure, which would make their costs lower. AFP costs are much lower than the costs of U.S. mutual funds that operate in emerging markets. They are much lower than mutual fund fees for voluntary saving in Chile, which, during the early 1990s, averaged around 6 percent per year for equity funds and 2 percent for bond funds, plus entrance and exit charges (Maturana and Walker 1999). AFP fees are also lower than those of mutual funds in most other countries, where the combination of front loads and annual fees exceeds levels in the United States. Chilean AFPs are therefore relatively inexpensive if the standard of comparison is fees in other financial institutions that invest individuals' savings in a diversified portfolio. However, they are more expensive than savings accounts in commercial banks, either in Chile or elsewhere (Valdes 1999).

The breakdown of costs among AFPs shows that over 45 percent of total expenditures was used for marketing costs, especially sales commissions. This proportion is similar to marketing expenses in the retail financial markets in the United States and other countries. In both cases, the number would probably exceed 50 percent if we included staff salaries involved in marketing. These similarities suggest that a study of U.S. mutual fund data might yield insights into the determinants of costs in IA systems and how these costs might be reduced.

Finally, AFP fees are much higher than are the fees paid by institutional investors (see sec. 3.4 below), and they have a substantial effect on ultimate pension amounts. This leads one to wonder whether it is possible to organize a mandatory IA system so that it captures the lower costs of the institutional market and, if so, what the trade-offs are.

3.3   Costs in the Retail Market of American Mutual Funds

The mutual fund in the United States has been a hugely successful financial institution. Assets have grown from less than $1 billion in 1949 to almost $140 billion in 1980 to over $4 trillion by the end of 1997 and now exceed the combined total of savings bank deposits and life insurance assets (Pozen 1998). The variety of fund objectives and ancillary services has also escalated, with equity funds expanding much more quickly than bond or money market funds over the last twenty years. Savers apparently feel that investing through mutual funds gives them advantages in terms of convenience, liquidity, and diversification that justify the fees.

Our object was to analyze the determinants of mutual fund fees and how they are spent in order to shed light on how costs might evolve or might be shaped in a reformed social security system with individual accounts. We used simple cross-tabulations, regression analysis, and frontier analysis based on a large data set of mutual funds (4,254 funds in 1997 and 1,300–2,000 each year for 1992–96) that we obtained from Morningstar. We also culled information from annual reports, fund prospectuses, and financial statements filed by the funds' investment advisers as well as surveys conducted by the association of mutual funds and discussions with fund officials and their transfer agents.[7]

In the United States, as in Chile, mutual funds are organized by sponsors, but they are not owned by these sponsors. Instead, the assets are owned by the shareholders who invest in them. A board of directors (most of whom are affiliated with the sponsor) chooses the investment adviser, who, in almost all cases, is the original sponsor of the fund. Often, the same sponsor starts multiple funds in a fund complex such as Fidelity or Vanguard. The adviser makes key strategic decisions, hires analysts and portfolio managers (who handle day-to-day investment activities), advertises the fund, and provides other administrative services. Competition takes the form of investors exiting and entering funds rather than funds choosing and reevaluating investment advisers (Baumol et al. 1990).

Marketing and service have been major instruments in the competition among funds for investors. In contrast, price competition seems to have played a relatively minor role, especially in the short run. Later, we interpret this as a consequence of product differentiation and a high noise-to-signal ratio in volatile markets, which makes it difficult to distinguish between random good luck that will not repeat and low costs that will repeat in the future.

3.3.1   Costs in the Mutual Fund Industry

The fund pays annual fees to the investment adviser and much smaller amounts to distributors (12b1 fees), lawyers, auditors, transfer agents, and others (table 3.5). By regulation, the charges are passed on to shareholders

---

7. Money market funds, which constitute about one-quarter of the fund universe, were largely excluded from this study because they involve short-term deposits, high transactions levels, and related costs that would not be applicable to IAs in social security systems. Mutual funds with missing data for important variables were also excluded. We included only "open-end funds" whose shares are bought and sold at net asset value—total assets divided by total shares.

Table 3.5   **Composition of Mutual Fund Expenses, 1997 (as percentage of assets unless noted)**

	Simple Average	Asset Weighted		
		Average	Active	Passive
Expenses included in expense ratio:				
Investment adviser	0.56	0.49	0.52	0.08
Distributor for 12b1 fees[a]	0.35	0.21	0.22	0.02
Transfer agent (R&C)	0.13	0.12	0.12	0.05
Other (legal, audit, etc.)	0.23	0.09	0.08	0.13
Reported expense ratio	1.27	0.91	0.95	0.28
$s per account[b]	320	228	238	70
Other investor costs:				
Brokerage fees (trading costs)	0.26	0.12	0.12	0.03
Annualized front-loaded sales				
charge paid by shareholder[a]	0.31	0.40	0.43	0.01
Total investor costs as % of assets	1.85	1.43	1.50	0.32
$s per account[b]	463	360	375	80

[a]The 12b1 fee is a fee that is paid annually by the fund, primarily for distribution of new shares and related service. It is financed by a charge paid by all shareholders, whether or not they have purchased their shares through a broker. It is part of the fund's expense ratio and is based on assets. The front-loaded sales charge is paid directly to the distributor by investors who purchase through brokers, as a percentage of their new investment. It is not included in the fund's expense ratio. The average front-loaded fee is 4.48 percent. It is charged by about one-third of all funds. In this table, this one-time fee has been annualized according to the procedure described in n. 8. These numbers are averaged over all funds, ignoring the big distinction in costs to shareholders between funds that impose sales charges and those that do not (see table 3.10 below).

[b]For average account size = $25,000.

proportional to their assets and determine the fund's reported "expense ratio," which it subtracts from its gross return to obtain the investors' net return. Thus (unlike in Chile), shareholder fees paid to the fund equal the costs of the fund, although they may yield large profits to the investment adviser. In addition, for many funds, front-loaded and back-loaded commissions are paid directly by individual investors to brokers on purchase or sale; these entry and exit fees are part of the price to relevant shareholders, although they are not received or paid by the fund and are not included in the expense ratio. Brokerage fees paid for securities transactions are also excluded from the expense ratio, although they are indirectly paid by shareholders in the form of reduced gross returns.

We have constructed a "total investor-cost ratio," which equals the reported expense ratio plus average brokerage (trading) costs and annualized front-loaded sales commissions (table 3.5).[8] In 1997, the total inves-

8. Average brokerage costs were estimated on the basis of a subset of funds that reported these data for 1997. The unweighted and weighted averages were twenty-six and twelve basis points, respectively.

Annualized front-loaded sales commissions were estimated as 0.2 times the front-loaded

tor cost was 1.85 percent of assets, compared to the reported expense ratio of 1.28 percent. Weighted by assets, these numbers fall to 1.43 and 0.91 percent (or $360 and $228 per average account), respectively. Asset-weighted numbers are more relevant for our purposes because they indicate the expense incurred by the average dollar invested. The lower asset-weighted figures are consistent with economies of scale and/or a selection of clients into low-cost funds. The variation in costs is also great. For example, the average dollar invested in passively managed funds incurs a cost ratio that is only one-fifth the expense of a dollar invested in actively managed funds.

Table 3.6 converts these numbers into the cost categories set forth in section 3.1—R&C costs, investment costs, marketing expenses, and fixed costs—both in terms of dollars per account and as a percentage of assets. Comparing table 3.6 with the hypothetical numbers in table 3.1 above for an average account size of $25,000, we see that the costs are somewhat larger than but very close in breakdown to panel C of table 3.1. Investment

---

commission on new sales. An annualization factor of 0.2 was used to convert a one-time fee into its annual present-value equivalent, assuming that the average investment is kept in the fund for seven years and that the discount rate is 10 percent. A high discount rate is used because the alternative for these investors may be an additional mutual fund purchase, over a period in which the three-year asset-weighted net return was 20 percent. The annualization factor and the annualized fee are not very sensitive to the discount rate; a discount rate of 5 percent would have made a difference of only three basis points.

The seven-year average holding period is a guestimate since good data are not available on this variable. A sample of redemption rates for equity funds purchased in 1974 showed that 50 percent of original shares were sold within five years, 76 percent within fifteen years, which is roughly consistent with our seven-year assumption (Wyatt Co. 1990). However, the mutual fund industry and its clientele have changed substantially since 1974, so it is likely that redemption behavior has also changed. An average holding period of ten to twelve years would have reduced the annualized fee by five to ten basis points, while an average five-year holding period would have increased it by a similar amount. Holding periods and therefore annualization factors may vary among funds. For example, evidence suggests that loads discourage movements out of funds, so the holding periods of funds with loads may be higher than average (Ippolito 1992; Chordia 1996). However, we did not have the disaggregated data that would allow us to take these differences into account.

Back-loaded sales charges are omitted from this calculation because they fall as a function of the time the shares are held. Investors self-select into funds with back loads if they expect to hold their shares for long periods. The average deferred load paid for assets held more than five years is negligible, and we do not have a more detailed distribution of holding periods. This omission slightly understates total costs.

The total fund-expense profile calculated here is very similar to the total shareholder-cost ratio calculated by Rea and Reid (1998), although they use slightly different data sets and definitions. The most important differences are that they deal only with equity funds (which are more expensive than bond funds) and that they do not include brokerage fees in their measure, probably because they are interested in changes through time and data on brokerage fees were not reported before 1996. These two effect may cancel themselves out in terms of a comparison with our numbers. Their simple average-cost ratio is 1.99 percent and their asset-weighted average 1.44 percent, very similar to our numbers of 1.85 and 1.43 percent, respectively. According to their calculations, marketing fees are 40 percent of total costs, while, in our calculations (which include brokerage costs in the denominator), the simple average is 36 percent and the weighted average 43 percent.

Table 3.6   **Mutual Fund Expenses by Cost Components, 1997**

	A. As a Percentage of Assets		
	Weighted Average	Actively Managed	Passively Managed
Investment	0.61	0.64	0.11
R&C	0.12	0.12	0.05
Marketing	0.61	0.65	0.03
Fixed and miscellaneous	0.09	0.08	0.13
Total	1.43	1.50	0.32
	B. In Dollars per Account		
Investment	153	160	28
R&C	30	30	13
Marketing	153	163	8
Fixed and miscellaneous	23	20	33
Total	360	375	80
	C. Percentage of Total Expenses		
Investment	43	43	34
R&C	8	8	16
Marketing	43	44	9
Fixed and miscellaneous	6	5	41
Total	100	100	100

Source: Table 3.5 above.

Note: For conversion into dollars, average account size = $25,000. Investment = investment adviser + brokerage fees. R&C = transfer agent. Marketing = 12b1 fees + loads. Fixed & miscellaneous = other. Marketing costs are understated and investment costs overstated because part of the investment adviser's fee is spent on advertising and organizing sales efforts. Totals differ slightly from some of subcategories owing to rounding errors.

costs far exceed R&C cost, and marketing cost is the largest component for many funds.

More than half the reported expense ratio is paid to the investment adviser, who then allocates the money among the factors of production. While, in our simple breakdown, we have allocated this to "investment expenses," actually some of it is spent on advertising, the development of new products and technologies, and other functions. This disaggregation is difficult to obtain since most fund sponsors are private companies, which are not required to disclose their records.

Other problems related to measuring and understanding mutual fund costs are the following (except for the last point, we do not believe that these problems bias our major results): (1) Disclosure of brokerage costs (for securities transactions) was not required until 1996, and brokerage costs are reported for only a subset of our funds for 1996 and 1997. (2) Some brokerage fees cover research or other expenses of the fund or its adviser (i.e., the "soft-dollar" issue), thereby reducing the reported cost that goes into the expense ratio and understating real expenditures on these items. (3) Some investment returns are reported net of cost, without data for the cost of producing them. (4) Income from securities lending operations is sometimes used to offset custodial and other expenses, which are therefore underestimated by reported fees. (5) Some funds do not report number of shareholders, and the growing use of omnibus accounts that consolidate many shareholders further complicates the use of this explanatory variable. (6) Investment advisers temporarily waive some fees, especially fees of new funds, as a business strategy to attract new customers but may later reinstate them; these temporary fees may not reflect real costs. (7) The data set includes only funds that were still operating in 1997, and it therefore suffers from survivorship bias. Many expensive or poorly performing older funds have terminated, which may lead to an understatement of costs or an overstatement of expected returns. (8) Many shareholders pay a front-loaded one-time sales charge directly to brokers or other sales agents. These charges are not reported as fund expenses. To include them, we had to annualize them on the basis of estimated holding periods for which we lack good data, so caution is needed to interpret these estimates of marketing expenses. (9) The invisible diseconomy of scale—the effect of a fund's buying and selling activities on security price—is not measured here. This may lead to an overstatement of scale economies, especially in small-cap and thin markets where the fund owns a large part of total capitalization. (10) Most funds are members of a mutual fund complex (e.g., Fidelity and Vanguard). Certain activities, such as advertising, research, and new product development, are jointly supplied to all members of the complex by the common investment adviser. The allocation of these expenses among the funds may be influenced by estimates of where the expenses can be absorbed with least loss of clients (see point 6 above). Thus, the relative fees paid by members of a fund complex do not necessarily reflect the real cost of producing them. Perhaps most important for our purposes, business strategy concerning joint cost allocation may be different in a mandatory system given its different clientele.

3.3.2   Specification of Regressions

The main dependent variable in our regressions is the "expense ratio"—reported expenses (excluding brokerage fees and loads) as a percentage of assets. We did not use the "total investor-cost ratio" as our dependent variable because reliable data were not available for holding periods by fund or on brokerage costs for most funds in the data set. Front-loaded sales commissions, a large portion of total marketing expenses, are not part of the expense ratio, but they are treated as an independent variable that may influence the expense ratio and are discussed as a marketing cost.

We sought to determine the extent to which cost variation is random or

Table 3.7   **Mean, Median, and Standard Deviation of Variables in Sample, 1997**

	Asset-Weighted Mean	Simple Mean	Simple Median	S.D.
Expense ratio (as % of assets)	0.91	1.28	1.17	0.61
Assets ($billions)	9.94	0.59	0.09	2.35
No. of shareholders (thousands)	453.62	23.55	2.19	115.38
Assets in family funds ($billions)	151.15	42.06	12.30	86.00
3-year net return (%)	20.16	14.30	11.44	9.22
3-year gross return (%)	21.79	16.16	13.45	9.19
3-year standard deviation	11.67	9.85	8.68	6.59
Turnover (%)	69.40	98.00	65.00	117.00
Fundage	19.90	8.97	5.35	9.58
Percentage of funds that are:				
Bond funds	30	51		
Small cap	5	6		
Specialty	7	7		
International	10	11		
Emerging market	1	3		
Institutional	5	7		
Initial investment ($10,000–$100,000)	1	1		
Index	6	2		
Low 12b1 fee (0.25 percent or less)	36	41		
High 12b1 fee (between 0.25 and 1 percent)	10	21		
Front load	42	35		
Back load	12	27		
Bank advised	5	16		

systematic, to identify the factors that lie behind the systematic variation, and to assess the implications for IA systems. Our independent variables fall into three main groups—a core group capturing economies of scale and scope for the key outputs (investment of assets and R&C services per account) as well as the possible relation between costs, returns, and risk; an asset-allocation group acknowledging that different real costs are implied by different portfolios; and a business- and marketing-strategy group reflecting decisions made by the fund's adviser, such as whether the fund should be actively or passively managed, whether it should seek large (institutional) investors, etc. (table 3.7):

Core Group
Assets (in billions of dollars)
Asset^2
Assets in entire fund complex
Number of accounts (in thousands) or, alternatively, average assets per account
Three-year gross return or, alternatively, three-year load-adjusted net return
Three-year standard deviation of returns

Asset-Allocation Group
Dummy variables for funds that specialize in bonds, small-cap stocks, special sector stocks, international (industrialized-country) funds, and emerging market funds, with large-cap stock funds as the omitted category

Business- and Marketing-Strategy Group
Minimum investment required
Stock turnover rate
Fund age
Dummy variables for funds that sell only to institutional (very large) clients, index funds, bank-advised funds, funds with high (equal to 1) or low (greater than 0 but less than 1) 12b1 fees, and funds with front loads and deferred loads

We ran the OLS regressions separately for each year from 1992 to 1997. We also conducted a frontier (envelope) analysis for 1992–97, which included a time trend as an additional variable. Tables 3.8 and 3.9 report results from the OLS regression for 1997 and the frontier analysis for 1992–97, which yield a consistent picture of the determinants of mutual fund costs. The OLS regressions explain 64 percent of the variance when all the variables listed above are included, with the business- and marketing-strategy group accounting for more than half the predictive power. Most of the variance in costs is therefore systematic rather than random. Costs faced by investors vary in large part because of business choices made by fund managers, and these same costs could be substantially influenced by policy choices in a mandatory IA system.

3.3.3   Economies of Scale and Scope

Expense ratios fall when total assets in the fund, assets in the entire fund complex, and assets per shareholder increase. For funds with assets under $10 million, the simple average expense ratio is 1.54 percent, while, for funds with assets over $1 billion, it is 0.96 percent. All funds need industry analysts, portfolio managers, computers, and access to electronic trading facilities. Large funds, however, can be managed with virtually the same staff and trading access as smaller funds. The scale economies come from marketing costs as well as investment management: large funds spread their advertising expenses (and, less important, their legal, accounting, and audit expenses) over a larger asset base. Partly for these reasons, the largest and fastest-growing mutual funds also experienced the greatest drop in operating expenses over the last twenty years (Rea and Reid 1998).[9]

---

9. For more on sources of scale economies, see Baumol et al. (1990) and Sirri and Tufano (1993).

Table 3.8   Regression Analysis: Determinants of Expense Ratios of Mutual Funds in the United States, 1997

	(1)	(2)	(3)	(4)	(5)
Core group:					
Intercept	113.7*	112.1*	111.0*	83.4*	125.0*
	(59.63)	(55.35)	(22.22)	(22.03)	(26.09)
Assets ($billions)	−9.2*	−7.9*	−9.1*	−3.9*	−5.2*
	(−9.55)	(−10.03)	(−9.61)	(−5.65)	(−5.67)
Asset^2	0.1*	0.1*	0.1*	0.1*	0.1*
	(5.22)	(7.20)	(5.48)	(−6.17)	(4.51)
No. of shareholders (thousands)	0.1*		0.1*	0.0	0.0
	(3.14)		(3.02)	(−1.48)	(0.89)
Assets/shareholders		−0.4*			
		(−4.9)			
Assets in fund complex ($billions)	−0.1*	−0.1*	−0.1*	−0.1*	−0.1*
	(−7.99)	(−7.61)	(−8.66)	(−7.31)	(−10.07)
3-year net return[a]	−1.5*		−0.9*	−0.7*	−0.7*
	(−13.73)		(−6.26)	(−6.37)	(−4.84)
3-year gross return		−1.1*			
		(−9.73)			
3-year standard deviation	4.6*	4.4*	3.5*	3.1*	3.3*
	(29.56)	(27.93)	(14.24)	(17.94)	(14.32)
Asset allocation:					
Bond			−1.9	−9.6*	−8.0**
			(−0.52)	(−3.71)	(2.35)
Small cap			3.2	11.6*	−0.2
			(0.76)	(3.98)	(0.05)
Specialty			23.0*	11.7*	16.4*
			(6.01)	(4.33)	(4.61)
International			28.9*	24.1*	24.5*
			(7.61)	(8.96)	(6.89)
Emerging market			37.6*	37.5*	39.9*
			(5.25)	(7.43)	(5.53)
(continued)					

Table 3.8   (continued)

	(1)	(2)	(3)	(4)	(5)
Investment and marketing strategy:					
Institutional				−15.4*	−52.8*
				(−4.23)	(−11.45)
Initial investment				−0.4*	−0.4**
				(−3.22)	(−1.9)
Index				−38.5*	−51.7*
				(−8.72)	(−8.86)
12b1 fee < 1, > 0				18.4*	
				(9.73)	
12b1 fee = 1				43.5*	
				(14.19)	
Front load				2.7	
				(−1.43)	
Deferred load				47.3*	
				(16.86)	
Turnover				4.3*	6.0*
				(8.21)	(8.65)
Bank advised				−8.1*	−18.7*
				(−4.44)	(−7.88)
Fundage				−0.2*	−1.1*
				(−3.26)	(−12.37)
Adjusted R^2	23.8	22.2	26.9	64.2	38.0
Dependent mean	127.6	127.6	127.6	127.6	127.62
N	3,609	3,609	3,609	3,610	3,610

Note: Brokerage fees and front and deferred loads are not included in expense ratios. The dependent variable is total expenses/total assets, in basis points (1 basis point = 0.01 percent). *t*-statistics are given in parentheses.

[a]Three-year net returns are gross returns adjusted for expense ratio and loads.

*Significant at the 0.2 percent level.

**Significant at the 5 percent level.

Table 3.9 **Frontier Analysis: Determinants of Expense Ratios of Mutual Funds in the United States, 1992–97**

	(1)	(2)	(3)	(4)
Core group:				
Intercept	22.6*	23.0*	26.4*	65.0*
	(12.73)	(12.31)	(9.17)	(31.91)
Assets ($billions)	−3.5*	−2.2*	−2.7*	−2.3*
	(−5.97)	(−5.97)	(−7.05)	(4.64)
Asset^2	0.1*	1.0*	0.1*	0.1*
	(5.77)	(5.33)	(6.18)	(6.21)
No. of shareholders (thousands)	0.03**			0.0
	(2.68)			(1.3)
Assets/shareholders		−1.0*	−0.1*	
		(−3.11)	(−3.17)	
Assets in fund complex ($billions)	−0.1*	−0.1*	−0.1*	−0.1*
	(−6.27)	(−8.47)	(−8.23)	(−12.94)
3-year net return[a]		−0.6*	−0.5*	
		(−16.25)	(−13.5)	
3-year gross return	−0.4*			−0.3*
	(−11.31)			(−8.89)
3-year standard deviation	0.13*	1.5*	1.0*	1.0*
	(16.79)	(19.2)	(−11.59)	(12.82)
Asset allocation:				
Bond			−12.6*	−23.8*
			(−7.57)	(−19.25)
Small cap			14.9*	11.5*
			(5.12)	(6.25)
Specialty			15.7*	6.8*
			(5.59)	(3.96)
International			18.5*	21.7*
			(7.65)	(13.72)
Emerging market			59.9*	48.2*
			(12.92)	(15.64)
Investment and marketing strategy:				
Institutional				−15.4*
				(−8.09)
Initial investment				−0.3**
				(−2.48)
Index				−38.6*
				(−14.18)
12b1 fee < 1, > 0				17.7*
				(13.84)
12b1 fee = 1				49.9*
				(23.16)
Front load				6.2*
				(4.71)
Deferred load				49.7*
				(25.3)
Turnover				2.0*
				(7.46)

(continued)

Table 3.9   (continued)

	(1)	(2)	(3)	(4)
Bank advised				−2.4**
				(−1.92)
Fundage				−0.4*
				(−8.95)
Time	2.3*	2.3*	2.3*	1.2*
	(11.17)	(10.66)	(10.96)	(6.41)

Note: Brokerage fees and loads are not included in expense ratios. The dependent variable is total expenses/total assets, in basis points (1 basis point = 0.01 percent). *t*-statistics are given in parentheses.
aThree-year net returns are gross returns adjusted for expense ratio and loads.
*Significant at the 0.2 percent level.
**Significant at the 5 percent level.

On the one hand, scale economies may be somewhat underestimated in these regressions because fund complexes may subsidize their new smaller funds, charging them less than full costs while they are "infants," and earning a higher profit margin on their large, well-established funds, where clients may be less responsive to small differences in fees. On the other hand, scale economies may be overstated for certain types of assets, such as small-cap and emerging market stocks. Reverse causation may also be at work: low-cost funds may have attracted large amounts of assets rather than vice versa. We were not able to distinguish between these two effects in this paper.

Perhaps most important, these economies from asset aggregation do not continue indefinitely. The positive sign on the coefficient of Asset^2 in the regressions brings to a halt the fall in expense ratio when fund size reaches the \$20–\$40 billion range. Other studies have found that scale economies stemming from the size of the entire fund complex may stop at \$20–\$40 billion in the United States and at Fr 2.9 billion, a much lower level, in France (Collins and Mack 1997; Dermine and Röller 1992). Price impact, not measured here, also places brakes on scale economies, especially in illiquid markets. The fact that many small funds coexist with larger ones is further evidence of the limits to scale economies and also of the gradualness of the market process in adjusting to these economies. Thus, aggregation brings economies that lead to industry concentration, but the limit to these economies nevertheless leaves space for multiple mutual funds (and pension funds), the exact number depending on the total market size of each country. A mandatory IA system in the United States would generate over \$60 billion of new contributions annually, even with a small contribution rate of 2 percent. Such flows are large enough to offer options among many fund managers at a cost-effective scale.

3.3.4   Fixed R&C Costs per Account

Holding aggregate assets constant, the expense ratio increases with number of shareholders, but this effect disappears once such strategy variables as minimum investment are controlled. The expense ratio decreases as average account size rises. The basic reason, as seen above, is that funds incur a cost per account for R&C; the larger each account, the smaller this cost will be as a percentage of assets.

R&C costs are $20–$25 for an average-size account, according to these regressions. According to corroborating evidence from periodic surveys of transfer agents (the organizations that provide these services for mutual funds), average R&C costs per account have been quite constant in this range during the 1990s. In 1995, the average cost was $21, and 80 percent of all funds reported R&C costs between $10 and $32 (see sec. 3.5 below).

Fixed costs per account associated with R&C pose a potential problem for IA systems if the accounts are small; $20 is 4 percent of a $500 account but less than 0.1 percent of a $25,000 account, approximately the current level for mutual funds. These fixed costs help explain the high expense ratios of new AFPs and mutual funds in developing countries. This raises the question of whether an investment option with lower R&C costs (basic service, limited transferability) should be used initially or whether these fixed costs should be amortized over a long time period, to avoid imposing a heavy burden on early cohorts, in new IA systems.

3.3.5   High Marketing Costs

Aggressive marketing strategies have been developed by mutual funds to maximize the assets under their management. Using brokers, other salespersons, and mass-advertising methods (media advertisements, direct mailings), the industry has successfully called to the attention of potential shareholders the advantages of equity investing, using mutual funds as the vehicle. This probably accounts for a large part of the industry's dramatic growth in assets and its access to scale economies. At the same time, marketing itself adds substantially to costs.

The major marketing expense incurred by shareholders consists of sales commissions. Over two-thirds of all funds are sold through third parties (brokers, insurance agents, financial planners) who receive some kind of commission (through front or deferred loads or annual 12b1 fees). However, the proportion of assets managed as no loads through direct marketing is larger and has been increasing through time (table 3.10).

How much do marketing fees add to total expenses? It is possible that sales commissions may substitute for other costs, such as advertising or communication costs. Our regressions, however, show little trade-off. Most of the 12b1 fee is passed on to consumers as an additional cost. A low 12b1 fee (usually 0.25 percent), which is included in the expense ratio,

Table 3.10   **Marketing Expenses of U.S. Mutual Funds**

	Unweighted		Weighted	
	1992	1997	1992	1997
Prevalence of commissions (% of total funds):				
Funds with 12b1 fees	55.00	61.00	49.00	46.00
Funds with front load	50.00	35.00	52.00	42.00
Funds with deferred load	9.00	27.00	9.00	12.00
Funds with no load or 12b1 fee	34.00	32.00	36.00	44.00
Expenses as % of assets (all funds):				
Average 12b1 fee	0.21	0.35	0.18	0.21
Average annualized front load	0.46	0.31	0.50	0.40
Reported expense ratio	1.16	1.28	0.87	0.91
Brokerage fees (trading costs)	0.27	0.26	0.15	0.12
Total expenses	1.89	1.85	1.52	1.43
Marketing expenses as % of total expenses	35.00	36.00	45.00	43.00
Expenses as % of assets (funds with either 12b1 or front load):				
Average 12b1 fee	0.38	0.52	0.36	0.37
Average front load	0.65	0.46	0.75	0.72
Reported expense ratio	1.27	1.46	0.98	1.09
Brokerage fees	0.28	0.28	0.15	0.11
Total investor cost ratio	2.20	2.20	1.88	1.92
Marketing expenses as % of total expenses	46.82	44.55	59.04	56.77
Expenses as % of assets (funds without 12b1 or front load):[a]				
Average 12b1 fee	0	0	0	0
Average front load	0	0	0	0
Reported expense ratio	0.94	0.89	0.68	0.68
Brokerage fees	0.29	0.23	0.17	0.12
Total investor cost ratio	1.23	1.12	0.85	0.80

Note: Average brokerage fees are taken from a subset of funds for which they were available.

For 12b1 fee, front load, and total expenses, see table 3.5 and n. 8 above. Deferred load is a back-loaded sales charge that is paid to the distributor by investors. Usually, the deferred load falls as a function of time the shares are held; therefore, the average deferred load paid by investors ends up being small (but we do not have precise data). Neither front load nor deferred load are included in the fund's expense ratio since they are paid by the shareholder, not the fund.

Annual marketing expenses are defined here as 12b1 fee + 0.2 (front load). 0.2 is annualized front load for reasons given in n. 8 above.

This table overstates marketing expenses if investors hold their front-loaded shares longer than assumed or if the discount rate is lower than assumed. On the other hand, given that deferred load is excluded (on the grounds that most people hold their investments long enough to avoid most of the deferred load) and advertising costs are excluded (because they are not reported), this table probably understates marketing expenses.

[a]These funds have no explicit marketing expenses in the form of sales commissions. Advertising costs are present but not reported.

raises the expense ratio by 0.2 percent, a high 12b1 fee (usually 1 percent) raises it by 0.4 percent, and the latter is usually found together with a deferred load, which raises it another 0.5 percent, implying that most of the 12b1 fee is an added cost. A front load (a one-time sales fee of 4–5 percent) that is paid by investors directly to brokers does not reduce the reported expense ratio paid by the fund. (For corroboration of the cost-raising effects of sales loads, see Ferris and Chance [1987] and Trzcinka and Zweig [1990].)

If we define *total annual marketing cost* (paid by the shareholder) as the 12b1 fee plus the annualized front load, it is 0.61 percent of assets—43 percent of all fund expenses (table 3.10). This is very similar to the marketing proportion of total cost in Chile's AFP system. For funds with front loads or 12b1 fees, total investor costs are over 1 percentage point higher than for funds that pay no sales commission, and more than half of total investor expenses can be attributed to marketing costs. These numbers undoubtedly understate true marketing costs as they do not include the salaries of the staff who manage the marketing efforts or the advertising costs that are paid for out of the adviser's fee. Marketing costs played an even more important role in the early years of the mutual fund industry, before no loads developed.

Investors have the option, of course, to purchase no loads. This implies that, rightly or wrongly, they believe that they receive value from the third-party intermediaries with whom they deal. (For corroboration, see Kihn [1996], and Capon, Fitzsimmons, and Prince [1996].) From a social point of view, marketing probably provides a mixture of useful information, misleading information, an impetus to good performance, and zero-sum game raiding. Other studies have shown that the funds that have gained the most are those that combine vigorous marketing with good performance (Sirri and Tufano 1997). The possibility of spreading favorable information by marketing probably acts as a spur to good performance and product innovation. Nevertheless, most methods to keep IA costs low involve a reduction in marketing expenses, under the assumption that it is zero or negative sum and not the most efficient way to provide useful information to new investors.

3.3.6   Lower Expenses for Institutional Funds

A small number of mutual funds or special classes within a large mutual fund are limited to institutional investors (i.e., bank trust departments, corporations, small pension funds, etc.). Usually, the minimum investment for these funds is $100,000 or higher. These funds have a significantly lower expense ratio as compared with funds for individual investors. The same assets can be amassed with much lower marketing and R&C costs from one large institution than from numerous small individuals. Institutions are much less likely to pay 12b1 (or front-loaded) fees to brokers because they have more efficient ways of gathering information. On the rare occasions when they do pay these fees, they obtain lower rates. As a result, the expense ratio of institutional funds is 0.6 percent lower than that of other funds in the regression specifications where sales commissions are not controlled, and the total investor cost (as a percentage of assets) for the average institutional fund is less than half that for retail funds (table 3.11).

Some funds have an initial investment requirement that is high (over $10,000), albeit not as high as that for institutions. These funds also have a significantly lower expense ratio (0.4 percent) than funds that cater to smaller investors, albeit not quite as low as institutional funds. These observations led us to investigate the institutional market in greater detail in order to determine whether IAs could also benefit from the low expense ratios that would result from the large aggregate amounts in the mandatory system.

3.3.7   Lower Costs of Passive Management—for Some Assets

Also important is the significant negative sign on passively managed funds, known as *index funds,* which do not have to pay the high fees that popular active managers command. Passively managed funds mimic or replicate a stated benchmark, such as the Standard and Poor's 500 or the Russell 2000. The manager does not engage in discretionary stock selection or market timing and therefore cannot claim a fee for superior information or judgment. Index funds generally benefit from low turnover, which reduces the expense ratio as well as brokerage fees. Their high correlation with the market (low nonsystematic risk) means that they are less likely to engage in heavy marketing and more likely to rely on price (cost) competition (see below). In the regressions, expense ratios of index funds are 0.5 percent less than those of other funds. On average, their fees are less than one-third those of actively managed funds in the retail market (table 3.11). Better-informed institutional managers realize this and hold a disproportionate share of index funds.

The low cost of index funds should be interpreted with some caution, however. It could mean that fund complexes view these funds as the products that are designed to capture price-sensitive consumers, and, for this reason, they may allocate much of their joint expenses (advertising, new product development) to the other members of their complex.[10] R&C charges also tend to be less for passively than for actively managed funds; this may be a business-strategy decision rather than a reflection of real cost differentials. The real cost savings to the economy and the potential savings in a mandatory IA system from index funds may therefore be

---

10. For example, in 1998–99 Fidelity waived part of its normal management fee on its Standard and Poor's 500 index funds in order to make them more competitive.

Table 3.11   Institutional versus Retail Mutual Funds: Average Expense Ratios and Total Investor Cost as Percentage of Assets, 1997

		All		Active		Passive	
	All	Retail	Institutional	Retail	Institutional	Retail	Institutional
A. Expense Ratio—Unweighted							
Domestic stock funds	1.43	1.47	0.91	1.50	0.98	0.71	0.37
Domestic bond funds	1.08	1.12	0.62	1.12	0.62	0.65	0.35
International stock funds	1.69	1.75	1.09	1.77	1.15	0.95	0.66
Emerging market funds	2.12	2.19	1.39	2.21	1.39	0.57	0.00
All funds in universe	1.28	1.31	0.79	1.33	0.81	0.72	0.42
B. Expense Ratio—Weighted by Assets							
Domestic stock funds	0.93	0.94	0.51	0.99	0.85	0.31	0.19
Domestic bond funds	0.80	0.82	0.53	0.82	0.54	0.25	0.31
International stock funds	1.18	1.19	0.96	1.20	0.97	0.42	0.68
Emerging market funds	1.75	1.77	1.25	1.81	1.25	0.57	0.00
All funds in universe	0.91	0.93	0.56	0.96	0.69	0.31	0.20
C. Total Investor Cost, Including Annualized Front Loads and Brokerage Fees—Weighted by Assets							
Domestic stock funds	1.44	1.47	0.63	1.55	0.97	0.35	0.22
Domestic bond funds	1.30	1.35	0.65	1.36	0.65	0.29	0.34
International stock funds	1.83	1.87	1.08	1.89	1.09	0.45	0.71
Emerging market funds	2.29	2.33	1.37	2.38	1.37	0.60	0.00
All funds in universe	1.43	1.48	0.68	1.52	0.71	0.35	0.23

Note: In this table, international stock funds include emerging market funds.

overstated by our regression results. If index funds become a larger share of the total market, opportunities for cost saving and cost shifting may decline. Finally, in separate regressions by asset class, the lower costs of index funds were not statistically significant for small-cap and emerging market funds. This suggests that IA systems in large-cap stock and bond markets in industrialized countries can keep their costs down and increase their net returns by using index funds, although this effect may be smaller than indicated by these regressions and less true of developing and transitional countries, where emerging markets and small-cap stocks dominate. Passive investment strategies would have the additional advantage in a mandatory system of reducing the variance in returns among participants.

3.3.8   Asset Allocation: International Funds

Asset allocation has a major effect on costs. The dummy variables for asset classes have large significant effects—although the total R^2 does not change much in comparison with the core group. Bond funds have lower costs, and small-cap or specialty funds have higher costs. Expenses are highest in international funds, especially emerging market funds—as a result of their smaller size, the greater difficulty in obtaining information in these countries, their high bid-ask spreads, transactions and custodial costs, currency-hedging costs, and the relative paucity of effective cost-saving passive investment opportunities. If brokerage fees and price impact were taken into account, this would increase their expenses still further. These factors would also apply to local funds operating in emerging markets, although such institutions need not hedge against domestic currency risk and may have an informational advantage over those that are based in a foreign country. It follows that IA systems in industrialized countries such as the United States can economize on costs if they concentrate investments in large liquid domestic instruments and that international diversification comes at the expense of higher costs. In contrast, developing countries are likely to have higher costs for domestic investments—although this effect could be mitigated for them by international diversification.

3.3.9   Brokerage Fees

Brokerage fees paid for securities transactions average 0.26 percent of assets for the subset of funds in our sample that included these data. Weighted by assets, average annual brokerage fees fall to 0.12 percent. Recall that these fees are not included in the reported expense ratio but are deducted from gross returns and are therefore part of total investor cost. Separate regressions on this subset show that, as do other expenses, brokerage fees exhibit economies of scale with respect to assets as large fund families use internal trading and spread the fixed costs of electronic trading over a larger base. Brokerage costs are higher for international funds, especially in emerging markets, and they are, of course, strongly dependent on securities turnover rates.[11]

3.3.10   Net Returns, Gross Returns, and Risk

Of course, the investor ultimately cares about net returns, not the expense incurred in earning them. If higher costs led to higher returns, they would be worth incurring. However, a large literature indicates that this is not the case (see Carhart 1997; Elton, Gruber, and Hlavka 1993; Malkiel 1995; Malhotra and McLeod 1997; *Washington Post,* 13 September 1998, B1). While this paper focuses on costs, we also carried out regressions on net and gross returns for 1992–97. These indicate that some of the same factors that increase costs actually reduced returns during this period (James et al. 1999).

Most important, larger assets under management increase both gross and net returns, although this effect stops after a point. Funds with front-loaded fees do not earn higher gross returns, so their load-adjusted net returns are lower than are those of no loads. Index funds earn significantly more than actively managed funds, overall, particularly in the large-cap stock and bond markets, but specifications that were disaggregated by asset class indicate that this effect is absent in the small-cap, international, and emerging market funds (see also Muralidhar and Weary 1998; and Shah and Fernandes 1999). Institutional funds have higher gross and net returns.

These results from separate equations and previous literature are consistent with the negative sign on gross and net returns as a control variable in our expense-ratio equations. Cost and returns, especially net returns, appear to be negatively correlated. Thus, strategies involving high administrative costs do not seem to be justified on the grounds that they raise returns.

3.3.11   Changes over Time: Will Price
Competition Reduce Investor Costs?

The question of whether expense ratios have been going up or down over time has been hotly debated (see Lipper 1994). This is an important question because it tells us whether policy makers can rely on market forces to reduce costs. In our regression analysis for 1992–97, time has a

---

11. The typical brokerage fees paid by mutual funds apparently exceed the "best execution fees" charged by deep-discount brokers or commissions paid by large institutional investors by a factor of three or four (see Livingston and O'Neal 1996; and table 3.12 below). One possible reason is that brokerage fees are not included in the expense ratio, which is the most widely reported expense figure. They were not even disclosed until 1996. Reported expenses could be reduced by covering some research and marketing services out of transactions fees paid to brokers—the controversial soft-dollar issue. It will be interesting to see whether disclosure and, in fact, a glaring spotlight will change fund behavior in this respect.

small significant positive effect on the reported expense ratio (one to two basis points per year), after controlling for all our other variables.

These estimates do not take into account changes in sales commissions that are included in the total investor-cost ratio but not in the reported fund-expense ratio. Between 1992 and 1997, a shift of investors toward no loads and a decrease in the size of front loads led to a small fall in the total investor-cost ratio, despite the rise in the reported expense ratio (table 3.10 above). Over a longer time period (1980–97), the average investor-cost ratio has fallen more substantially (by about one-third), for the same reasons (Rea and Reid 1998). But the picture remains mixed because the total dollar cost per account (expense ratio times average assets per account) has gone up dramatically over the same period, primarily as a result of asset growth and secondarily as a result of the rise in nonmarketing expenses. More recently, investors have been shifting into cheaper passively managed funds, but, in 1997, these still held only 6 percent of all assets.

The movement to lower-cost and better-performing funds generally occurs through the flow of new money to the funds rather than the reallocation of old money. The process, therefore, has been very gradual, and some poorly informed investors have not participated in it (Ippolito 1992; Patel, Zeckhauser, and Hendricks 1994; Sirri and Tufano 1997; Gruber 1996). The slowness may be due, in part, to the generally robust stock market since 1980. Costs have been small relative to returns, and the vast majority of investors in diversified mutual funds have fared well, even those in high-cost funds. Costs may become more important as a determinant of net returns and peoples' investment decisions when gross returns decline. Nevertheless, it appears that, in the short run, we cannot count on competition to bring price down for the individual investor.

Why is this the case? We hypothesize that competition through marketing rather than through price cuts may be a consequence of volatility combined with the nonseparability between cost and benefit in equity markets (where the "benefit" is the net return and the "cost" is one of the ingredients of net return).[12] High volatility creates a high noise-to-signal ratio that makes it difficult for investors to distinguish between random luck versus skill and low costs that are likely to repeat, in predicting net returns, and leads funds to spend on marketing rather than to cut price. A small example will illustrate this point.

Suppose a fund manager has a low expense ratio that, ceteris paribus, leads to an alpha (i.e., a net return above the fair return given the risk involved) that is 0.1 percent per month or 1.2 percent per year. This incre-

---

12. In financial markets, consumers are basically purchasing an expected net return, which equals the gross return minus the expense ratio. They will be willing to pay a higher expense ratio (price) if this is correlated with higher gross and net returns, and stock market volatility enables some high-cost funds to argue that this is the case (even though our regressions show that, on average, this is not the case).

ment to net return will ultimately increase accumulations of lifetime investors by 24 percent, but, given the volatility of the portfolio, it is realized with a monthly standard deviation (of the nonsystematic risk) of 1 percent. In any given month or year, some other managers will outperform this manager, although, over time, he will outperform the market. How do investors distinguish the true ability of this manager to yield excess returns over the long run, owing to his lower costs, from the random short-run gains that accrue to other managers? If we take each month as an independent observation, regress this fund's return on the market return, and are fortunate enough to secure the true alpha as the estimated alpha, 384 observations, or almost twenty years, are needed to convince investors that this alpha is significantly higher than zero, at the 5 percent significance level.[13]

In the intervening years, other funds will be advertising their performance, choosing some convenient time period when they experienced above-average returns, and arguing that these superior returns more than justify their higher fees. Given the wide divergence between price and marginal cost in the industry and the fertile possibilities for shaping information in a favorable way, each fund has an incentive to spend substantially on marketing to increase the assets under its management. The proliferation of new funds that are kept alive if they randomly experience high returns at their beginning exacerbates the difficulty in separating noise from signal and the long time periods needed to do so. In view of these calculations, it is not surprising that it has taken no loads twenty years to gain barely half the market and that low-cost index funds are still only a tiny fraction of the market.

The more volatile the fund-specific returns and the greater the product (portfolio) differentiation, the more difficult it is to isolate true cost savings from random luck; we would expect marketing expenses to play a larger role relative to price competition in these circumstances. Bank deposits and money market funds, therefore, would be expected to depend less on marketing and more on price competition, and the same is true of bond and equity index funds. The movement toward low-cost funds might accelerate with a mandatory IA system that includes many low-income investors who are interested in low cost. But, more basically, when returns are volatile, true cost saving that yields higher long-run returns cannot be distinguished from short-run random luck until many years of observations have elapsed. This poses a problem for IA systems as an entire generation of workers may pass through the system before low-cost, high-performing funds have been identified. The difficulty that small investors have in processing financial information will only exacerbate this situation. An IA system that constrains investment options to funds with low nonsystem-

13. $1.96 = (0.1 \text{ percent}) (\sqrt{384/.01})$ (adapted from Bodie, Kane, and Marcus 1989).

atic risk will encourage price competition relative to marketing competition because such funds will be able to demonstrate their cost-based superiority more quickly than funds with greater fund-specific volatility.

3.4 Costs in the Institutional Market

Mutual funds are limited in their ability to charge lower fees for large investors. Regulations require funds to charge all investors the same expense ratio—unless they create separate classes of shares that incur different expenses. Thus, institutional investor classes are usually not charged for shareholder services or distribution because it can be demonstrated that they do not incur these costs, but they are charged for a pro rata share of the investment adviser and other fees. This treatment makes it possible for mutual funds to compete for small institutional accounts (e.g., of $1–$20 million, owned by bank trust departments or corporations). However, it puts them at a disadvantage when competing for larger accounts. Larger institutions (e.g., defined-benefit [DB] plans of major corporations and public employers) can get better rates elsewhere.

3.4.1 How Much Do Institutional Investors Pay for Asset Management?

Table 3.12 presents illustrative sliding-scale data on costs of money management provided by a large manager of assets for institutions. It also shows median costs for 167 large and 10 of the largest U.S. pension funds (median large fund = $1.5 billion; median assets per money manager = $113 million; median largest fund = $42 billion; median assets per money manager = $543 million). These rates show clear evidence of scale economies, the cost efficiency of passive management, and the effect of asset allocation.

Fees as a percentage of assets decline over large ranges with volume of assets managed. Marginal fees are as low as 1 basis point for passive management of large-cap stocks and 2.5 basis points for small and mid caps, once assets in an account reach $200 million. Fees for active management are higher but still far less than mutual fund rates. For large-cap domestic equity exceeding $25 million, investors must pay 35 to 50 basis points. Not surprisingly, fees for emerging market investments are much higher than those for domestic investments, but advantages to large institutional investors remain. For active management, they pay a marginal fee of 0.8 percent and, for index funds, only 0.4 percent. The largest pension funds pay still less. But even these funds use multiple money managers (an average of thirty-four) and allocate less than $1 billion on average to each active manager, evidence that diversification benefits eventually outweigh scale economies. There appears to be no strong cost reason for aggregating assets per manager beyond $1 billion.

Table 3.12 **Marginal and Average Asset-Management Fees for Institutional Investors: How They Vary with Amount of Investment (in basis points)**

	Large Cap	Small and Mid Cap	
Passive domestic equity:			
< $5 million	20.0	25.0	
$5–$10 million	10.0	15.0	
$10–$25 million	8.0	10.0	
$25–$100 million	6.0	7.5	
$100–$200 million	3.0	5.0	
Balance	1.0	2.5	
Average fee for $100 million	7.2	9.1	
Average fee for $500 million	2.6	4.3	
Median cost, large U.S. pension funds[a]	4.0	7.0	
Median cost, largest U.S. pension funds[b]	1.0	6.0	

	Value	Growth	Small Cap
Active domestic equity:			
< $5 million	65.0	80.0	100.0
$5–$25 million	35.0	80.0	100.0
Balance	35.0	50.0	100.0
Average fee for $100 million	36.5	57.5	100.0
Average fee for $500 million	35.3	51.5	100.0
Median cost, large pension funds		37.0	69.0
Median cost, largest pension funds		25.0	55.0

	Index	Active
International equity:		
< $10 million	25.00	90.0
$10–$25 milion	25.00	70.0
$25–$40 million	20.00	70.0
$40–$50 million	20.00	60.0
$50–$100 million	15.00	60.0
Balance	10.00	60.0
Average fee for $100 million	18.75	66.0
Average fee for $500 million	11.75	61.2
Median cost, large pension funds	12.00	54.0
Median cost, largest pension funds	8.00	34.0
Emerging market:		
< $50 million	40	100
Balance	40	80
Average fee for $100 million	40	90
Average fee for $500 million	40	82
Median cost, large pension funds	23	77
Median cost, largest pension funds	12	70
Fixed income:		
< $25 million	12.0	30
$25–$50 million	8.0	24
$50–$100 million	5.0	17
Balance	3.0	12
Average fee for $100 milion	7.5	22

(*continued*)

Table 3.12   (continued)

	Index	Active
Average fee for $500 million	3.9	14
Median cost, large pension funds	6.0	24
Median cost, largest pension funds	5.0	25

	Other Asset-Management Costs for Institutional Investors[c]
Internal administrative costs:	
Median cost, large pension funds	6
Median cost, largest pension funds	2
Brokerage costs (trading costs):	
Median cost, large pension funds	10
Median cost, largest pension funds	7

Note: Sliding-scale fees for institutional commingled funds, the BT Pyramid funds, were graciously supplied by Bankers Trust, a large money manager of indexed and actively managed institutional funds. Data on large U.S. pension funds is from CEM (1997).

[a]These are median costs of external money management for given type of assets, reported by 167 large U.S. pension funds ranging in size from less than $100 million to over $100 billion. Median fund = $1.5 billion. Average of 14 external money managers per fund, managing $194 million each; median amount managed per manager = $113 million.

[b]These are median costs for the 10 largest U.S. pension funds, excluding Calpers, ranging in size from $29 to $65 billion. Average of 34 external money managers per fund managing $646 million each ($543 million median).

[c]This includes brokerage (trading) costs plus internal administrative costs of money management, such as executive pay, consultants, performance measurement, custodial arrangements, trustees, and audits. The breakdown by passive and active is not available, but brokerage costs are estimated to be much lower for passive.

If we add to these asset-management costs another 3 to 10 basis points for brokerage fees and internal administrative costs that are incurred by large institutions, this brings the total cost to 0.04–0.65 percent, depending on investment strategy. This may be compared with retail costs ranging from 0.3 percent to 1.5 percent for the average passively and actively managed mutual fund, respectively.

3.4.2 Why Do Institutions Get Better Rates?

In an imperfectly competitive market, large investors have greater reasons and resources to seek out asset managers who will provide good performance at low cost. They are better able to separate noise from signal, to evaluate whether a particular fee is warranted by the expected returns, and, therefore, to respond sensibly to price differentials. They also have the credible threat of managing their money in house if they do not get good terms from an external manager. Thus, if marginal costs are less than average because of fixed costs, to attract an institutional investor the asset manager is likely to charge only a small fee above marginal cost per unit invested; this adds up to a large contribution toward total fixed costs where large sums are involved.

Besides possessing greater information and bargaining power, institutional investors also require lower R&C and marketing costs by the asset manager. It is easier and less labor consuming for the asset manager to deal with the financial staff at a few large institutions than with numerous small, uninformed households. To reach individual retail investors, advertising expenses must be incurred, numerous brochures and statements sent to households, and follow-up with personal communications must be made to convince them to invest and to choose a particular fund. Often, commissions are paid to motivate sales agents to spend the time and effort needed to carry out this task. In contrast, marketing in the institutional marketplace is likely to consume fewer resources because of the concentration of investors, their greater financial expertise, and their price sensitivity; sales commissions are rare. And, once the contract is secured, only one investor need be served in the institutional market. Even if the billion-dollar investor gets better service than the thousand-dollar investor (as is likely the case), total R&C demands relative to assets are much smaller for one institution than for a million small investors.

These factors lead to costs for institutional investors as low as 0.04–0.65 percent of assets, depending on asset category and investment strategy chosen. These would be the costs in a centrally managed social security fund—if it is well run.

3.5 Capturing Institutional Rates for a Mandatory IA System: Constrained Choice

Mandatory IA systems can also be structured to obtain scale economies in asset management without high marketing costs. In other words, they can offer workers an opportunity to invest at much lower cost than would be possible on a voluntary basis. To accomplish this requires aggregating numerous small accounts of a mandatory system into large blocks of money and negotiating fees on a centralized basis, through a competitive bidding process with limited entry or open entry with price ceilings. Limited entry avoids high start-up costs in the early years of a new system. Low fees create a disincentive for high marketing expenses. The lowest fees are obtained when worker choice is constrained to low-cost investment portfolios and strategies, such as passive investment. Still, enough choice could be retained to satisfy individual preferences and avoid political control. We call this an institutional approach to IAs or a system of *constrained choice.* (For a description of constrained-choice systems in Bolivia and Sweden, see James, Smalhout, and Vittas [1999].)

3.5.1   How Would It Work?

The exact number of asset managers in a constrained-choice system would depend on the volume of contributions as well as the desired amount of choice per worker. Initially, the number might range from two to three in countries with a small contribution base to five to ten in larger countries. This number would gradually increase with the growth of assets in the system. If a competitive bidding process is used, as in Bolivia, issues related to the auction process include selection criteria, term of contract, frequency of rebidding, and fee structure (performance based, asset based, or otherwise). For countries with weak financial markets, an auction would provide an incentive—a guaranteed or quasi-guaranteed market share—for international companies with financial expertise to enter the industry. To produce this outcome, these countries would need to avoid the temptation to corrupt or politically manipulate the bidding process.

Initially, the options might be restricted to a variety of passive investment choices indexed to different diversified benchmarks. Again, this may not be feasible or desirable in developing countries where such benchmarks do not exist, asset holdings are concentrated and illiquid, the rapid entry of new firms makes it difficult to build a stable benchmark, and inefficient markets give an edge to active managers who can obtain private information. But, where feasible, the bidding process and passive investment strategies would help avoid high start-up costs and large expense deductions from small accounts.

Later, as aggregate assets increase, entry could be opened up to a larger number of asset managers, including active managers who agree to operate below a specified price ceiling. The ceiling would be set high enough to cover marginal cost plus part of fixed costs but low enough to discourage marketing expenses—not an easy target to achieve. It might vary according to benchmark chosen: higher for small caps and emerging market portfolios than for domestic large caps. (If only one price ceiling is set, this is tantamount to restricting the available portfolios and strategies to those that are profitable at low cost.) For example, the ceiling might be set at the mean or median money-management cost, by asset class, of the largest pension funds in the country. R&C services would be provided elsewhere to keep small accounts attractive to asset managers and to avoid service deterioration under incomplete contracts. The Swedish system of fee ceilings moves directly to this second stage: it involves numerous mutual funds and centralized R&C. This scheme is also consistent with the two-tiered plan for the United States outlined in Goldberg and Graetz (chap. 1 in this volume). Their plan would initially give workers a choice among six index funds (SPIFs, or simple personal investment funds) but would allow workers to opt out into a broader set of qualified options (Q-funds, or qualified private funds) once their accounts reach a specified size.

3.5.2   Marketing Expenses

One intended consequence of this method that accounts for much of the cost saving is reduced marketing expenditures. Limited entry and low fees reduce the incentive for marketing. Given the large fixed costs and declining average costs in the industry, it will always be tempting for funds to spend more on advertising and sales commissions to increase their market share so long as the attainable fee is higher than marginal cost. When the fee is decreased, the incentive to spend on marketing will similarly decline, and this helps sustain the low fee.

Is this attempt to reduce marketing expenses efficient? This depends on whether the cuts come mainly from the informational content of marketing or its zero-sum game competitive elements. It seems likely that the socially optimal amount of marketing is less in a mandatory IA system than in the voluntary market. First, since the total investable amount is predetermined by law, marketing is not needed to induce people to save or to invest in financial markets. Second, mandatory centralized collections can aggregate savings into large blocs for efficient investment without marketing expenses. Third, while information is imparted by marketing, investment companies and brokers have a clear incentive to impart misleading information that is in their rather than the consumer's interest. For example, broker-salespeople may lead clients to "their" funds rather than to the "best" or the "least-cost" funds. This could be a big problem in a new mandatory system with many small, inexperienced investors. Such a system should include other, more cost-effective ways to impart less biased information relevant to investment choices, such as government publications and the popular media. The incentives for good performance and innovation imparted by marketing could continue to be provided in the voluntary marketplace. Reducing marketing expenses may be less efficient in countries with low tax-collection capacities and fewer sources of information, particularly those that wish to use marketing as a tool to increase coverage and reduce evasion. However, for others, the potential savings from cutting marketing costs seems to be about 0.4–0.5 percent of assets.

3.5.3   Constrained Choice of Investment Portfolios

A second consequence of this cost-cutting method is restricted choice regarding investment portfolios and strategies. The institutional approach to IA systems limits the range of options available to workers in order to obtain better rates from fund managers. In developed financial markets, this is likely to mean ruling out expensive portfolios in illiquid assets such as small-cap stocks and foreign emerging markets and directing workers toward index funds in liquid domestic instruments instead. The Thrift Savings Plan (TSP) in the United States does this directly. Sweden's new IA system does it indirectly by setting price ceilings that will restrict the supply of "expensive" funds and cross-subsidies that will push consumers toward cheaper funds. In James, Smalhout, and Vittas (1999), we show that most of the cost saving achieved by these systems is due to the portfolio and strategy changes that they require or induce.

Constraining investment choice in this manner has certain disadvantages. It increases the probability of corruption or collusion and decreases the adaptability to individual risk-return preferences—although not as much as a single centralized fund. Individuals may have a smaller sense of "ownership" and a larger sense of being taxed if their choice of investment manager is constrained. The risk to the government of being responsible for a bailout in case of investment failure may be greater when it has "endorsed" or participated in the process of choosing a small number of asset managers. The constraint on choice and these consequent dangers would be particularly great in countries with a small contribution base and a tradition of inefficient government control. Greater choice could be allowed, and hence the trade-off between low cost and low political risk would be less serious, in economies with larger investable resources—from higher contribution rates or wages. As we have seen, a large country such as the United States could allow considerable choice, and Sweden plans to allow substantial choice.

Constrained choice has an additional value at the start of a new system. It facilitates learning by doing, which is probably the most effective form of education, by limiting the mistakes that people can make. It makes government guarantees of benefits potentially less costly by diminishing moral hazard problems. Constrained choice can represent an efficiency gain if these advantages, together with the real cost reduction, are valued by participants more than the flexibility that they would have had in retail markets. This is most likely to be the case if the constraints on choice are not too great.

We estimate that asset-management costs in this system of constrained choice would be similar to those in a single centralized fund—0.04–0.65 percent of assets, depending on the range of strategies allowed—with a small addition for advertising costs. R&C costs would, however, be considerably larger in an IA system since numerous individual accounts, rather than one big pension fund, would have to be tracked. We move on now to discuss how this could be handled in a cost-effective manner.

3.5.4   How to Keep R&C Costs Low

While R&C costs are a small component of total costs in mutual funds, they are likely to be a relatively larger cost component in an IA system that has successfully cut its marketing and investment expenses. The magnitude of these costs are, to a substantial extent, a policy choice, a function

Table 3.13   **Transfer Agent (R&C) Costs in Dollars per Account**

	1991	1993	1995
Cost per account	21.55	22.77	20.93
80 percent range	$8–$38	$10–$36	$10–$32
Cost per open account	24.76	25.92	25.09
If external	23.08	24.56	23.42
If internal	25.34	26.39	25.64
If equity	20.31	22.52	21.89
If money market	31.27	30.28	28.83
If sales through affiliated broker	13.63	15.07	16.57
If direct market/retail	29.31	34.01	32.61
Cost per account (all):			
If dividends paid annually	17.12	20.77	19.30
If dividends paid monthly	23.94	24.94	22.29

Source: ICI and Coopers Lybrand (1995, 1997).

of level and types of services provided, rather than an exogenously given variable. In this section, we consider some of the policy choices that can keep R&C costs low.

According to periodic surveys of transfer agents (i.e., the organizations that provide these services for mutual funds), average mutual fund cost per account and per open account has been quite constant, at $21 and $25 per account, respectively (table 3.13). However, they are not uniform across all funds. They tend to be lower for funds that contract out the transfer-agent function rather than performing it internally. This may result because pricing in internal arrangements is not an arm's-length competitive transaction and because internal control is designed to provide more personalized service, to inculcate loyalty to the fund. Costs per account are 33 percent higher for money market than for equity funds because of the greater transaction volume and check-writing facilities offered by the former. They are twice as high for direct market retail funds as for funds that sell through brokers, who perform some of the customer-communications functions that are otherwise provided by the fund ($33 vs. $17). Transfer-agent costs are 20 percent higher for accounts where dividends are paid monthly rather than annually. Size of account does not appear as a factor influencing R&C costs.

Competition in the U.S. mutual fund industry has resulted in a high and expensive level of R&C service, in part because shareholder service and building shareholder loyalty (a form of marketing) are closely intertwined. Service innovations include the ability to make frequent telephone exchanges, to wire funds, to write checks, and to speak to a representative twelve or even twenty-four hours per day. Each of these services costs, but the costs are hidden.[14] They are free of charge to the individual user—although, of course, not to users as a group.

Despite these incremental costs for each transaction, the most common method that transfer agents use for charging funds is a flat fee per account. Mutual funds, in turn, rarely charge shareholders special fees for check writing, exchanges, or telephone inquiries (ICI and Coopers Lybrand 1995, 1997). This is due in part to the cost of measuring and charging for transactions and in part to the strong desire of funds to avoid antagonizing high-asset consumers. The net result is a cross-subsidy from nonusers to heavy users and the absence of incentives for shareholders to economize on these services. A lower basic service level, with incremental services available at a charge, may be appropriate for a mandatory IA system that has many small investors.

To accomplish this, the R&C function could be separated from the asset-management function and centralized—either in a public agency or in a clearinghouse run jointly by all participating funds or contracted out to an independent private company. In fact, the mutual fund industry has been moving toward outsourcing the transfer-agent function and concentrating it in two or three large companies. So this would merely accelerate and standardize this process.

Centralization immediately reduces systemwide costs by avoiding the setup and systems-integration problems that occur when members switch their accounts from one fund complex to another. It allows workers to divide their money among two or more funds without the cost of maintaining duplicate records. It keeps a single record of a worker's lifetime contributions and returns. This is particularly important in a mandatory system, where such a record should be readily available, error free, on retirement. The separation of R&C from the asset-management function would actually increase the choice of asset managers available to small accountholders since R&C costs, which are relatively expensive for such accounts, would be covered elsewhere.[15] It would facilitate a cross-subsidy

14. Processing the application for a new account costs about $10; a personal telephone call costs $7; check writing costs $5 to set up and $1 per draft thereafter. Technology (the Internet, automated phones) is ostensibly being used to reduce costs, but so far the savings have not materialized. Instead, the greatest effect has been to increase investment costs and improve service still further. Additional electronic options are available, while the utilization of expensive personal services has not diminished. This helps explain why, in the regressions for 1992–97, a period that has seen great technological strides, expense ratios rose slightly and total expenses (expense ratio times assets) rose dramatically.

15. Most mutual funds would not be interested in small IA accounts or would charge them a very high annual fee (thereby cutting benefits commensurably) unless some new means is developed of handling R&C costs. For the small accounts currently under consideration in the United States, average mutual fund fees of 1.4 percent would not cover the real marginal R&C cost of the bottom half of the worker population for more than five years. Fees in low-priced index funds would not cover these costs for more than twenty years. So these funds or their counterparts are unlikely to serve as asset managers for small accounts if the R&C

to small accounts, which may be socially desirable, without competitive pressures that might oppose this. Moreover, centralization would allow personalized services to be reduced without generating inefficient competitive pressures to upgrade. (But note that government capacity and trust in public agencies are necessary preconditions for centralized R&C, and these are lacking in many developing countries.)

A second step concerns setting the level of basic service as well as the charges for incremental service in an unbundled system. The basic service level should be low enough to pass a benefit-cost test, given the small average size of the account for the first few years of the new system. It should focus on keeping accurate, timely records and processing transactions efficiently. At the same time, different service levels could be chosen by those willing to pay for more.

For example, services such as check writing could be ruled out, dividends and capital gains could be credited annually, and fund transfers or other transactions could be restricted or discouraged by a fee that covers the cost. Most important (because most expensive), personalized services, especially telephone discussions with representatives, could be minimized by encouraging members to use automated phones or the Internet instead. A possible strategy here would be to make telephone service available only for limited hours per day and build in probable waiting time to encourage members to switch to automated techniques. Less palatable is the use of toll calls instead of 800 numbers to pass the phone-company charges on to consumers or the use of 900 numbers to impute the representative's time as well. Costs could be cut further by sending statements annually instead of quarterly. The costs and performance of each fund could be reported in a brief (one- to two-page) summary rather than the lengthy and detailed prospectus that is required of all mutual funds today. In fact, the short statement may be more educational than the lengthy prospectus, which few people read or understand. In-person workshops provided by many 401(k) plans would be avoided and replaced by brochures introducing investors to concepts such as risk-return trade-offs, diversification, and indexing, published for mass distribution. Market competition for high-income investors does not allow mutual funds to use these strategies, but centralized record keeping in a mandatory system does.

Additional economies may, in some case, be achieved by piggybacking on existing tax-collection facilities. Contributions to IAs could be sent in together with other payroll taxes, thereby saving on incremental collection costs. This might also facilitate compliance checks, as a central agency knows whether the contribution has arrived while a decentralized fund may have little reason to report this information to the government accu-

---

function is decentralized. They might, however, welcome their asset-management business if R&C is carried out and paid for elsewhere.

Table 3.14   Hypothetical Annual R&C Cost per Account—Breakdown of Services ($)

	Typical Direct Market Mutual Fund	IA System with Central Records
Account setup (annualized)[a]	2.00	0.10
Annual record keeping and update	1.00	1.00
Personal phone calls[b]	7.00	2.00
2 automated phone calls per account	2.00	2.00
4 quarterly statements	6.00	. . .
1 annual statement or tax statement	1.50	1.50
2 transactions with written confirmation	5.00	5.00[c]
1 dividend + capital gains distribution with statement	2.50	1.00[d]
Distribution of prospectus, semiannual and annual reports	3.00	1.00[e]
Queries and mailing about other funds in complex	2.50	. . .
General educational material	. . .	2.50
Total	32.50	16.60

Source: State Street Bank, mutual fund representatives, and authors' own calculations.

[a]We assume that the investor switches to a new mutual fund every seven years but would stay in the centralized records of an IA system for forty years.

[b]We assume one phone call per year per account in a mutual fund, one-third per account in the IA system.

[c]Possible fee for additional transactions.

[d]Dividends and capital gains are credited to account in the IA system and are included in the annual statement.

[e]Two-page statement substitutes for prospectus.

rately. However, utilizing existing tax agencies must be approached with caution as it involves hidden costs such as long delays (as much as nine months) before the worker's contribution is allocated to his or her account and money manager. If the new contribution loses, say, an incremental 3 percent rate of return in the interim, this is equivalent to a loss of 0.15 percent of assets per year over a worker's lifetime. Moreover, this approach may not be an option for countries that have weak tax-collection mechanisms and a distrust of public agencies. In these countries, workers may be more likely to contribute if they can put the money directly into their own accounts. This was the case, for example, in Chile at the time of its reform; only a decentralized approach was feasible under those circumstances. Piggybacking, however, can greatly reduce collection costs as well as facilitate compliance and record keeping in countries that have the capacity.

Table 3.14 compares the R&C composition of a high-cost mutual fund account and a modest-service account proposed for an IA system that exploits all these cost-saving opportunities. It seems likely that collection and R&C costs will total less than $20 per account, which is at the low (but not the lowest) end of the mutual fund spectrum.[16]

3.5.5   Comparison with the TSP

Our $20 figure is also consistent with R&C costs of the TSP, a retirement savings plan for federal employees in the United States. The TSP began in the late 1980s. It now has 2.3 million participants, approximately $65 billion in assets, and an average account size of $27,000 (table 3.15). TSP R&C costs have remained fairly stable, at $18–$21 per account, since 1988, although total administrative costs have increased to $30 per account as assets have grown. (These numbers are in 1998 dollars, and they cover gross costs, including trading and other investment costs, although these are partially offset on TSP books by account forfeitures.)

R&C costs are low in part because much of the communication with participants takes place through the federal agencies where members are employed, at an additional (but unknown) cost. In a mandatory IA system, information would have to be distributed directly from the funds or public agencies to the individual, at some monetary cost. However, the TSP provides certain expensive services that would not be included in a mandatory IA system, such as loans and withdrawals. Moreover, an IA system would benefit from much greater economies of scale. For example, the TSP numbers given above include systemwide fixed administrative costs that would disappear per account in the much larger social security system.

But the biggest cost saving for the TSP is due to the constraints that it places on portfolio choice and investment strategy: workers must choose among a money market fund, an equity fund indexed to the Standard and Poor's 500, and an indexed long- and medium-term bond fund. (For comparison, Standard and Poor's 500 index funds are available in the retail

16. This $20 figure may be contrasted with the $50 per account figure in Diamond (chap. 4 in this volume), which is much higher than either the TSP or mutual funds. The $50 number is Diamond's estimate of the political equilibrium, under the assumption that political pressures will drive up service levels and costs. While we do not try to estimate a political equilibrium—which is highly subjective—it should be noted that the equilibrium service level and cost can be influenced by process and disclosure. For example, if the charge is prominently displayed on the annual statement, if the basic service is financed by cross-subsidization from large to small accounts via an asset-based fee, and if services are unbundled so that incremental services are paid for by the user, the political equilibrium may result in a relatively small common service charge.

Also, Diamond's $50 may include some of the costs that we cover in a different category. Our total dollar cost for an average account in steady state, including money-management and brokerage fees that are tied to money management, is $31–$39 for passive management and $106–$172 for active management. These costs would hold when the average account size is $22,000 (in 1999 dollars).

Table 3.15   Administrative Costs of the Thrift Savings Plan, 1988–98

Year	Expense Ratio (basis points) (1)	Average Size Account ($thousands) (2)	Administrative Cost per Account		Investment Cost per Account ($) (5)	R&C Cost per Account	
			$ (3)	1998 $ (4)		$ (6)	1998 $ (7)
1988	.70	2.4	16.8	22.7	1.0	15.8	21.4
1989	.46	3.7	17.1	22.21	1.5	15.5	20.2
1990	.29	5.1	14.81	18.00	2.0	12.8	15.6
1991	.26	6.7	17.4	20.71	2.7	14.7	17.6
1992	.23	8.5	19.6	22.53	3.4	16.2	18.6
1993	.19	10.7	20.3	22.81	4.3	16.1	18.0
1994	.16	12.8	20.6	22.39	5.1	15.4	16.7
1995	.14	16.5	23.1	24.57	6.6	16.5	17.6
1996	.13	20.1	26.2	27.01	8.0	18.1	18.7
1997	.12	25.3	30.3	30.61	10.1	20.2	20.4
1998[a]	.11	27.4	30.1	30.10	11.1	19.2	19.2

Source: TSP publications and authors' calculations.

Note: Expense ratio in col. 1 is gross expense ratio as reported in TSP publications (before adjustment for forfeitures) plus three basis points imputed by authors for brokerage (trading) fees. Cols. 5 and 6 are authors' estimates separating R&C from investment expenses. Investment expenses are assumed to be three basis points of trading costs plus one basis point for asset management, custodian, legal, and auditing fees related to investments. R&C costs are the remainder. TSP does not report its brokerage costs or breakdown of other expenses between investment and R&C.

[a]Based on January–August annualized.

market for twenty-two basis points, but most investors choose higher-cost funds.) Moreover, the right to manage these funds has been auctioned off to only one company, on a monopoly basis. Marketing costs therefore are virtually absent, and investment costs are minimal—estimated by us to be four basis points, including brokerage (trading) fees. Total administrative costs (including R&C) have fallen to only 0.11 percent of assets as average account size has grown. (For a more detailed analysis of the TSP, see James, Smalhout, and Vittas [1999].)

3.5.6   Cost Implications for a New IA System

Suppose that, in the year 2000, the United States were to institute a similar structure (but preferably with greater choice, corresponding to the greater volume of assets in the system) for a mandatory IA system with an annual contribution of $500. If this amount were put in escrow pending tax reconciliation and establishment of the new information system, three to four years of contributions and interest would accumulate before the IAs became operative. By that time, the $20 R&C cost would be only 1 percent of assets for the average account. Following panel A of table 3.1 above, in steady state forty years later it would be only nine basis points.

After adding these nine basis points to the investment cost derived in section 3.4 above, the total cost for an IA system based on constrained choice is projected to be 0.14–0.18 percent if passively managed or 0.49–0.79 percent if actively managed. In constant dollars, the steady-state cost for the average-size account would be $31–$172. This cost is much lower than an IA system run through the retail market with unconstrained choice among investment portfolios, resulting in a pension accumulation that is 15–25 percent larger. It is lower than that of similar portfolios in the voluntary market to which individual investors have access, primarily owing to reduced marketing and secondarily to bulk buying power and no-frills service.[17] It is slightly more than a single centralized fund would

17. It may be useful to compare the cost of passive management under constrained choice with the cost of the Standard and Poor's index funds offered by Vanguard and Fidelity to individuals and institutions. These are among the lowest-cost mutual funds available, marketing themselves to a cost-conscious clientele and making business-strategy and cost-allocation decisions accordingly. Their marketing expenses are kept low by the absence of 12b1 fees, front loads, or back loads. The Vanguard institutional fund has a six-basis-point expense ratio, and we impute three basis points in brokerage fees, bringing the total cost to nine basis points. The Vanguard and Fidelity Standard and Poor's index funds have an expense ratio of nineteen basis points plus an imputed three basis points for brokerage fees, bringing the total to twenty-two basis points. (Actually, Fidelity's fees are higher, but fees above nineteen basis points have been waived to enable Fidelity to compete with Vanguard. Asset management for Fidelity's index fund has been contracted out to Banker's Trust for less than one basis point.)

In contrast, for an IA system under constrained choice, we have estimated a cost of fourteen basis points for passive management of large-cap stocks, including brokerage fees. The IA system would be five basis points more expensive than the institutional fund because of the greater R&C costs associated with numerous IAs. The IA system would be eight basis

cost but, in exchange, offers much greater adaptability to individual preferences and insulation from political risk (table 3.16).

3.6 Conclusion

We started this paper by asking, What is the most efficient way to set up an IA component of a social security system, and how do we compare the cost effectiveness of investing social security funds through (1) the retail market with open entry and choice, (2) the institutional market with constrained choice among investment companies, and (3) a centralized fund without IAs or choice?

The evidence in this paper demonstrates that large cost savings can be realized by investing IAs through the institutional market with constrained choice. This would involve moving money in large blocs rather than as small individual investments while still giving workers considerable choice among asset managers. In the early years of a new system, a competitive bidding process could be used in which a limited number of managers are chosen for differentiated portfolios. Subsequently, an open-entry process could be used in which companies agree to restrict their fees in exchange for the right to participate. Further economies might be achieved by centralized R&C and collections. The cost savings to participants come partly from reducing marketing expenses, economizing on R&C costs, and exploiting bargaining power regarding the distribution of the fixed-cost burden. Limiting investment strategies to passive management in the early phase would produce the largest cost reduction.

The evidence indicates that many of the same factors that reduce costs will also raise returns. The price paid for lower costs is therefore not lower expected returns but rather other, less quantifiable factors, such as greater risk of corruption, collusion, a weaker sense of worker ownership, and problems stemming from incomplete contracts. The importance of these factors will vary among countries and will decrease as the number of asset managers in the system increases. A contribution base that is large enough to allow meaningful choice among multiple asset managers, together with long-run contestability, will go far toward diminishing these dangers.

---

points cheaper than the index funds for individual investors because of the lower level of service provided by centralized R&C, the spreading of fixed costs across a larger asset base, and the bulk buying power of large money blocs.

Importantly, for the first fifteen years of the IA system, most accounts will be below the $10,000 minimum investment required by Fidelity and Vanguard for these funds. This minimum investment was set by Fidelity and Vanguard precisely because of the R&C cost per account (discussed in the text). Smaller investors are either excluded or required to pay an additional $10 fee, equivalent to another ten to one hundred basis points depending on account size, to help cover R&C. In getting access to a similar index fund without this fee, small investors have an investment opportunity under a constrained-choice IA system with centralized R&C that they did not have, or that would have been much more expensive for them, in the retail market.

Table 3.16 **Costs of Retail, Centralized, and Institutional IAs with Constrained Choice Compared (in basis points per unit of assets unless specified otherwise)**

	Retail		Centralized		Constrained Choice, Institutional	
	Passive	Active	Passive	Active	Passive	Active
Asset management	8	52	1–5	25–55	1–5	25–55
Marketing	3	65	…	…	1	5
R&C	5	12	…	…	9	9
Brokerage fee and other	16	20	3	10	3	10
Total cost	32	150	4–8	35–65	14–18	49–79
$ cost per average account of $22,000 in steady state (see panel A of table 3.1 above)	70	329	9–18	77–142	31–39	106–72

Note: Retail costs are taken from tables 3.5 and 3.6 above. Centralized costs are taken from table 3.12 above. Institutional constrained-choice costs are taken from tables 3.12–3.15 above. Marketing costs under constrained choice are based on the assumption that fee ceilings or the competitive bidding process will keep them low.

As to the relative cost effectiveness of a constrained IA system versus a centralized fund with no choice, we have seen that the extra costs associated with IAs are negligible, providing that a modest level of service is chosen for record keeping and communicating with participants. At the same time, optional services might be unbundled so that those who use them pay for them.

The most expensive service involves communication and education. It is not reasonable to expect consumers to make complicated financial choices without information. Our R&C cost estimate included an allocation for preparing and distributing published materials. However, we would argue that, especially for workers who are saving for the first time in their lives, the best education will come from practice—with small amounts. This is another reason for simplifying and limiting choice, especially at the beginning of the new system. By the time accounts have grown and greater choice is permitted, most workers will already have learned from experience. No doubt the popular press (newspapers, magazines, television talk shows) would also play a significant role in educating the public as it would surely face a huge demand once everyone had an IA.

In sum, the structure of an IA system matters. Administrative costs need not make IAs prohibitively expensive. The cost of managing savings in a mandatory IA system can be significantly less than the cost of voluntary saving. By using the institutional market, an IA system that gives workers some choice can be structured to cost only slightly more than a single centrally managed fund with no choice. Decisions about whether to fund and whether to manage the funds publicly or privately should therefore depend on other factors, such as the economic benefits of funding and the risks and returns associated with public and private management of funds.

References

Baumol, William J., Stephen M. Goldfeld, Lilli A. Gordon, and Michael F. Koehn. 1990. *The economics of mutual fund markets: Competition versus regulation.* Boston: Kluwer Academic.

Bodie, Zvi, Alex Kane, and Alan J. Marcus. 1989. *Investments.* Homewood, Ill.: Irwin.

Capon, Noel, Gavan J. Fitzsimmons, and Russ Alan Prince. 1996. An individual level analysis of the mutual fund investment decision. *Journal of Financial Services Research* 10:59–82.

Carhart, Mark M. 1997. On persistence in mutual fund performance. *Journal of Finance* 52, no. 1:57–82.

CEM. 1997. Cost effectiveness pension fund report. Sacramento: CALPERS (California Public Employees' Retirement System).

Chordia, Tarun. 1996. The structure of mutual fund charges. *Journal of Financial Economics* 41:3–39.

Collins, Sean, and Phillip Mack. 1997. The optimal amount of assets under management in the mutual fund industry. *Financial Analysts Journal* 53, no. 5:67–73.

Dermine, Jean, and Lars-Hendrik Röller. 1992. Economies of scale and scope in French mutual funds. *Journal of Financial Intermediation* 2:83–93.

Elton, E. J., M. J. Gruber, S. Das, and M. Hlavka. 1993. Efficiency with costly information: A reinterpretation of evidence from managed portfolios. *Review of Financial Studies* 6, no. 1:1–22.

Ferris, Stephen P., and Don M. Chance. 1987. The effect of 12b-1 plans on mutual fund expense ratios: A note. *Journal of Finance* 42, no. 4:1077–82.

Gruber, Martin J. 1996. Another puzzle: The growth of actively managed mutual funds. *Journal of Finance* 51, no. 3:783–810.

Investment Company Institute (ICI) and Coopers Lybrand. Various years. *Mutual fund transfer agents.* Washington, D.C.

Ippolito, Richard A. 1992. Consumer reaction to measures of poor quality: Evidence from the mutual fund industry. *Journal of Law and Economics* 35:45–70.

James, Estelle, and Robert Palacios. 1995. Costs of administering public and private pension plans. *Finance and Development* 32, no. 2:12–16.

James, Estelle, James Smalhout, and Dimitri Vittas. 1999. Administrative costs and the organization of individual account systems: A comparative perspective. Paper presented at the World Bank conference New Ideas for Old Age Security, Washington, D.C., 14 September.

Kihn, John. 1996. To load or not to load? A study of marketing and distribution charges of mutual funds. *Financial Analysts Journal* 52, no. 3:28–36.

Lipper, Michael. 1994. The third white paper: Are mutual fund fees reasonable? New York: Lipper Analytical Services.

Livingston, Miles, and Edward S. O'Neal. 1996. Mutual fund brokerage commissions. *Journal of Financial Research* 19, no. 2:273–92.

Malhotra, D. K., and Robert W. McLeod. 1997. An empirical analysis of mutual fund expenses. *Journal of Financial Research* 20, no. 2:175–90.

Malkiel, Burton G. 1995. Returns from investing in equity mutual funds, 1971 to 1991. *Journal of Finance* 50, no. 2:549–72.

Maturana, Gustavo, and Eduardo Walker. 1999. Rentabilidades, comisiones, y desempeno en la industria Chilena de fondos mutuos. *Estudios Publicos* 73: 293–334.

Mitchell, Olivia. 1998. Administrative costs in public and private retirement systems. In *Privatizing social security,* ed. M. Feldstein. Chicago: University of Chicago Press.

Muralidhar, Arun S., and Robert Weary. 1998. The greater fool theory of asset management; or, Resolving the active-passive debate. WPS98-020. Washington, D.C.: World Bank.

Patel, Jayendu, Richard J. Zeckhauser, and Darryll Hendricks. 1994. Investment flows and performance: Evidence from mutual funds, cross-border investments, and new issues. In *Japan, Europe, and international financial markets: Analytical and empirical perspectives,* ed. Ryuzo Sato, Richard M. Levich, and Rama V. Ramachandran. New York: Cambridge University Press.

Pozen, Robert. 1998. *The mutual fund business.* Cambridge, Mass.: MIT Press.

Rea, John D., and Brian K. Reid. 1998. Trends in the ownership cost of equity mutual funds. *Perspective* (Investment Company Institute) 4:1–15.

Shah, Ajay, and Kshama Fernandes. 1999. The relevance of index funds for pension investment in equities. Paper presented at the World Bank conference New Ideas about Old Age Security, Washington, D.C., 14 September.

Sirri, Erik R., and Peter Tufano. 1993. Competition and change in the mutual fund industry. In *Financial services: Perspectives and challenges,* ed. Samuel B. Hayes III. Boston: Harvard Business School Press.

————. 1997. Costly search and mutual fund flows. Harvard Graduate School of Business Administration. Mimeo.

Trzcinka, Charles, and Robert Zweig. 1990. *An economic analysis of the cost and benefits of S.E.C. rule 12b-1.* Monograph Series in Finance and Economics. New York: New York University, Salomon Brothers Center for the Study of Financial Institutions.

Valdes, Salvador. 1999. Las comisiones de las AFPs: Caras o baratos? *Estudios Publicos* 73:255–91.

Wyatt Co. 1990. Investment company persistency study conducted for the National Association of Securities Dealers. Washington, D.C.

Comment   David A. Wise

The authors have presented an enormous amount of information on the cost of operating mutual funds. The data are drawn from a broad range of sources. Some of the information is, I believe, especially relevant with respect to the projected administrative cost of operating a social security individual account system. Given the information provided by the authors, I am inclined to believe that the costs of operating individual account programs—which might evolve as part of social security reform—are likely to be very low. Indeed, it seems to me that, whatever the pros and cons of individual accounts, a proper interpretation of the data on administrative costs suggests that such costs should not be a determinant of whether such accounts are adopted.

The data on Chile I found interesting in that these data show that it can be done, but perhaps the costs are not so relevant to prospective costs in the United States.

Much of the information about the cost of operating "retail" mutual funds in the United States is presented in the form of regressions showing the relation between mutual fund expense ratios and attributes of the fund. The results confirm that there are economies of scale with respect to the size of the fund, that actively managed funds (with substantial turnover) are associated with large administrative costs (especially emerging market funds), that funds for institutional investors (with large minimum investments) incur lower costs, and that index funds operate with very low administrative cost.

But the most relevant information, in my view, pertains to the cost of operating specific funds. As far as I can tell, no one expects that individual

David A. Wise is the John F. Stambaugh Professor of Political Economy at the John F. Kennedy School of Government, Harvard University, and the director for Health and Retirement Programs at the National Bureau of Economic Research.

accounts would have participants choosing from the thousands of mutual funds available in the United States. Instead, it seems to me that investment options would likely be limited. It also seems to me that individual contributions could be "bundled" in some way to reduce the number of very small transactions, although I was not exactly clear what the authors had in mind in this respect. In addition, there is enormous room for varying the "services" that funds provide, as the authors emphasize.

The authors conclude that competition with respect to client service has resulted in high administrative cost among many "retail" mutual funds. Many of these services would appear to be unnecessary in the case of universal compulsory contributions.

Thus, it seems to me that the information most relevant to social security individual accounts is the cost of operating specific types of plans like the federal employees' Thrift Savings Plan or index funds in general. For such options, the administrative cost is very low.

Exactly how to "keep the records" would have to be solved, but it is hard to believe that, in this world of technical capacity, that infrastructure cannot be worked out. Indeed, I believe that the computer facilities that the NBER uses to keep track of medicare and employer-provided medical insurance claims records could handle the job.

It seems to me, however, that, even without the evidence of specific very low-cost plans, competition for individual accounts would tend to produce many more low-cost options. And more index funds are an obvious example. If there is money to be made—and surely there will be with so many participants—I believe that firms will compete for it.

But, what is more, I believe that what is happening independent of social security reform is likely greatly to facilitate the adoption of individual social security accounts. In the early 1980s, few people were actively involved in the equity market. That is no longer true, and it will be even less true in coming years. Now, perhaps 45 percent of *families* participate in a 401(k) plan, and these plans are still spreading rapidly. Including IRAs, an even larger number of families are gaining acquaintance with the equity market and, in particular, with mutual funds. Poterba, Venti, and Wise (1998) suggest that the cohort retiring in 2025 will have 401(k) assets at least as large as social security assets (under current provisions) and probably much more. Those retiring in 2035 will have even greater 401(k) assets.

There are two things that are important about the spread of individual retirement saving, independent of social security. One is that individual accounts are less and less a new thing with which most families do not know how to deal. Indeed, there is a substantial amount of "investment" education provided by firms to employees. This education is just as applicable to social security individual accounts as to 401(k) accounts. Second, I suspect that, as a larger and larger proportion of persons become more sophisticated about investing and investment returns, there will be increasing competition to provide low-cost mutual funds, as many firms already do (although the authors here do not seem to see that, thus far, their data are really not appropriate for addressing this issue). Thus, I would look for lower administrative costs in response to greater awareness on the part of the rapidly growing number of IRA savers. I would guess that social security individual accounts would work in the same direction. In addition, it seems to me that there is substantial room for piggybacking on the 401(k) infrastructure. For example, employees in a firm with a 401(k) plan might choose the individual account investment from the same menu of options provided for the 401(k).

Finally, assuming that a logical way to run individual accounts is through the IRS, this provides substantial possibility for increasing saving, especially among low-income households. It would be easy—once the system is set up—to allow tax filers to increase their contribution beyond the "minimum" requirement. In Canada, for example, each tax filer now receives a letter each year from the minister of national revenue advising the recipient of the allowable registered retirement saving plan contribution—which could be described as a combination of U.S. IRA and Keogh plans—for the year. Although this practice was adopted because of the complex Canadian contribution limits, it is evident that the practice may also serve to promote the program and thus increase saving. My guess is that any similar arrangement operated through our IRS would have the same effect.

Reference

Poterba, James M., Steven F. Venti, and David A. Wise. 1998. Implications of rising personal retirement saving. In *Frontiers in the economics of aging,* ed. David A. Wise. Chicago: University of Chicago Press.

Discussion Summary

Michael Graetz expressed doubt regarding the ability of a system of individual accounts to "piggyback" on the existing 401(k) infrastructure, noting that, while 62 percent of wage earners earned less than $15,000, only 8.3 percent of workers held 401(k) accounts. Consequently, Graetz reiterated the claim of the Graetz and Goldberg paper that the system should piggyback on the social security and IRS infrastructure. He also commented that he was not as sanguine as David Wise regarding the potential for reduction in marketing costs as a result of competition between fund managers under a system of individual accounts. Graetz claimed that one advantage of the Goldberg and Graetz paper's two-tiered approach (i.e., offering both a default plan and an opt-out plan) would be to hold down costs in the opt-out plan (Q-fund, or qualified private fund) as a result of the low-cost alternative of the default (SPIF, or simple personal investment fund) plan. *Fred Grauer* added that the marketing costs of passively managed funds are significantly lower than those of actively managed funds.

James Poterba offered a comment regarding the proper interpretation of the James et al. paper's regressions analyzing the determinants of expense ratios of mutual funds. In general, he cautioned that looking cross-sectionally at the effect of various *currently permissible* activities on expense ratios is quite different from analyzing the likely effect on expense ratios of restricting the mutual fund market's set of permissible activities. He noted that the exact relation between the regressions and this latter question is not clear.

Olivia Mitchell cited evidence from a recent Lipper study (Lipper Analytical Services 1998) suggesting that, on average, older mutual funds have lower costs than newer ones. She suggested that James et al. may want to focus on the older funds as a benchmark, not the newer funds, which may still be amortizing start-up costs. *Estelle James* agreed, noting that the authors had performed regressions in which the age of the fund was included and had a negative coefficient. James also suggested that the older funds' lower costs may reflect a survival bias.

Echoing James Poterba's cautionary note on the interpretation of the expense-ratio regressions, *Stephen Zeldes* noted that the negative coefficient on fund size had a causality problem. That is, large size may be driving lower costs, but lower costs may also attract investors and thus lead to large size. He cited Vanguard as a possible example of this latter effect.

Peter Diamond cited a recent ICI report (Rea and Reid 1998) that examined average administrative costs of mutual funds with some equity component. Based on a dollar-weighted (on deposits) average, they arrived at a mean figure of 150 basis points for 1997. Diamond suggested that it would be interesting to contrast this analysis with that of the James et al. paper.

References

Lipper Analytical Services. 1998. The third white paper: Are mutual fund fees reasonable? New York, September.

Rea, John, and Brian Reid. 1998. Trends in the ownership costs of equity funds. *Perspective* (Investment Company Institute), November, 2.

4

Administrative Costs and Equilibrium Charges with Individual Accounts

Peter Diamond

Individual account proposals come with a vast variety of different structures and details. There are many different ways in which a discussion of individual accounts might be organized. For analytic discussion of administrative charges, a central distinction is between *government-organized accounts* and *privately organized accounts.* The term *government-organized accounts* will be used to denote individual account systems in which the government arranges for both the record keeping for the accounts and the investment management for the funds in the accounts—whether these functions are performed by government agencies or by private firms under contract to the government. An example of government-organized accounts is the federal Thrift Savings Plan (TSP), a pension plan that contracts with a government agency to perform record keeping and with a private firm to do fund management. The term *privately organized accounts* will be used to denote individual account systems in which individuals directly select private firms to do the record keeping and investment management. An example is IRAs, where individuals select their own private financial institution.

With government-organized accounts, two questions are how much it costs to run the system and how the government allocates those costs

Peter Diamond is institute professor and professor of economics at the Massachusetts Institute of Technology and a research associate of the National Bureau of Economic Research.

This paper draws heavily on the material developed by the Panel on the Privatization of Social Security of the National Academy of Social Insurance (see NASI 1998). The author is grateful to his colleagues on the panel and its staff for illumination on these issues. They are not responsible for his interpretations. While he has marked extensive quotations from the report, he has also drawn liberally and verbatim in smaller doses, with permission and without repeated acknowledgment.

among the different accounts (and possibly to outside sources of revenue). There are also costs that may fall on employers and workers. With privately organized accounts, we must ask about equilibrium prices and their relation to selling costs as well as the costs of record keeping and investment management. Again, there are also costs that may fall on employers, workers, and the government. Since the government may be purchasing services from private providers, another way to see this distinction is that government-organized accounts are organized on a group basis while privately organized accounts are organized on an individual basis. As with financial and insurance products generally, the group and individual markets function very differently and yield different pricing structures.[1]

A central element in thinking about costs is the quality of services offered with the accounts. With government-organized accounts, the central question for this element is what Congress might legislate and, underlying that, what services are likely to be requested by constituents. With privately organized accounts, Congress will legislate a minimum standard of quality of services, but the market is likely to offer an array of services, extending above the minimum. In turn, this equilibrium is likely to be influenced by the details of the regulations that are placed on these accounts for these accounts are likely to be subject to a new set of regulations, possibly administered by a new regulatory body or possibly handled by one or more existing bodies, such as the SEC. These regulations will affect the costs of providing services and may include regulation directly of charges, either in level or in form.

There are many steps in organizing and running individual accounts. The costs of different steps might be paid by different sources: workers, employers, charges against the accounts, the rest of social security, the non–social security portion of the federal budget. In comparing different cost estimates, it is important to be clear about which tasks, and their costs, are included in a given estimate and which are assumed to be borne elsewhere. To help with such comparisons, the National Academy of Social Insurance (NASI) Panel on Privatization of Social Security prepared a list of many of the tasks associated with having accounts. That list is reproduced here as appendix A.

The paper proceeds by first describing how a low-cost/low-services government-organized plan might look, how it differs from the TSP, and what it might cost. For this purpose, I rely heavily on NASI (1998). My estimate of the cost of such a system is in the range of roughly $40–$50 per worker per year. I suspect that there would be pressure for more services, which would raise costs. After this discussion, the paper turns to

---

1. The paper does not consider the use of employers to organize groups for some workers, as would follow with a mandate on employers rather than on workers. The Australian system is a mandate on employers (see, e.g., Edey and Simon 1998).

privately organized accounts and the nature of equilibrium. My conclusion is that, for the small accounts that are the current focus of political discussion (financed from 2–3 percent of payroll), the costs of private organization would be very high compared to the cost of government organization, given the perceived advantages of such a system.

4.1 Government-Organized Accounts

The creation of mandatory government-organized individual accounts would involve setting up nearly 150 million individual accounts, with a system to produce a flow of deposits into the accounts and a mechanism for investing, reporting, and changing portfolio choices.[2] To put the scope of a possible new system in perspective, the TSP maintains fewer than 3 million individual accounts, the largest number of existing individual accounts handled by a single firm has under 6 million accounts, and there are fewer than 10 million IRAs with multiple investment options. No existing system could handle the administrative complexities of a program with this scope of individual accounts; creating one would take time and resources.

In addition to needing a structure for accumulation in individual accounts, a structure is needed for the provision of retirement-income flows. This issue is considered below after the structure and cost of the accumulation phase are considered.

Since the present structure of social security would be preserved for the remaining defined-benefit retirement system as well as disability insurance and survivors insurance for young families, any introduction of individual accounts would add to the costs of social security. Currently, social security costs about $16 per person (workers and beneficiaries) per year. Excluding the costs of the disability program, OASI costs about $10 per person per year. A cost of $10 per participant is a cost of $14.50 per worker.[3]

4.1.1 Measuring Costs

Setting up and administering a system of individual accounts involves a variety of types of costs. Some would be one-time costs to set up the system, independent of the size of the system. Other setup costs would depend on the number of participants. In terms of ongoing costs, most are

---

2. One can have a defined-contribution system without any individual portfolio choice. While such a construct is useful for analytic purposes (see, e.g., Diamond 1998), this is not on the agenda of proposals being taken seriously currently.
Much of the presentation in this section is drawn verbatim from NASI (1998).
3. The estimates for costs are based on the 1997 administrative cost of $3.4 billion for the total program divided by 198.7 million participants (145 million workers and 43.7 million beneficiaries). The cost for only the retirement and survivors part of social security is based on an administrative cost of $2.1 billion and 182.6 million participants (145 million workers and 37.6 million beneficiaries) (Board of Trustees 1998, 97, 105; SSA 1997, 167, 183).

fixed costs per account, while some depend on the size of the account. Since the bulk of ongoing costs would likely be fixed costs per account, estimating costs is approached in those terms (e.g., x dollars per account per year). That is, the cost of managing the aggregate portfolio is small relative to the costs of record keeping, including communication with account owners. With the TSP, investment-management fees are roughly one-tenth of total costs borne by the TSP (with the costs borne by federal agencies also fixed costs per account). Dividing an annual dollar cost by annual deposits converts this to a percentage front load.

It is also useful to express these costs in other ways. One familiar method of stating costs is as an annual management fee in percentage terms (e.g., y percent of the accumulated balance in the account per year). Once the size of the accounts has been estimated, a dollar cost per year and a percentage of balances per year can be related by calculations that equate the present discounted value of costs over the career of a worker. If charges are imposed to cover the costs under these two methods, the charges will be equal on a lifetime basis but will likely differ in any given year or stage of life. With balances that grow relative to wages, a constant percentage of balances is a smaller charge in early years and a larger charge in later years. A third way in which to report on the costs is in terms of the percentage decrease in the accumulation in an account at retirement age as a consequence of the administrative charges, called the *charge ratio*. The relation among percentage front load, annual management fee, and charge ratio, based on continuous-time calculations, are presented in appendix B, which is reproduced from Diamond (1998). Some examples are shown in table 4.1.

The costs of organizing the accounts depend on the level of services provided with the accounts. Examples of variation in the level of services include variations in the frequency of deposits of withheld funds into the accounts, the number of alternative investment options available, the fre-

Table 4.1   Decline in Value of Accounts due to Fees after a 40-Year Work Career

Type and Level of Fees	% Decline in Account Value due to Fees	Type and Level of Fees	% Decline in Account Value due to Fees
Front-load fees (% of new contributions) of:		Annual management fees (% of account balance) of:	
1%	1	0.1%	2.2
10%	10	0.5%	10.5
20%	20	1.0%	19.6

Note: I assume real wage growth of 2.1 percent and a real annual return on investments of 4 percent. With a larger difference between the rate of return and the wage growth rate, the charge ratio with annual management fees is slightly larger, and conversely.

quency of interfund transfers that is allowed, the frequency of reporting on balances, the availability of information (e.g., an 800 number), the ease of communication (e.g., the presence of people who can speak different languages), and the amount of education made available to workers.

I begin by considering government-organized accounts that have relatively low costs and provide a relatively low level of services. The following description is taken from NASI (1998), with a few modifications. In particular, using round numbers and reflecting diverse opinions, the panel described a range of costs as being $25–$50. I use a range of $40–$50 because I consider this range more plausibly centered.

4.1.2   An Illustrative Low-Cost/Low-Services Plan

Transmission of Funds

At present, employers pay social security taxes to the Treasury shortly after each pay period, with a frequency depending on the size of the employer. However, these payments are not individually identified to the Treasury; that is, the Treasury knows the employer but not the individual employee associated with any tax payment. Once a year, employers file W-2 forms that show the annual taxable earnings of individual workers, which are needed for the eventual determination of benefits. Until 1978, firms reported on individual earnings quarterly, but that frequency was reduced to hold down costs, particularly for employers with few workers.[4] At present, of the 6.5 million employers that report to the Social Security Administration (SSA) each year, 5.4 million file their W-2 reports on paper; these include more than 4 million employers with ten or fewer employees.

While shifting to more frequent reporting might not be costly for employers with electronic record keeping, doing so would represent a significant cost for small businesses. Therefore, in the low-cost/low-services version of individual accounts, it is assumed that these taxpaying and reporting practices of private firms would not change. With this structure, the Treasury could place the portion of aggregate payroll-tax revenues that was allocated for individual accounts in a separate trust fund, which would earn interest. Such a fund could hold Treasury debt, but it might be better to hold the estimated average portfolio, based on existing allocations and previous earnings. This would permit an allocation to individual accounts that reflected individual portfolio choices (which would have been made before the year began). Moreover, the allocation to individual accounts might go more smoothly in the capital market if assets were allocated to the accounts rather than funds to buy assets. Without a direct

---

4. Olsen and Salisbury (1998, 15) cite a 1972 estimate of the cost savings to small employers from dropping quarterly reporting that, "adjusted to 1997 dollars, . . . would amount to about $900 million a year."

adjustment, there would be some difference between the total investment returns of the separate trust fund and the amounts to be credited to individual accounts. This difference could be averaged over time, or allocations could be adjusted each year, but something would need to be done. However, the allocation could not recognize the actual timing of payments by different workers; all workers would be treated as if the timing of their withheld tax payments were the same as the timing of aggregate withholdings.

Once a year, the Treasury would allocate the accumulated separate trust fund to individual accounts. To process almost all the accounts without greater cost than at present would probably require seven to nine months after the end of the year in which the taxes had been collected.[5] More time would be required for those cases in which there was a mismatch between the reported W-2 information and social security records as well as for the self-employed, who can file as late as 15 April (and later if they file for an extension). In a system this large, even a small percentage of errors adds up to a large number of errors. Currently, roughly 3 percent of W-2 forms (6 million cases) require direct contact with employer or employee to match the W-2 and social security records. With the additional element of portfolio allocation, more errors would have to be resolved.

Portfolio Choice

Under this structure, individuals would inform social security about the division of their deposits among the available portfolios. Workers might do this directly or through their employers, but, in either case, it would have to be done before the start of the calendar year, with the allocation unchanged from the previous year unless the worker requested otherwise. Presumably, a chosen allocation would be unchanged until a worker selected a different one. Thus, a worker changing employers would not need to report a portfolio choice to social security; only newly covered workers and workers wanting to change their allocations would need to report. Since many new and changed allocations would be reported on paper if done by a firm or on paper or by phone if done by workers, there are likely to be errors and a need for both an error-correction mechanism and a record-keeping function to provide evidence for sorting out errors.[6] Some individuals, particularly newly covered workers, would not have selected an allocation, and there would have to be a default portfolio for these workers. This could be legislated to be similar to the current portfolio of the Social Security Trust Fund, or the average portfolio in individual

5. Mitchell (1998, 417) reports, "Only 70 percent of earnings were posted within six months of the tax-year end in 1991."
6. As an example of the difficulties present in error correction, Olsen and Salisbury (1998, 25) cite unpublished SSA data (1998) that "approximately 10 percent of employers reporting wages to SSA go out of business each year."

accounts, or a prudently selected portfolio. In addition to directing the flow of new deposits among different index funds, workers would be allowed to shift existing account balances on a limited basis, such as once a year. Again, if this were allowed, a record-keeping mechanism would be needed to deal with possible mistakes or claims of mistakes. Similarly, information on the level of their accounts would be provided directly to workers only once a year. Workers could infer the value of their accounts by knowing the number of units held in each account and checking the values of those units, which would likely be presented regularly in the media.

To keep costs low, worker education about portfolio choices would be limited to providing pamphlets on investment strategy. It should be noted, however, that experience with worker education in 401(k) plans shows that considerably more substantial (and expensive) worker education is needed to have a noticeable effect on workers' investment choices (Bayer, Bernheim, and Scholz 1996). Moreover, the covered population includes many people who have not considered investment choices, making this low level of education an important issue. As reported by Arthur Levitt (1998), SEC research indicates that half the public do not know the difference between a stock and a bond. In addition to this minimal outreach providing education, the SSA would need to respond to questions asked by covered workers. Presumably, this would be a major source of cost, particularly reflecting the education and language difficulties of part of the population.

Handling and managing the aggregate funds would probably require only a small management fee. Currently, the TSP is charged roughly one basis point by the fund managers handling the bond and stock funds.

Benefits

The cost of paying retirement benefits from individual accounts must also be considered. Assuming that annuitization is mandated, the least-cost approach would be automatic annuitization of these funds according to rules set by legislation, with the payments added to the payment of whatever defined benefits were maintained. Information would be provided to beneficiaries on the source of each payment.

4.1.3   Cost

A starting place for estimating the additional costs to social security for adding such a low-cost/low-services individual account plan is the portion of the costs of the TSP that fall on the TSP (i.e., excluding the costs that fall on federal agencies that educate workers, answer questions, and report earnings records to the TSP and excluding the administrative costs coming from the payment of annuities [which are paid by retirees and reflected in the price of privately supplied annuities]). The TSP cost is currently roughly $20 per worker per year, although the costs were lower when fewer services were provided.[7] With 140 million accounts, a cost of $20 per worker would be an aggregate cost of $2.8 billion per year. The start-up costs of the TSP in 1987 were $5.25 million; if the start-up costs were the same per participant, the 1998 cost would be $1.08 billion (Olsen and Salisbury 1998).

There are a number of issues involved in comparing TSP costs with the incremental costs of the low-cost/low-services system just described. On the one hand, the TSP provides better services (in terms of frequency of reporting, frequency of portfolio change, and frequency of deposit), must deal with loans against workers' accounts, and has fewer economies of scale. In addition, social security would have some economies of scope. For example, a single annual statement can contain information on both parts of the system. These factors tend to lower the costs of social security individual accounts relative to TSP costs. On the other hand, there are factors that tend to raise the cost of social security individual accounts relative to TSP costs. First, many costs of the TSP system are borne by federal agencies as employers. They handle the education of participants (providing more education than described in the low-cost plan), respond to their questions, enroll them in the plan, transmit their portfolio choices electronically, and make employees whole when reporting errors cause them to lose investment returns on their contributions. If employers do not fill the roles that they fill with the TSP, these costs will likely fall on social security. Many of the 140 million workers have more limited education and less proficiency in English than is typical of federal employees, and direct contact would be needed to handle the tasks outlined above. For example, the cost of providing account information over the Internet is 1 percent of the cost of providing the information by an operator responding to an 800 number and 4 percent of the cost of providing it by an automated 800 number (Joel Dickson, personal communication, 1998). The social security population would make less use of the Internet, on average, than the 401(k) population. Second, social security covers many small employers that report social security records on paper rather than electronically, which would add to the cost and risk of errors in record keeping. While error correction for earnings needs to be done for the continuing defined-benefit system, adjusting individual accounts for the same errors would be an additional cost. Also, correction of errors in reported portfolio choice would have additional costs. Third, social security covers part-time, intermittent, and highly mobile workers, many of whom have multiple employers, whereas federal employees have low labor mobility.

7. The estimate for the TSP is based on its 1997 balance sheet and includes administrative costs of $44.1 million, investment-management fees of $2.3 million, and fiduciary insurance of $0.2 million, divided by 2.3 million participants (Arthur Anderson 1998).

Table 4.2   **Percentage of Workers with Social Security Earnings below Specified Levels (wage and salary workers, 1996)**

Annual Taxable Earnings of Less Than:	No. of Workers	% of Workers
$5,000	29,554	22
$10,000	46,438	35
$15,000	61,816	46
$20,000	76,178	58
$25,000	88,900	67
$30,000	99,458	73
$40,000	114,629	85
$50,000	123,641	91
$60,000	128,591	95
$63,000	129,578	96
$63,001	136,689	100

Source: Office of the Actuary, SSA.

Fourth, there are likely to be mandatory adjustments on divorce and account sharing between spouses. Finally, there will be costs of providing benefits, whether annuitized or paid out regularly, that are not part of TSP costs. A range of $40–$50 per worker per year seems to me a reasonable rough order of magnitude for a low-cost/low-services plan. A bit lower or somewhat higher cannot be ruled out. I note that this is a considerably higher cost than the 10.5 basis points for accounts financed by 1.6 percent of payroll assumed by the Advisory Council on Social Security (1997).

While the bulk of the costs would be fixed per account, their effect on the accumulation in individual accounts would depend on how charges for these costs were allocated across accounts of different sizes. The charges could be proportional to deposits or to account sizes, implying that all workers with the same portfolio choice would receive the same rate of return. Alternatively, the charges could include a fixed component reflecting the underlying structure of the costs, implying that workers with higher accumulations would have better rates of return net of charges. The importance of this choice depends on the dispersion in earnings for the covered population. In 1996, 22 percent of workers covered by social security earned less than $5,000, while 58 percent earned below $20,000 (table 4.2). Presumably, government-organized accounts would follow the approach of uniform percentage charges.

How would these added costs affect the retirement income of covered workers? The relative significance of a cost range of $40–$50 per worker per year would depend on the proportion of workers' earnings being deposited in the accounts and the size of their earnings. In 1997, mean social security taxable earnings were approximately $23,000. If 2 percent of workers' earnings went to individual accounts, the mean deposit would be

$460. A $40–$50 cost charged to the account would be equal to 9–11 percent of the new contribution (equivalent to a "front-load" charge) for the mean earner. Presumably, the cost would rise roughly in step with average wages, keeping the front load roughly constant in percentage terms. These calculations would be the same for workers at any earnings level if charges were the same percentage for all workers. If charges reflected some of the fixed costs of accounts, the load would be larger for low earners and smaller for high earners. The calculation for accounts financed from larger or smaller percentages of payroll would be proportional.

Another way to describe these charges is to ask what charge as a fraction of assets under management would cover these costs on a lifetime basis, assuming that the cost grew with average wages. Using table 4.1 above, with 2 percent accounts an annual $40–$50 change would be roughly equivalent to a forty- to fifty-basis-point charge on assets under management over a forty-year career.

Note that the distribution of earnings of workers covered by social security is very different from that of earnings of current 401(k) participants. In contrast to table 4.2, of workers participating in 401(k) plans in 1993, only about 20 percent earned less than $20,000 (EBRI 1994).

4.1.4   Level of Services

Costs would be raised by the provision of additional services, such as more frequent reporting on accounts, more frequent deposits into accounts, more frequently allowed reallocations of existing portfolios, more readily available information on account balance, more resources devoted to answering questions, or more worker education. Thus, a critical question is what level of services would be a political equilibrium. A low-cost/low-services plan would provide far fewer services than a typical 401(k) account, with which much of the public is familiar. That might be one source of pressure for more services. In addition, unless voters make a good connection between services and costs, there might be pressure for more services that Congress might be inclined to satisfy since it does not have to legislate a tax increase to finance the higher services, the higher cost just coming out of the individual accounts without explicit pricing by Congress. Thus, a steady rise in services and costs might well be the political equilibrium, as it has been with the TSP.

4.1.5   Payment of Benefits

The cost of paying retirement benefits from individual accounts also depends on legislative decisions. Assuming that annuitization is mandated, the least-cost approach would be automatic annuitization of these funds according to rules set by legislation, with the payments added to the payment of whatever defined benefits were maintained. Information would be provided to beneficiaries on the source of each payment. Such a system would add little to the total costs of social security. However, this method for providing services might not be the political equilibrium. An important issue with mandated annuitization of accounts that are individually owned and managed is the political stability of such a proposal as the public's view of social security shifts. For example, would an individual with limited life expectancy or extraordinary immediate needs be forced to annuitize? Indeed, proposals for individual accounts sometimes propose alternatives, including some degree of choice as to how benefits are received. Another reason why this might not be the political equilibrium is that it would involve social security's directly holding the assets that back the annuity promise. Some of the reasons that some people favor individual accounts have them favoring private market provision of annuities, unless the backing is fully in indexed Treasury debt. First, I consider private market–provided annuities for government-organized accounts with mandated annuitization. Then I consider possible alternatives for benefit provision.

Annuity Provision

Annuitization of individual accounts might be accomplished in three different ways. First, the federal government could decide what benefits to pay for given accumulations, with social security bearing the risk inherent in projecting mortality and selecting a portfolio. Second, the federal government could contract with private providers to receive accounts from the government in return for paying the annuities. These annuities would be priced on a group basis. These payments could go directly to beneficiaries or to the government for transmittal to beneficiaries; in the latter case, the government would provide the payments directly to beneficiaries along with defined benefits. The private providers would bear the mortality and return risks, although there would be residual risk that a private insurance company would be unable to meet its obligations for annuity payments. It would be undesirable and probably politically untenable to put that residual risk on individuals, particularly those late in life. Therefore, the government should absorb that residual risk. Currently, insurance companies receive oversight from state governments, not the federal government; with such a residual risk for the federal government, there would be a call for federal oversight instead of or in addition to state oversight. Third, individuals could be left free to contract with insurance companies on their own, purchasing annuities from their accounts. This approach would employ individual rather than group purchase of annuities. In insurance markets generally, group products are considerably less expensive than individual products. This outcome reflects both lower costs for insurance companies in dealing with groups and greater competition for large group accounts than for smaller individual accounts. Costs with the third approach would be considerably higher than with either of the other two.

The costs of private market annuitization are discussed elsewhere (see Poterba and Warshawsky, chap. 5 in this volume; and also Mitchell et al. 1999).

Like many insurance products, annuities are offered far more cheaply on a group basis than on an individual basis. In order to have private provision on a group basis with a large national program, some mechanism would be needed. One issue is the sheer size of the program, calling for the use of multiple groups and multiple providers rather than a single provider of annuities for all retirees. If multiple groups are used, then, to preserve as much of the advantage of group purchase as possible, the government needs to allocate people to different groups rather than allowing the market to form the groups (Diamond 1992). Since there is little reason for a geographic concentration of benefit recipients, people could be allocated to different groups randomly, giving everyone roughly the same opportunities, which could be adjusted by cross-subsidization between groups receiving slightly different bids. While such group provision is likely to be somewhat more expensive than government provision provided the same portfolio were held for backing for the annuity promises, there is probably not a great deal of difference in cost. What is likely to be more of an issue is the determination of benefits. With private provision, the political outcome is more likely to be to accept the prices offered by the market. With government provision, there may be pressures for intervention when the pricing implied by mortality projection and current interest rates involves a drop in benefits.

Benefit Alternatives

Proposals take three different forms with regard to allowing choice about retirement income. Some proposals allow lump-sum withdrawals, leaving the worker free to choose the extent of annuitization of that portion, whatever rules apply to the remaining balances. While providing a lump sum is not expensive to social security, retirees who do want to annuitize are then left with the private annuities market in which to annuitize. Private market annuitization on an individual basis is considerably more expensive than is provision of retirement benefits by social security, making this option costly for those who might annuitize. Those who did not annuitize would be bearing the risk of outliving their retirement wealth. An intermediate position is to give workers a choice between annuitization and periodic withdrawal (e.g., monthly), with a limit on the size of the allowed withdrawal to limit the risk of outliving the retirement wealth. Other proposals mandate annuitization of the entire accumulation. An important issue with mandated annuitization of accounts that are individually owned and managed is the political stability of such a proposal as the public's view of social security shifts. For example, would an individual with limited life expectancy or extraordinary immediate needs be forced to annuitize? Moreover, with mandated annuitization, the issue remains of the extent to which any mandate is for inflation-adjusted annuities and/ or for joint-and-survivor annuities for married couples.

4.1.6   Conclusion

While individual accounts and annuitized benefits could be provided at a cost of around $40–$50 per year, a critical question is what the political equilibria would be for the level of services during accumulation and for the structure of benefit provision after retirement. Cost estimates need to recognize the uncertainty in what will be legislated for the accounts.

4.2   Privately Organized Accounts

To consider the charges for government-organized accounts, I followed three steps. First, I described the level of services likely to be provided if there are government-organized accounts. Second, I estimated costs for that plan, noting that additional services increase costs. And, third, I suggested that the costs would be allocated to different workers in proportion to either deposits or account balances, or some combination of both. To consider privately organized accounts, I discuss the level of services that might be provided and how the costs differ from those of government-organized accounts. In addition, we must consider the issues raised by competition among private firms. In doing this, I keep in mind a realistic picture of competitive markets, not an idealized one. Charges differ from the costs identified because of marketing costs and markups (which interact in equilibrium).

4.2.1   Deposit of Funds

There are three methods of deposit of funds to consider. In parallel to the low-cost/low-services government-organized plan described above, I consider a system under which the government continues to collect all taxes and transmits them once a year to private financial firms, with workers directly informing the government as to which private firm to use. Second, I consider having employers directly transmit the funds to financial firms. Third, I consider direct deposit by workers, keying off a tax credit. We need to keep in mind costs that fall on all three players in this scenario—workers, employers, and the government.

If the government transmits the funds once a year to firms, then there are some additional costs for the government beyond having it transmit the funds to itself. The actual transmission is not likely to have significant costs, but there are additional steps. Workers must inform the government as to the destination of the funds. There is a major design issue at this stage. Is a worker restricted to keeping his or her account at a single financial institution, or are workers allowed to have accounts at several institutions? If it is the former (as in Chile), then the government must enforce such consistency. When a worker, particularly a worker with a new employer, selects a financial institution, the government must check for consistency with the location of the existing account. With a centralized deposit plan, this is readily accomplished. Without a centralized system, restricting workers to a single account is probably not feasible, and we would have, as Australia does, a problem of many very small accounts, particularly as some low earners might start many accounts. This will be a problem for the workers who start multiple accounts in the absence of regulatory restrictions and/or subsidies since the earnings on small accounts would not cover the costs of maintaining them. If firms are required to charge all accounts the same percentage amounts (and to accept all workers), this cross-subsidization of multiple accounts is part of the cost for everyone. In Australia, this is a significant problem and is one reason for preferring the centralized transmission of funds. I assume that workers are restricted to a single account each. Otherwise, costs per account must be multiplied by accounts per worker to estimate costs per worker.

With government transmission of funds, the costs include verifying and correcting mistakes in the choice of firm, verifying and correcting mistakes in the deposits with financial firms (e.g., do the social security number and the name in the firm's records match those given in the incoming deposit information?), and overseeing transfers between firms. It seems plausible that many workers would shift financial firms from time to time. In Chile, turnover is roughly 20 percent per year. Transmission would not cost much since all communication between the government and firms would be electronic and would be likely to be accurate. The problems would come from errors at either end.

Direct deposits from employers would be significantly more expensive for both employers and financial firms. Financial firms would have to process many paper transactions (duplicating the same paper transactions being handled by the SSA) and would have to deal with many employers separately. Similarly, employers would have higher costs, whatever the frequency of transactions, from dealing with many financial firms as well as with the government. In Chile, there are a small number of AFPs (*administradoras de fondos de pensiones*), so the process is not so bad. In the United States, there would be a vast array. While there would arise private clearinghouse arrangements (which have not arisen in Chile) to help particularly small firms, this is another layer of costs and markups. Moreover, there would be the usual tensions in a naturally increasing-returns activity between costs and competitive pressures depending on how many firms survived as clearinghouses. Financial firms would still have the problem of communicating with both workers and the fund transmitter (employers rather than the government), which adds to costs. Since this seems to add significantly to costs and has little in the way of benefits that are apparent to me in the U.S. context, I will not consider such transmissions further. While there would be some economies of scope from combining these accounts with 401(k)s, it is important to recognize that only a fraction of workers have 401(k)s, that regulations covering 401(k)s are likely to be different from those covering mandated accounts (requiring separate record keeping), and that it is unlikely that workers would be required to use only the options provided by the employer that provides their 401(k)s. So, while there is an advantage here, it is unlikely to offset the sizable cost disadvantage of this approach.

Direct deposit by individual workers has the advantage for financial firms that the firms are dealing with only a single entity, although they would still need to keep the government informed, as with mutual funds currently. The agent with whom they must communicate anyway is the one who makes the deposit and whose job it is to check that the deposit is properly handled. With many workers without financial sophistication, the government is likely to play a larger role in policing accuracy than it does when dealing with voluntary accounts with financial firms currently. This would follow both from the difference in populations from those currently dealing with financial firms handling retirement savings and from the presence of a mandate. In addition, deposits would be overwhelmingly on paper, making for considerably higher costs and error rates than with a single electronic transmission from the government. This seems to me likely to be noticeably more expensive than government deposit. Moreover, it involves issues of some workers filing for refundable tax credits who would not otherwise file taxes. So I conduct the analysis on the basis of government collection of taxes and transmission to private firms.

4.2.2   Alternative Investments

One of the major arguments in favor of privately organized accounts is the presence of a wider choice of investment options. In particular, one would expect that all three of the banking, insurance, and mutual fund industries would be active participants in this market. Banks would offer CDs and a vast array of locations. Insurance companies would offer accounts with insurance features attached to them. Mutual funds would offer managed as well as indexed funds and possibly individually designed portfolios.

Several issues arise from this array. One is the currently diverse regulation of these different institutions. In particular, mutual funds and banks have different federal regulatory agencies, while insurance companies are regulated at the state level. Presumably, this would change in a significant way under a system of privately organized accounts.

A second major issue is how to think about the value of this diversity as well as the increased diversity just within mutual funds. As economists, we normally consider increased options to be advantageous, provided that the increased options do not come with adverse price changes as part of the adjustment to a new equilibrium. This need not be the case here for two reasons, both related to the purpose of and motivation for social security. First, the purpose is to have retirement income. Insofar as workers (implicitly) trade off current services (including possibly kickbacks) for a lower rate of return (and so lower retirement incomes), the increase in options in privately organized accounts is cutting against the primary purpose of the mandate. Second, insofar as the mandate comes from a concern that individuals do not do a good job of looking out for themselves when it comes to retirement planning, it seems right to recognize that many people will not do a good job of choosing a financial intermediary for retirement savings as well. The current financial market is marked, as are almost all retail markets, by a diversity of prices for similar, sometimes seemingly identical products. Some people end up with high-cost options. Since individual accounts would involve an ongoing relationship, with little at stake in any particular month, workers, particularly low earners, would not have much incentive to stay on top of the changing array of alternative investments and alternative charges. In the absence of detailed regulations limiting pricing alternatives, we might see a dizzying array of prices and arrangements in this market.

In this setting, it is important to move beyond an "average" worker and to recognize the allocation of workers across different options and the relations between different worker characteristics, particularly earnings level and options selected. Thus, it would not be an adequate analytic approach to consider the availability of some low-cost option as the basis for evaluation, with an assumption that everyone choosing some higher-cost option is gaining from making that choice. Both positive political economy and normative considerations suggest that this would be a tightly regulated market, with both the benefits and the costs of tight regulation.

Comparing Costs

In some settings, private firms have lower cost functions than the government because they have access to better technologies, are able to generate better incentives for workers, or can pay lower wages, perhaps by avoiding unionization. The potential for these opportunities depends on the nature of the task being fulfilled. As Wilson (1989) has argued, some bureaucratic tasks have outputs that are easy to measure, so it is easier for a government bureaucracy to do a good job. Current social security is in this category. The tasks are well defined (collect money, keep records, distribute money, provide information). Indeed, the costs of social security are very low compared to private firms involved in similar activities. Moreover, this is not a special U.S. outcome but a common feature of many national pension systems in advanced countries. (On costs in other advanced countries, see Mitchell [1998].) It seems to me that organizing a TSP-type system has similar characteristics from the perspective of ease of bureaucratic management. I would not expect private firms to have lower cost functions than the federal government. In addition to considering the cost functions, there are issues of returns to scale since the government system would be vastly larger than the average private system. While some firms may have economies of scope from combining their share of social security individual accounts with other fund-management activities, social security has economies of scope as well. I conclude by suggesting that record-keeping and investment-management costs are likely to be higher with privately organized than with government-organized accounts.

Charges

If the world were like an idealized competitive market, then all we would need to know is costs since, in the absence of regulation, charges would equal costs. But observation of other countries that have national (mandated or voluntary) privately organized individual accounts (Chile, Argentina, the United Kingdom) makes it clear that this model does not apply. Similarly, consideration of the voluntary individual capital market in the United States shows considerable advertising expenses and charges that do not have the structure of costs.

There are two aspects to thinking about equilibrium in such a market. What will be the structure of charges, and what will be the levels of pricing parameters in the structure? Currently, the most common bases for charges in mutual funds are proportional to the amount in an account or a combination of the amount in an account and the amounts being deposited— in 1997, load funds accounted for more than half of all new sales of equity funds (Rea and Reid 1998). The market has higher charges for people with lower accounts, minimum account balances, and some flat charges. It is plausible that, without regulations on the structure of charges, mandatory accounts would see a similar structure. I am not aware of analyses as to why this structure has evolved. I suspect that a charge in basis points is less psychologically aversive than one in dollars—it is harder to think about how much it is actually costing. Since the advantage of having "better" management of funds increases with the size of the funds, charges that vary in this way may take advantage of the way in which charges will be viewed and the extent to which investors will shop and switch. Presumably, this is a market with considerable inertia as to switching, even though switching costs are very low (except from firms that have back loads or to firms that have front loads on transfers).

Looking across different portfolios, it does seem to be the case that those funds with higher costs have higher charges, but there is considerable spread in charges within portfolio categories, indeed, even within index fund categories that are tracking the same index. Spreads in prices for the same services are widespread phenomena in retail markets and suggestive of imperfections in perceiving and acting on alternatives that exist in the market. This suggests that, without regulation to the contrary, charges on average will be higher (in percentage terms) for accounts that are financed with a smaller fraction of taxable payroll. It also suggests that charges on average will be higher (in percentage terms) for lower earners than for higher earners.

This view of markets as having markups and variation primarily because of consumer lethargy is clearly different from a perspective that consumers are choosing the best option in an array of competitive firms that offer different qualities of services at different prices. It is the case that firms offer different services in terms of the nonreturn aspects of services. But I find it hard to accept the competitive market model. This would be particularly an issue with mandatory accounts where people may not know how services vary across firms or how to value such services. In particular, it is very difficult to assess whether some portfolio managers are better than others even if one understands the concept of a risk-return trade-off. Given the difficulty in doing this with sophisticated analysis, most workers would have considerably greater difficulty, even though *Consumer Reports* would be giving ratings to the small fraction of the public that would follow such information. I conclude that equilibrium is likely to have substantial markups, together with the selling costs that are encouraged by such markups.

This possibility has led some analysts to call for a cap on allowable charges for handling privately organized accounts. Our experience with price regulation leaves it unclear how well such regulation would work. In addition, caps would be somewhat difficult to enforce. Some types of accounts (e.g., CDs) do not have separate charges. Currently, charges from brokerage fees are treated separately from other charges. And costs are different for different types of accounts (bond vs. stock, domestic vs. international, index vs. managed).

Current Examples

One approach is to consider existing market alternatives and their costs. While this might give some idea of average charges, it is more difficult to consider the degree of matching of different workers with different institutions. It also needs to be recognized that the average size of accounts may well be different from any particular example and that the population whose demand reactions affect pricing would be different.

A key point is that individuals will be seeking out firms on an individual basis. Thus while quotations of charges made by financial firms on an institutional basis are relevant when considering costs with government-organized accounts, they seem to me irrelevant when considering privately organized accounts. We therefore need to consider the market for individual choice or the market that deals with small firms. It is natural to look at four pieces of evidence. What has happened in other national systems with individual accounts organized individually? What are charges for mutual funds and other investment vehicles? What are charges with IRAs and 401(k)s? It is also important to look at the entire market, not just the offerings of one or a few firms. Since other papers in this volume also consider the available information, I will be brief.

Costs in Chile (which are front-load costs of roughly 15–20 percent) are roughly equivalent to seventy-five to one hundred basis points on accounts that are 10 percent of taxable wages (which seems to me relevant since the labor costs of the financial firms will resemble the average labor costs in an economy). Argentina, with smaller accounts, has larger charges. Mexico, which has amounts put in the accounts by the government as well as amounts withheld from workers, has higher charges relative to the deposits of workers' withholding but lower charges relative to total deposits. The United Kingdom has considerably higher charges than Chile.[8]

Some people have argued that costs are high in Chile because of the nature of regulation there. Regulations require uniform pricing for all workers, preventing the formation of groups that might bargain for lower prices, with an unclear implication for charges to the remaining population. Regulation on the structure of charges (only front loads and only a combination of flat and proportional charges) would not prevent competitive pressures, if they are as in the idealized market, from keeping charges, on average, close to costs and so holding down the incentive for sales efforts. The high markups over production costs and the high fraction of costs devoted to sales suggest that it is inherent in individually organized markets for this type of product to have high markups. The similarity of costs in Chile to those in markets without such price-structure regulations also suggests that the details of the regulation are not the prime reason for the level of costs.[9]

A recent Investment Company Institute study of equity mutual funds (Rea and Reid 1998) argues that the average dollar invested in individual funds in 1997 was charged around 149 basis points, not including any brokerage charges that go with many of these products. The calculation includes balanced and other hybrid funds. This calculation includes both annual maintenance charges and an annualization of front-load charges.[10]

---

8. For more details, see Diamond (1998).

9. Australia has a mandate on firms, not workers. Thus, evidence from the large-firm section of that economy does not seem relevant for the typical proposal in the United States.

10. The study argues for the importance of including front loads since roughly two-thirds of retail investors buy mutual funds through sources offering load funds and load funds accounted for more than half of all new sales of equity funds in 1997 and represented 60

The study also reports that this average charge has fallen from 225 basis points in 1980. The study does not report the average account size, which would help for comparison with individual social security accounts.[11]

I do not know what the implicit charges would be with bank CDs. Similarly, I have not looked into insurance company charges.

I do not examine IRA and 401(k) charges—for discussions of the literature, see Mitchell (1998) and Olsen and Salisbury (1998). As these authors note, some data sources (e.g., form 5500) report only part of the charges made by financial firms. We need to recognize that both IRA and voluntary accounts may well have lower costs than mandatory accounts because financial firms deal only with the depositor in these cases but would deal with both the government and the individual with mandatory accounts. On the other hand, 401(k)s have considerable regulation for tax qualification and have financial firms deal with both employers and employees. Thus, the costs for providing services to small firms may well be higher than with mandatory accounts organized with direct government deposits. Larger firms have economies of scale and bargaining power in negotiating individual deals rather than accepting a take-it-or-leave-it offer in the market—so their charges and costs are probably not relevant for thinking about privately organized accounts.

I see no reason to think that the nature of equilibrium with privately organized individual accounts would be dramatically different from these examples. The accounts would be smaller and the population dealing with the financial community more diverse and less sophisticated on average. I suspect that the costs for the typical worker choosing a mutual fund would be at least one hundred basis points with accounts from a large percentage of payroll and larger, possibly considerably larger, if we are considering accounts financed with only 2 percent of payroll. I note that this is roughly consistent with the 1 percent cost for accounts financed by 5 percent of payroll assumed by the Advisory Council on Social Security (1997).

Implications of Charges

For example, with one hundred basis points of accumulations per year charged over a full career, and assuming that wage growth exceeds the interest rate by 2 percent, the final accumulation in privately organized accounts would be reduced by 19.6 percent. Other examples were reported

percent of equity fund assets at the end of 1997. The study does not seem to deal with the complication in annualizing front loads owing to the fact that the interest rate relevant for the individual depends on the charging structure. I suspect that this would not be a significant change in the calculation, but it should be examined.

11. Mitchell (1998) reports on expense ratios without front loads separately for different types of mutual funds and does report on average account sizes. For fiscal years ending in 1994–95, calculations show expense ratios varying from 0.324 for equity index funds to 1.043 for growth funds and 1.250 for global funds. From average account sizes, these translate into $67.9 for index funds and $137.5–$302.5 for the other funds.

in table 4.1 above. Thus, privately organized accounts are likely to deliver accumulations at retirement that are at least 10–15 percent lower than could be delivered by government-organized accounts and quite possibly even lower. In addition, the provision of annuitization would be more difficult and would likely be more expensive.

4.2.3   Conclusion

My conclusion is that privately organized individual accounts are very expensive for satisfying the basic purpose of social security. Since I think that government-organized accounts can be reasonably insulated from political interference, that the increased choice that would be present with privately organized accounts may be as likely to be harmful to the worker as helpful, and that greatly increased regulation is likely with the uncertainties created by the introduction of a new regulatory structure, I consider privately organized accounts to be dominated by government-organized accounts.

Appendix A
Tasks in Implementing Individual Accounts

This list first considers tasks in implementing government-organized accounts, and then notes tasks that would be different with privately-organized accounts.

Government-Organized Accounts

This list assumes that contributions are received throughout the year, and are linked to individual taxpayers after the end of the year, when W-2s are filed. It also assumes that the government receives the money, arranges for investment, recordkeeping and benefit payments. An asterisk (*) indicates tasks now done by the Social Security Administration or Treasury, or similar tasks. In some cases, the tasks become more complex because of differences in timing or other concerns.

1. Collect Contributions from Employers

   a. Receive and record money from employers shortly after each payday.*

   b. Reconcile amounts received with quarterly 941 and annual W-2 reports to detect missing or discrepant payments.*

   c. Segregate account contributions from other taxes paid by employers.

2. Invest Funds

a. Select a private fund manager(s).

b. Invest new contributions during the year according to government policy.

c. Designate a default investment portfolio for individuals not selecting one.

d. Report investment returns to the recordkeeper—annual average for new contributions, monthly/quarterly for account balance valuations.

3. Credit Workers' Accounts with New Contributions

a. Find missing or inconsistent reports from employers by reconciling annual and quarterly reports and correspond with employers to fix it.*

b. Record new contributions to individual accounts. Identify discrepancies between W-2s and SSN files and correspond with employers or employees to fix mistakes.

c. Set up new information system of records needed to administer accounts: workers' ID, portfolio choice, effective date of choice, interfund transfers and date of interfund transfer, death beneficiary designation, marital status, spouse ID, and spousal consent code (depending on policy), current address.

4. Enroll Workers and Get Portfolio Choice
(and Other New Information)

Depends on employer involvement (either mandatory or voluntary). Options include: (i) ongoing requirement that employers enroll new employees and report portfolio choices annually (on W-2s or W-4s); (ii) one-time employer responsibility to enroll workers in the plan and send data to the record keeper; (iii) do not involve employers—deal directly with workers through 1040s, correspondence, phone, website or in person.

5. Educate and Communicate with Workers

a. "Wholesale" tasks (such as in the TSP) include developing educational brochures, videos, training courses for employers to use to enroll workers.

b. "Retail" tasks (performed by employers in the TSP) include one-on-one communication with workers—via Social Security (or IRS?) field offices, an 800 number, website.

6. Pay Death Benefits

a. Determine policy for death benefits including registry of state laws on inheritance rights and rules for determining jurisdictions, if relevant.

b. Set rules of evidence for determining correct death beneficiary and maintain record system to support it.*

c. Resolve competing claims when they occur.*

7. Implement Policy on Treatment of Accounts at Divorce

Possible policies include: (i) let courts decide; (ii) automatically divide 50/50 changes in account balances that occurred during the marriage; and (iii) automatically divide contributions each year between spouses. Depending on policy, tasks include:

a. Set policy for treatment of QDRO (qualified domestic relations order from court).

b. Maintain historical records that can be used to retroactively combine and split two individuals' change in account balances for a period of years or each year, link accounts of husbands and wives and transact a split.

c. Set up systems for verifying marital status and spouse ID, and policies for resolving disputes, discrepancies, and informing each party of transactions made on their accounts.

8. Pay Retirement Benefits

a. Determine policies about nature of withdrawal options.

b. With annuities, determine whether government or insurance companies will: (i) assume mortality and investment risk; and/or (ii) administer the annuities.

c. If insurance companies, determine policy for their involvement— e.g., standards for participation, competitive bidding for group contract, some sort of reinsurance.

d. Policy on joint-and-survivor annuities and beneficiary designation for non-annuitized funds (or period certain annuities).

9. Retirement Benefit Counseling (assuming a number of withdrawal options are available)

a. Explain to retirees what the choices are and what terms mean and run scenarios of how different choices would affect the particular retiree and spouse.

b. Set policies (if any) on who will provide the information and who will pay for it.

10. Early Access (if loans or withdrawals end up being allowed for "hardship.")

a. Determine hardship rules and how they will be applied.

b. *If loans,* set up systems for how they will be repaid.

Privately-Organized Accounts: Additional Tasks

This list assumes that funds are withheld and paid by employers to the government (as they are now) and that employers report annually on W-2s the amounts belonging to each worker. The government's tasks in collecting contributions would be the same as in government organized accounts.

When W-2s are in, the government would send each worker's funds to a financial institution chosen by the worker. The financial institution would be responsible for all further dealing with the account holder. It would be responsible for: investing funds, crediting workers accounts with new contributions, getting information about the worker's portfolio choice and other data needed to pay benefit to the worker or his/her beneficiaries, educate and communicate with workers about investment choices, pay death benefits, implement policy on treatment of divorce, pay retirement benefits under applicable rules, and provide retirement benefit counseling. It would also be responsible for enforcing whatever policy applies with regard to early access.

New issues and tasks that arise under this model:

a. Government would maintain a default plan or default institution for workers who fail to designate a financial institution.

b. Government would set rules on financial institutions eligible to hold Social Security accounts.*

c. If workers would be required to hold their funds in only one institution at a time, government and financial institutions would put systems in place to ensure that happened.

d. Once money is sent to the financial institution, it would be responsible for receiving portfolio choices from workers, sorting out mistakes and making employees whole under whatever rules apply.

e. Government policies might regulate fee arrangements of financial institutions, terms on which accounts are accepted by institutions, and possibly, marketing practices.

f. Government policies might regulate allowable portfolios.

g. Government would monitor institutions' compliance with whatever rules apply to the accumulation and distribution of account funds.*

h. Auditing, trustee, legal and related functions, to the extent not included above.

Appendix B

I do the calculation in continuous time. Consider a worker who earns w_s at time s, assumed to grow exponentially at rate g:

$$(1) \qquad\qquad w_s = w_0 e^{gs}.$$

The tax rate on these earnings is t. There is a proportional front-load charge of f so that $t(1 - f)w_0 e^{gs}$ is deposited at time s. This accumulates until retirement age, T. The accumulation occurs at the rate $r - c$, where r is the rate of return, and c is the management charge per dollar under management. Thus, deposits made at time s have accumulated to $t(1 - f)w_0 e^{gs}e^{(r-c)(T-s)}$ at time T. The total accumulation at time T is the integral of this expression from time 0 until time T. Integrating, the accumulation depends on f and c and (for $g + c \neq r$) is equal to the following:

$$(2) \qquad A[f,c] = t(1 - f)w_0 e^{(r-c)T}\{e^{(g+c-r)T} - 1\}/(g + c - r).$$

For $g + c = r$, the accumulation satisfies

$$(3) \qquad\qquad A[f,c] = t(1 - f)w_0 e^{(r-c)T}T.$$

For r unequal to both $g + c$ and g, the ratio of the accumulation to what it would be without any charges satisfies

$$(4) \qquad \mathrm{AR}[f,c] = A[f,c]/A[0,0]$$
$$= (1 - f)e^{-cT}\{(e^{(g+c-r)T} - 1)/(e^{(g-r)T} - 1)\}$$
$$\times \{(g - r)/(g + c - r)\}.$$

The charge ratio is one minus the accumulation ratio:

$$(5) \qquad\qquad \mathrm{CR}[f,c] = 1 - \mathrm{AR}[f,c].$$

Sample calculations are shown in table 4.1 above.

References

Advisory Council on Social Security. 1997. *1994–1996 Advisory Council on Social Security: Findings and recommendations: Volume I and II.* Washington, D.C.
Arthur Anderson LLP. 1998. Financial statements of the Thrift Savings Fund, 1997 and 1998. Available through the Thrift Savings Plan, Washington, D.C.
Bayer, P., B. D. Bernheim, and J. Scholz. 1996. The effects of financial education in the workplace: Evidence from a survey of employers. NBER Working Paper no. 5655. Cambridge, Mass.: National Bureau of Economic Research.
Board of Trustees. Federal Old-Age and Survivors Insurance and Disability Insurance Trust Funds. 1998. *1998 annual report.* Washington, D.C.: U.S. Government Printing Office.
Diamond, P. 1992. Organizing the health insurance market. *Econometrica* 60: 1233–54.
———. 1998. Economics of social security reform. In *Framing the social security debate: Values, politics, and economics,* ed. R. D. Arnold, M. J. Graetz, and A. H. Munnel. Washington, D.C.: Brookings.
Edey, Malcolm, and John Simon. 1998. Australia's retirement income system. In

Privatizing social security, ed. Martin Feldstein. Chicago: University of Chicago Press.

Employee Benefit Research Institute (EBRI). 1994. Employment-based retirement income benefits: Analysis of the April 1993 Current Population Survey. Special report no. SR-25/Issue Brief no. 153. Washington, D.C.

Levitt, Arthur. 1998. The SEC perspective on investing social security in the stock market. Speech presented at the Kennedy School, Harvard University, 19 October.

Mitchell, Olivia. 1998. Administrative costs in public and private retirement systems. In *Privatizing social security,* ed. Martin Feldstein. Chicago: University of Chicago Press.

Mitchell, O., J. Poterba, M. Warshawsky, and J. Brown. 1999. New evidence on the money's worth of individual annuities. *American Economic Review* 89 (December): 1299–1318.

National Academy of Social Insurance (NASI). 1998. Evaluating issues in privatizing social security: Report of the Panel on Privatization of Social Insurance. Washington, D.C. Available at www.nasi.org.

Olsen, Kelly A., and Dallas L. Salisbury. 1998. Individual social security accounts: Issues in assessing administrative feasibility and costs. Special Report no. SR-34/Issue Brief no. 203. Washington, D.C.: Employee Benefit Research Institute.

Rea, John D., and Brian K. Reid. 1998. Trends in the ownership cost of equity mutual funds. Washington, D.C.: Investment Company Institute.

Social Security Administration (SSA). 1997. *Annual statistical supplement to the Social Security Bulletin.* Washington, D.C.

Wilson, James Q. 1989. *Bureaucracy.* New York: Basic.

Comment   Martin Feldstein

Peter Diamond has made an important contribution to the general analysis and design of social security reform by calling attention to administrative costs. His earlier writing (Diamond 1997) and our personal discussions in the past have also caused me to reconsider the appropriate way to finance individual investment-based supplementary social security accounts and to change my own proposal (Feldstein 1997) to an alternative structure with significantly lower administrative costs. I return to this below.

In the present paper, Diamond emphasizes the distinction between two types of individual investment-based accounts: *government-organized accounts,* in which the government does the record keeping and investment management (as it does for the federal employees' Thrift Savings Plan [TSP]), and *privately organized accounts,* in which private firms do the record keeping and investment management. Diamond's conclusion is that government-organized accounts would cost about $40–$50 per account

Martin Feldstein is the George F. Baker Professor of Economics at Harvard University and president of the National Bureau of Economic Research.

per year while privately organized accounts would cost about twice as much. For an average-size account, Diamond translates the $40–$50 charge into a reduced yield of forty to fifty basis points, implying that the individual's accumulation at retirement would be 10 percent less than it would be if there were no administrative cost. The privately organized accounts would therefore, according to Diamond, reduce final accumulation by about 20 percent. From these calculations, Diamond concludes that government-organized accounts would be desirable (or at least acceptable) while privately organized accounts would be "prohibitively expensive."

I do not agree. In this comment, I make four basic points: First, centrally administered accounts raise fundamental problems that make them politically unacceptable as an alternative to part of the pay-as-you-go social security system. Second, even if we accept Diamond's estimate that government-organized accounts involve a forty- to fifty-basis-point administrative cost per year, the benefit of such accounts would outweigh the cost. Third, the same is true of individually organized accounts; their benefits would outweigh their costs even if those costs were the one hundred basis points assumed by Diamond. Fourth, privately organized accounts would not cost as much as one hundred basis points and could well become less expensive than government-organized accounts.

Centrally Administered Accounts

Diamond's estimate that a government-organized account costs forty to fifty basis points is relative to a system of investment-based social security with no administrative cost at all. The notion of an investment-based component of social security with no administrative cost can only be approximated by putting private securities into the Social Security Trust Fund or some other centrally administered single account as proposed in the Ball plan (Advisory Council on Social Security 1997) and the Aaron-Reischauer (1998) plan.

As a practical matter, I believe that such a central account is not a politically relevant option. Recall that, even with a mixed system that combines the current pay-as-you-go taxes with investment-based saving equal to 2 percent of payroll, the net accumulation after thirty years would then be equal to about 40 percent of the GDP in that year. In today's economy, that would be more than $3 trillion of private securities owned by the government. The political process, for good reason, would reject giving the government control over such a large pool of assets. Advocates like Aaron and Reischauer (1998) go to great lengths to emphasize that the funds would be administered by an independent administrative authority. Opponents reject claims of such independence since any authority, as a creature of legislation, is ultimately responsive to the Congress and/or the administration.

There are two broad concerns about the power that such an administrative authority would exercise. First, a government administrative authority would introduce political considerations into portfolio-investment decisions. The most obvious of these would be political prohibitions on investing in companies that make certain products (e.g., cigarette companies), companies that have been found to violate certain laws (antitrust rules, environmental rules, etc.), foreign-owned companies, U.S. companies whose foreign investments "take jobs away from American workers," etc. A second distortion would be geographic distribution requirements of the type that cause the defense budget and other public works to be distributed among states and congressional districts in response to political considerations rather than economic efficiency. A third problem would be distortion to risk decisions because of the politically asymmetrical reactions to gains and losses that would make investment managers likely to be excessively cautious to avoid the criticism that they gambled and lost retirees' money.

These concerns about the role of the government as an owner of equities also apply to corporate bonds. How would the government deal with companies that are in bankruptcy? Would its decision be the same as that of a private investment manager, or would it be concerned about employment effects, etc.?

The second broad concern is that government ownership of corporate stocks and bonds, even if in a nominally independent administrative authority, would bring with it control over corporations. Ownership conveys the right to vote shares. Even if this power were initially disavowed, it might eventually be assumed by the federal fund manager, just as state pension funds do now. How would the administrative authority vote on issues like takeovers, foreign takeovers, or poorly performing managers? A promise to be a passive investor that does not interfere in the management of the companies that it owns might change, rationalized by the argument that active management could lead to better investment performance, a decision that many state pension plans have made.

My impression from conversations with congressional leaders of both parties is that such a central account system is politically unacceptable. This view has been expressed publicly by Senator Daniel Patrick Moynihan, the ranking Democrat on the Senate Finance Committee, by Democratic senator Bob Kerry, and by a variety of Republicans in both the Senate and the House.

I conclude from all of this that, if there is to be an investment-based component of social security, it must take the form of individual accounts. If so, a forty- to fifty-basis-point administrative cost, relative to a centralized investment with no administrative cost (to use Peter Diamond's estimate of the effect of the "low-cost" government-organized accounts), is inevitable if there is to be an investment-based component to social security.

Government-Organized Accounts

That raises the question of whether such an investment-based strategy to replace part of the pure pay-as-you-go system is desirable if it does involve an administrative cost of fifty basis points. The simplest way to think about that question is to rephrase it as, If an investment-based social security system causes the nation to increase saving and investment above what it would otherwise be, is this desirable if the return on that investment must be reduced by fifty basis points? The real pretax return to increments to the capital stock is about 8.5 percent (Poterba 1997), implying that the real return to the increments caused by an investment-based social security program would be 8.0 percent if done through government-organized accounts. That is a substantially higher rate of return than the return that savers now receive after corporate-profits taxes, property taxes, and individual taxes on interest, dividends, and capital gains. This difference suggests a prima facie case for the desirability of increased saving through social security accounts.

Another way of judging whether an investment-based system of individual accounts with an administrative cost of fifty basis points would be desirable is to consider the way in which such a system would affect social security taxes and benefits over time. Andrew Samwick and I (Feldstein and Samwick 1998) present estimates of the effect of saving 2 percent of payroll in such accounts and receiving a return equal to 5.5 percent (the postwar average real return on a portfolio of 60 percent stocks and 40 percent bonds net of a forty-basis-point administrative cost). We show that, with new saving equal to 2 percent of payroll until 2030, and using the corporate tax receipts on the incremental capital stock that results from these individual accounts after that, it is possible to maintain the benefits provided in current law without raising the future payroll tax, thus avoiding an increase from the current 12 percent tax rate to a rate that is permanently more than 18 percent. My judgment is that that is a very attractive trade-off between current saving and permanently lower taxes.

My conclusion, in short, is that, if using an investment-based system requires a fifty-basis-point administrative cost, the investment-based system is very much worth doing.

Privately Organized Accounts

Government-organized accounts may not be politically acceptable for the same reason that a centrally administered account is not acceptable. Although government-organized accounts would provide a defined-contribution system in which individuals might have some influence on the extent of the risk that they take, a government-organized system in which the government is responsible for investment management would still leave many decisions in the hands of the government fund managers. As with any mutual fund, the government fund managers would be responsible for voting proxies, deciding whether to tender stocks in a takeover situation, etc.

With privately organized accounts, the government would be responsible for regulating what investments are eligible and for the prudential supervising of investment managers. But individuals would retain the choice among eligible private managers, and those managers would be responsible for exercising the rights of shareholders.

If the choice is between a pure pay-as-you-go system and a system of privately organized accounts for which, to use Peter Diamond's estimate for now, the cost is one hundred basis points, should the privately organized accounts be regarded as "prohibitively expensive"? I think not. The question again can be restated by asking whether an increased national investment is desirable if it earns a real return of 7.5 percent. That is again much more than the real after-tax return that individuals can earn in their private capacity, suggesting that such a return is a desirable investment. Indeed, unless the general consensus that the United States should save and invest more is true for a real return of 8.5 percent but would not be for a return of 7.5 percent, this is a desirable investment decision for the nation. That this return would accrue to the social security system in a way the avoids a permanent increase in the payroll-tax rate of more than 6 percentage points—from the current 12.4 percent to more than 18 percent—is an extra advantage.

To be more specific about the nature of individually organized accounts, I will now describe what I believe would be a cost-effective way to administer such accounts. A key aspect of the cost is how the money is collected and transferred to individual accounts. In my November 1997 *Wall Street Journal* article, I suggested that each individual would establish an account similar to an IRA, send 2 percent of his or her wage up to the maximum social security taxable earnings to that account, and receive a refundable income-tax credit for that amount. The net result would be that the individual added 2 percent of income to the account at no personal cost. These tax credits could be financed out of the projected budget surpluses, assuring that those surpluses would not be spent on public or private consumption.

After publishing that article, I was persuaded by Peter Diamond and others that this method of depositing funds in individual accounts would be too expensive because of the large number of individuals with multiple jobs, small incomes, etc. I now believe that a better way is to use the Social Security Administration (SSA) to transfer 2 percent of wage income from the Treasury (i.e., from the budget surplus) to individual fund managers selected by the individual employees. The SSA has the information on the total earnings of each individual up to the social security taxable maximum. Although that information is available only with a lag, individuals can hardly complain since the money being deposited is the government's.

Costs could also be limited if each individual could have only one fund manager (although multiple investments with that manager) and could change fund managers no more than once a year. Individuals would indicate the identification number of their chosen fund manager on their tax return when they establish the account and whenever they want to change fund manager. The SSA would then wire the money and the names and social security numbers to the fund managers.

There is no cost of collecting the individual savings in this system since all the money is provided by the government. The biggest potential cost of individually organized accounts is thereby eliminated.

A potentially useful option is to have a government-managed fund as a "default option," for anyone who does not choose a private company or prefers a government fund manager. I say *potentially* useful option because, while such a manager could act as a low-cost standard that disciplines private providers, there is a danger that the government would subsidize this fund manager so that it comes to be so attractive that it has most of the money, the very problem that individually organized accounts are designed to avoid.

How Expensive Would Privately Organized Accounts Be?

I return now to Peter Diamond's assertion that privately organized accounts would cost about one hundred basis points, equivalent to $100 per account per year at the present time. As I look at the evidence, I think that that estimate is much too high for the following reasons.

The TSP Benchmark. The TSP run by the federal government now costs $20 per worker per year. That includes (1) collecting funds from each individual in a system that allows individuals to select different percentages of their salary to be contributed and (2) managing a loan program that uses TSP as collateral. Many of the extra costs that Diamond associates with going from TSP to general government-organized accounts (thereby increasing the cost from $20 to $40–$50) would be avoided or offset by centralized collection and crediting of deposits as part of the ordinary social security payroll operations in the way that I described above. The government-organized accounts would be no more costly than the TSP, that is, about $20 per account per year or about twenty basis points for the average-size account.

Private Mutual Fund Benchmark. Major mutual fund managers offer equity index funds at about thirty basis points and fixed income funds at an even lower cost. These mutual funds have to collect funds and make payments, a major expense that would be avoided by the centralized finance using government funds.

Foreign Experience. Diamond and others cite the high costs in Chile, Mexico, and the United Kingdom. I believe that that experience is irrelevant given the very efficient and low-cost system demonstrated by U.S. mutual fund providers.

Selling Costs, Markups, and Managed Funds. Mutual funds now provide indexed investments at thirty basis points despite their advertising expenses. Some individuals would prefer managed funds to index funds despite their higher charges. Perhaps such managed funds would cost one hundred basis points, adding about $50 a year or $1 per week to the cost of the account. Diamond does not like that idea, considering it wasteful and frivolous, despite the fact that a large fraction of current mutual fund investors have shown a preference for such funds. More generally, Diamond does not like the prospect of individuals having a large number of choices, noting that the current phone-service market with its "dizzying array of options" is a good parallel to the problem that would face individuals with privately organized accounts. Does that mean that the government should not allow competition among phone companies with multiple options? And what about automobiles or household detergents? It would be ironic if the government prevents people from spending $1 a week extra to get managed funds rather than indexed funds while encouraging those same individuals to buy state lottery tickets.

Technical Progress and Innovation. The next decade will see enormous changes in communications technology, making the ability to access information over phone lines virtually free. The technology that will soon be widely available will make it possible to use phones (as well as personal computers) to review investments and make changes among the options offered by fund managers.

All this will reduce the cost of individual accounts. It is wrong to assume, as Diamond does, that administrative costs will rise in the future in proportion to wages (and therefore to account deposits). It is far more likely that this technological service will see the kinds of cost-reducing gains that will cause its relative cost to decline significantly.

I am convinced, moreover, that competition among private fund managers is much more likely to achieve faster technical progress and more innovative and user-friendly service for individuals than would occur with a government monopoly.

References

Aaron, Henry, and Robert Reischauer. 1998. *Countdown to reform: The great social security debate.* New York: Century Foundation Press.
Advisory Council on Social Security. 1997. *Report of the 1994–96 Advisory Council on Social Security.* Washington, D.C.

Diamond, Peter. 1997. Macroeconomic aspects of social security reform. *Brookings Papers on Economic Activity,* no. 2:1–89.

Feldstein, Martin. 1997. Don't waste the budget surplus. *Wall Street Journal,* 4 November, A22.

Feldstein, Martin, and Andrew Samwick. 1998. Potential effects of two percent personal retirement accounts. *Tax Notes* 79, no. 5 (4 May): 615–20.

Poterba, James. 1997. The rate of return to corporate capital and factor shares. Working Paper no. 6263. Cambridge, Mass.: National Bureau of Economic Research.

Discussion Summary

Peter Diamond began with two additional points on costs and a rebuttal to Martin Feldstein's comments on his paper. Diamond first noted that the possibility for individuals to open and hold multiple social security individual accounts could be a significant driver of costs and that a mechanism should exist to limit individuals to one account. Second, he noted that many individuals currently incur the (out-of-pocket) cost of employing personal investment advisers and that there is no inherent reason to believe that this would not continue under a system of individual accounts. In response to Feldstein's comments, Diamond first took issue with Feldstein's comparison of the rate of return to the current social security system to the rate of return to a system of individual accounts, arguing that it is not legitimate to compare the "return" on funds in a pay-as-you-go system to a portfolio rate of return. Second, Diamond questioned the legitimacy of Feldstein's claim that political considerations make government management and investment of funds infeasible. Diamond argued that it is just as likely that large corporations would be able to exert enough influence on Congress to stave off the type of government meddling that Feldstein suggested may occur. Third, he clarified his characterization of the costs of private management of individual accounts as "prohibitive" as meaning that private management would be higher cost without any significant offsetting benefit. And, finally, he noted that his comparison of a privately managed system of individual accounts to the current, fragmented phone-service provider market was intended to suggest simply that the market will be complex and that we should focus not just on the low-cost provider but also on the mean and distribution of the level of costs across the system as it is likely to be quite heterogeneous.

Sylvester Schieber began the discussion by questioning Diamond's contention that no current reform plan is proposing a 10 percent benefit cut (which is the amount by which individual account accumulations would be decreased by having them privately managed as opposed to government managed, according to Diamond's paper). Schieber noted that the Kerrey-Moynihan plan required benefit cuts of at least 10 percent and that Kerrey had been clear in stating this. Diamond acknowledged that this was a fair point.

Estelle James suggested that Diamond's estimate of an annual communications cost of \$40–\$50 per person seemed too high. She noted that the comparable figure for the Thrift Savings Plan is roughly \$20 per person and that much of that comes from supporting its loan activity, which would not be an issue for social security individual accounts. She also noted that mutual fund transfer agents charge only roughly \$25 per head and that they offer a relatively high level of service. Diamond countered that neither of these systems deals with as large and heterogeneous a population as the one with which the managers of social security individual accounts would be dealing. James agreed that the different population would imply different costs, especially with respect to accommodating multiple languages, but she emphasized the point that Diamond's conclusions are sensitive to the \$40–\$50 figure and that, if true communications costs are actually \$20–\$25, the effective reduction in account accumulations would be much lower.

Leonard Glynn inquired into the incremental benefit to the social security system of investing a portion of the social security funds in the capital markets. Specifically, he asked whether the tax increases and/or benefit cuts needed to save the current system would be lower if social security funds were invested in capital markets. *Peter Diamond* noted that there are two separate elements to this question. First, it is true that, if, in fact, the Social Security Trust Fund can accrue more money over time through investment in the capital markets, the tax hikes and/or benefit cuts needed to meet future obligations would be lower. The second issue is the risk associated with the change in portfolio and on whom this risk would fall.

Alan Gustman suggested that it may be possible to get some empirical evidence on demand for an individual account option and likely administrative costs by "red-circling" a certain group of current workers to be eligible to opt out of social security and invest in individual accounts. *Diamond* disagreed, noting that a large part of the cost dynamics and cost-saving potential of management of individual accounts comes from uniformity. If an institution had to perform special functions to service the experimental group, it would not shed much light on the likely cost issues in a completely new institutional framework.

Responding to Gustman's point, *Olivia Mitchell* noted that many private pensions do effectively red-line certain groups of people—for example, individuals below a certain age and/or job tenure do not have to participate—and there may be some useful evidence there on demand for pension instruments. Mitchell also voiced disagreement with Martin Feldstein's contention that foreign countries' experience with moving to individual accounts is irrelevant to the American experience. She argued that the foreign experience shows us that it is possible to implement a system of individual accounts. *Feldstein* responded that he meant that the foreign experience was irrelevant to our ascertaining the cost of implementing such a system in the United States. *John Shoven* suggested that foreign costs ought to be an upper bound on the costs. But *Peter Diamond* disagreed, asserting that, while it may be an upper bound on costs, it would not necessarily provide an upper bound on equilibrium pricing, which would depend on demand elasticities and other factors. Finally, *Mitchell* left as an open issue the comment that, if we believe that administrative costs of individual accounts are too high, perhaps we ought to be considering individual accounts that are based on larger contributions than just 2 percent of payroll.

Responding to Peter Diamond's earlier comment on social security's unfounded liability, *Sylvester Schieber* suggested that perhaps we should view this as a sunk cost and pursue the goal of reforming the system to be efficient in the steady state separately from the issue of how this sunk cost will be paid off. He suggested that combining the issues could result in our rejecting a reform that would be optimal in the steady state because it entailed a transition cost that fell disproportionately on one group. *Peter Diamond* agreed that the sunk cost is a separate issue and commented that his quarrel was with the attempt *directly to compare* the returns in a status quo system to the returns to a system of individual accounts. *Martin Feldstein* countered that, even if one drops the direct comparison, it is still the case that, if the market earns 7.5 percent (8.5 percent with a 1 percent reduction for administrative costs), that is inherently attractive. And, if the only way to access that return is to replace some of the pay-as-you-go element with an individual account element, then there is an *effective* comparison in favor of the individual accounts, if not a direct one.

Michael Graetz argued that the central issue in private as opposed to government management of individual accounts is the overriding political risk inherent in government-managed accounts. He asserted that, although in theory the government-management option would unquestionably imply lower administrative costs, it could produce prohibitively high costs from politically motivated investment strategies. He also suggested that any analysis of the attractiveness of individual accounts should take into account the possibility of early withdrawal of funds, which would decrease accruals. Finally, Graetz emphasized the importance of including a low-cost default option in any individual account system. The alternative to offering such an option, he argued, will be considerable price and product regulation of the funds that are offered.

5

The Costs of Annuitizing Retirement Payouts from Individual Accounts

James M. Poterba and Mark J. Warshawsky

One of the crucial questions about the operation of "individual accounts" systems of retirement saving is how participants will draw down their account balances when they reach retirement. Most defined-contribution plans do not specify how accumulated assets will be drawn down. By contrast, most defined-benefit plans sponsored by private companies or by the government provide retirees with mandatory life annuities. Private pension plans purchase these annuities as part of a group annuity contract with an insurance company or underwrite the annuities themselves. In public pension plans such as social security, the government underwrites the annuities.

Some, but not all, current participants in defined-contribution plans wish to obtain life annuities. Roughly one-third of 401(k) plans and most 403(b) plans currently offer participants a voluntary life annuity payout. The annuities purchased with funds from accounts in these pension plans are individual annuities purchased through the group plans. If an individual participates in a pension plan that does not offer life annuities and nevertheless desires such a distribution method, it is necessary to purchase an individual life annuity through an agent or a broker representing a commercial insurance company. The costs of such annuities, including

James M. Poterba is the Mitsui Professor of Economics at the Massachusetts Institute of Technology and the director of the Public Economics Research Program at the National Bureau of Economic Research. Mark J. Warshawsky is director of research at the TIAA-CREF Institute.

The authors are grateful to Jeff Brown, Edwin Hustead, Martin Feldstein, and conference participants for assistance and helpful discussions. Poterba thanks the National Institute on Aging and the National Science Foundation for research support. Opinions expressed are those of the authors and not necessarily of the institutions with which they are associated.

both administrative and sales costs, the "adverse-selection" costs associated with voluntary purchase behavior, and return on capital for the insurance company offering the annuity policy, affect the retirement income that the participant receives for a given level of wealth accumulation.

Questions about the cost of annuitization also arise in discussions of individual account social security reform proposals. Under the present social security system, the federal government provides life annuities to all retirees. Because these are compulsory annuities, the adverse-selection problems that may arise in private, voluntary annuity markets are not a concern. In addition, the existing social security arrangement involves none of the sales or marketing costs that might be charged by insurance companies that sell individual annuities, although there are some administrative costs associated with the current social security system.

Most proposals that suggest the use of individual accounts as a supplement to, or partial substitute for, the existing social security system would mandate some type of annuitization when the accountholder retires. This is true, for example, of the proposals advanced by the Committee on Economic Development, the CSIS (Center for Strategic and International Studies), and a subset of participants on the 1994–96 Social Security Advisory Council ("the IA proposal"). While the mandatory annuitization aspects of these proposals reduce concern about adverse selection, structuring annuity options to achieve equitable payouts, at low cost, is nevertheless an important issue.

Previous research on annuity markets provides only limited guidance on the potential operation of an annuity mechanism involving the purchase of individual annuity contracts within a defined-contribution "group" system. Most existing research has focused on the very limited agent-dominated individual annuity market in the United States. Previous studies, including Warshawsky (1988), Friedman and Warshawsky (1990), and Mitchell et al. (1999), have calculated the expected present discounted value of annuity payouts, relative to policy premiums, for individual annuity policies. Because the sales and administrative costs of current individual annuity policies are likely to be substantially greater than those of individual annuities provided in a group plan or a reformed social security system, existing calculations probably provide a lower bound on potential payouts in a system of "private accounts."

The PSA (personal security account) proposal put forward by a subset of the Social Security Advisory Council (see Gramlich 1996) would not mandate annuitization from individual social security accounts or create any group mechanism for providing life annuities. Rather, individuals who desired to convert their account accumulations to a life annuity would have to purchase an annuity from an insurance agent. Calculations of the expected discounted present value of payouts from private annuities therefore provide information that is likely to bear on an evaluation of the PSA proposal. It is possible, however, that administrative costs per policy and the degree of adverse selection in the market would change if wealth accumulation in individual accounts became universal.

In this paper, we present new findings on the costs of individual annuities, both in the individual annuity market and in two large defined-contribution pension systems, the federal government's Thrift Savings Plan (TSP) and TIAA-CREF. While we do not assess directly the cost of annuitization for any particular individual accounts social security system, we report background information that should be helpful in evaluating such costs. We provide a detailed summary of the structures employed by the TSP and by TIAA-CREF to offer individual annuities to their participants. Our goal is to inform discussion of potential options and structures for providing annuities under individual account systems that might be considered as part of a social security reform plan.

The paper is divided into four sections. Section 5.1 presents updated information on the expected present discounted value of annuity payouts in the market for individual single-premium-immediate annuities. These calculations draw on data for annuity premiums and payouts in June 1998 and extend the analysis in Mitchell et al. (1999) to consider individual annuities purchased through agents and brokers as part of qualified retirement-saving plans (like IRAs) as well as in nonqualified accounts. The results in this section indicate that the present value of annuity payouts, relative to premium costs, has increased in recent years.

Section 5.2 examines the annuity options that are available to individuals who participate in the federal government's TSP. This is a large, voluntary, 401(k) plan that is available to federal employees. We present information on the structure of the "request for proposals" that the TSP issues when it solicits bids from private insurance companies that may wish to provide life annuities to TSP participants. We also present information on the payouts associated with individual annuities purchased through this plan.

Section 5.3 describes the annuities offered by TIAA-CREF, which provides basic and supplementary pension plans to the employees of universities and other nonprofit educational and research institutions. TIAA annuities, which include a nonguaranteed element, offer payouts that are among the highest in the individual annuity market owing to their superior investment returns and low expenses. TIAA-CREF variable annuities offer payouts that reflect, on at least an annual basis, the investment experience of various underlying equity, fixed-income, and real estate investment portfolios.

The conclusion provides a summary and suggests several topics related to the cost of annuitization that require further investigation and analysis.

5.1   Individual Annuities Offered through Agents
by Commercial Insurance Companies

With individual nonparticipating, single-premium-immediate life annuities offered by commercial life insurance companies, individuals make an initial premium payment and typically begin receiving annuity payouts in the month after their purchase. We focus on nonparticipating annuities, which provide a fixed and guaranteed benefit payment.

Premiums for life annuities are reported each year in A. M. Best's publication *Best's Review: Life and Health*. We analyze data from the August 1998 issue, which presents the results of an annuity market survey carried out at the beginning of June 1998. The *Best's* data correspond to single-premium annuities with a $100,000 premium. Ninety-nine companies responded to the survey, reporting information on the current monthly payouts on individual annuities sold to men and women at ages fifty-five, sixty, sixty-five, seventy, seventy-five, and eighty. Companies also reported their payouts for similar annuities purchased with funds in qualified retirement-saving plans. Qualified annuities must begin payouts by age seventy, so there are no data for qualified annuities that start at ages seventy-five or eighty. Roughly two-thirds of the companies reported the same payout value for both the qualified and the nonqualified annuity, while one-third reported different values. Virtually all companies reporting differences between qualified and nonqualified annuities at a given age reported the same qualified annuity payouts for men and women of the same age, reflecting their use of a "unisex" mortality table in pricing the qualified annuities, in contrast to gender-distinct pricing of nonqualified annuities.

Table 5.1 provides summary information on the monthly annuity payouts associated with a representative set of annuity products. Each entry in the table shows the monthly payout per $100,000 of annuity premium. Because earlier research has documented wide dispersion in the annuity payouts offered by different companies, we report both the average payout across companies and the average payout for the ten firms that offered the highest payout products. A sixty-five-year-old man purchasing a $100,000 single-premium annuity would receive, on average, a monthly payment of $733, or $8,793 per year, for life. Because women live longer than men on average, a sixty-five-year-old woman paying the same $100,000 premium would receive about 10 percent less, $662 per month or $7,939 per year. These average payouts are roughly 8 percent lower than the payouts in the 1995 *Best's* survey, which provided the basis for the analysis in Mitchell et al. (1999). This presumably reflects the decline in interest rates since 1995.

One important feature of annuity prices, which is present in the June 1998 data as well as in those for earlier dates, is the substantial variation in the payouts offered by different insurance companies. The average

Table 5.1   **Monthly Payments ($) per $100,000 Premium for Annuities Available from Commercial Insurers in June 1998**

Buyer	All-Policy Average		Average for Ten Policies with Highest Payouts	
	Qualified	Nonqualified	Qualified	Nonqualified
Male, age 55	596.22	606.44	671.60	675.70
Male, age 65	719.91	732.73	809.30	806.58
Male, age 75	N.A.	988.84	N.A.	1,084.69
Female, age 55	568.46	563.04	639.70	630.62
Female, age 65	671.47	661.62	748.77	728.35
Female, age 75	N.A.	857.69	N.A.	948.58

Sources: Data are drawn from *Best's Review: Life and Health* (August 1998) and authors' tabulations.
Note: N.A. = not available.

monthly payout for the ten companies with the highest payout for a sixty-five-year-old man, for example, is $807, which is 10 percent higher than the average payout for all firms. There are similar differences in the prices offered to annuitants at other ages. In Mitchell et al. (1999), a variety of possible explanations for these payout differences were explored, such as apparent differential riskiness of different insurance companies, but no systematic pattern in the payouts was found. (The companies offering the "ten highest-payout" annuities in table 5.1 generally are small and medium-size life insurers.) Payout differences across firms may reflect different assumptions about mortality rates, different rate-of-return assumptions in pricing policies, and differences in administrative costs and expense ratios. The heterogeneity in annuity prices suggests that, if individuals were allowed to purchase their own annuity contracts in a system of "individual accounts," different individuals might receive substantially different annuity benefits.

Unfortunately, we do not have data on the volume of annuities sold by different firms in the *Best's* database, which would help judge the actual extent of payout dispersion in the annuitant population. In addition, such information would help determine whether the surveyed rates represent active lines of business or are just used to bolster illustrations in sales materials for deferred annuities. The calculations presented below focus on cases in which individuals purchase annuities that offer the average payout.

Table 5.1 presents information on nonqualified as well as qualified annuities. For men, the average monthly payout on qualified annuities is below that on nonqualified annuities, as a result of the use of "unisex" mortality tables in pricing the qualified annuities offered by some insurance companies, as mentioned above. For a sixty-five-year-old man, a qualified annuity offers payouts that average about 1.8 percent less than payouts on nonqualified annuities. For women, the pattern is reversed. The average payout from qualified annuities is greater than that from nonqualified annuities. For a sixty-five-year-old woman, qualified annuities offer an average payout that is roughly 1.5 percent greater, each month, than the average payout for nonqualified annuities.

To provide insight on the administrative and other costs associated with individual annuity products, we compute the expected present discounted value (EPDV) of payouts for the average annuity product. We compare this EPDV with the premium cost of the annuity. This yields a measure of the "money's worth" of the individual annuity, as in Warshawsky (1988), Friedman and Warshawsky (1988, 1990), and Mitchell et al. (1999).

The formula that we use to calculate the EPDV of a nominal annuity with monthly payout A, purchased by an individual of age b, is

$$(1) \qquad V_b(A) = \sum_{j=1}^{12\times(115-b)} \frac{A \times P_j}{\prod_{k=1}^{j}(1 + i_k)}.$$

The upper limit of the summation, $12 \times (115 - b)$, is the number of months that a person of age b would live if he or she reached age 115. We assume that no one survives beyond this age. P_j denotes the probability that an individual of age b years at the time of the annuity purchase survives for at least j months beyond this purchase.

The term i_k denotes the one-month interest rate k months after the annuity purchase. In our baseline calculations, we measure these interest rates using the term structure of yields for zero-coupon Treasury "strips." We estimate the pattern of monthly interest rates that is implied by these yields. The data on the zero-coupon yield curve are published each Thursday in the *Wall Street Journal,* and we use the data from the first Thursday in June 1998 to coincide with the timing of *Best's* annuity-price data. This approach to measuring discount rates differs from that in previous studies of the EPDV of nominal annuities. Friedman and Warshawsky (1990) assumed a constant nominal discount rate for all periods. Mitchell et al. (1999) used a term structure of riskless government bond yields, but they did not use the yields on zero-coupon bonds to construct this yield curve. We used the zero-coupon yields because they seem the best available information on the discount rates for the present-value calculations.

We also consider a second set of discount rates that correspond to a risky corporate bond. To construct these discount rates, we measure the difference between the yield on a BAA corporate bond and that on a ten-year Treasury bond in early June 1998. This yield spread was 137 basis points. We then add this "risk premium" to the entire term structure of riskless interest rates that we estimate from the Treasury yield curve.

We evaluate equation (1) using two sets of projected survival probabilities. Projections are needed because P_j describes the *prospective* survival experience of today's annuity buyers. The first set of survival probabilities corresponds to the population at large. We use cohort-mortality-rate projections developed by Bell, Wade, and Goss (1992) at the Office of the Actuary of the Social Security Administration (SSA). One of the key difficulties in evaluating the effective cost of purchasing an annuity, however, is that the pool of actual annuity purchasers has different mortality experience than the population at large. There is "adverse selection" in this market; annuitants tend to have longer life expectancies than individuals in the broader population. From the standpoint of an insurance company writing annuities, the annuitant mortality table must be used to determine the relation between premium income and the EPDV of payouts. Adverse selection is a "cost" of annuitization from the perspective of an individual in the population at large.

One important question about the potential effect of expanding individual account retirement-saving vehicles is how this expansion would affect the degree of adverse selection in the annuity market. A universal system of individual accounts, coupled with mandatory annuitization, would reduce adverse selection, although it would not eliminate it entirely because individuals would still presumably be allowed choices among annuity options and the age of settlement. The account-balance-weighted mortality table might also differ from the population mortality table because of income-related differences in mortality rates.

The second set of projected mortality rates that we use corresponds to that for current annuitants. Mitchell et al. (1999) develop an algorithm that combines information from the new Annuity 2000 mortality table (Johansen 1996), the older 1983 individual annuitant mortality table, and the projected rate of mortality improvement in the SSA's population mortality tables. The algorithm generates projected mortality rates for the set of annuitants who purchase annuity contracts in a given year. There are substantial differences between the population and the annuitant mortality rates. Mitchell et al. (1999) show that, in 1995, the annual mortality rate for annuitants between the ages of sixty-five and seventy-five was roughly half the mortality rate for those in the general population. This translates into a substantially larger EPDV of annuity payouts when we use the annuitant mortality table, rather than the population mortality table, for valuation.

We focus exclusively on valuing annuities in a pretax environment. While this follows in the tradition of most previous studies, Mitchell et al. (1999) also report information on the after-tax value of annuity payouts, recognizing that payouts from nonqualified annuities are partially taxable, and using an after-tax nominal interest rate for discounting. The EPDV of annuity payouts relative to premium costs was very similar in the pretax and posttax cases, however, so we focus on the simpler pretax case in this analysis.

Table 5.2 reports our estimates of the expected discounted value of annuity payouts using the all-company average payout rates from table 5.1 above. The first column shows calculations based on our estimate of the 1998 cohort mortality table for the general population, while the second column presents calculations based on the 1998 cohort mortality table for annuitants. The first panel presents results using riskless Treasury bond discount rates, while the second panel corresponds to our "risky interest-rate" discount factor. We report the EPDV of annuity payments per premium dollar. Using the general population mortality tables for a sixty-five-year-old man and the Treasury yield curve, the value per premium dollar for a life annuity is 0.849 for a nonqualified annuity. For a woman of the same age, the average value is 0.875. When we value the same annuities using the annuitant mortality table, the EPDV of payouts rises to 0.970 for men and 0.952 for women. These values are closer to unity than the estimates in previous studies that have used the riskless yield curve to discount annuity payouts.

The lower panel of table 5.2 reports our findings using riskier interest rates. In this case, the expected discounted value of payouts is lower than in the first panel. The calculations using the population mortality table suggest that the EPDV of payouts is between seventy-five and eighty cents per premium dollar. Using the mortality table for annuitants raises this

Table 5.2   **EPDV of Annuity Payouts, per Dollar of Premium Payment, Individual Annuity Policies Offered by Commercial Insurers, June 1998**

Age and Gender of Annuity Buyer	EPDV/Premium Using Population Mortality Table		EPDV/Premium Using Annuitant Mortality Table	
	Qualified	Nonqualified	Qualified	Nonqualified
Treasury discount rates:				
Male, age 55	.873	.888	.953	.970
Male, age 65	.835	.850	.953	.970
Male, age 75	N.A.	.815	N.A.	.966
Female, age 55	.902	.893	.959	.950
Female, age 65	.888	.875	.966	.952
Female, age 75	N.A.	.815	N.A.	.940
"BAA discount rate":				
Male, age 55	.773	.786	.835	.849
Male, age 65	.759	.772	.856	.871
Male, age 75	N.A.	.794	N.A.	.891
Female, age 55	.790	.782	.833	.825
Female, age 65	.797	.785	.860	.847
Female, age 75	N.A.	.794	N.A.	.861

Source: Authors' tabulations based on data in table 5.1 above and information described in the text.

Note: N.A. = not available.

estimate to between eighty-two and eighty-seven cents per dollar. Whether it makes more sense to use the riskless or the risky discount rate is open to some question. The historical default risk on annuity payouts has been extremely low, so annuity purchasers probably view their annuity income stream as riskless. Yet the portfolio held by insurance companies that offer annuity products is not restricted to riskless Treasury securities. It is clear from the results in table 5.2 that assumptions about the risk premium that should be included in the discount factor have an important effect on the estimated level of annuity payouts relative to premium costs.

In table 5.2, payout values per premium dollar that are less than unity imply that an annuity purchaser would effectively face a "transaction cost" when purchasing an annuity from a commercial insurance carrier. This is equivalent to purchasing an actuarially fair annuity, defined as one for which the EPDV of payouts equals the policy's premium cost but one that involves having to give up a fraction of one's wealth before investing the remainder in this annuity product. An annuity with payouts that have an EPDV equal to the premium cost is likely to be unattainable since this does not allow for any administrative costs, premium taxes, corporate taxes, commissions, advertising, overhead, assumption of risks, or other costs on the part of the insurance company selling the policy.

The difference between the EPDV calculations based on the population mortality table and those based on the annuitant mortality table provides some insight into the costs of adverse selection in the individual annuity market. For example, for an annuity sold to a sixty-five-year-old man, the cost of adverse selection is 12.1 percent of the annuity premium (97.0 − 84.9). This is roughly the same magnitude as the estimated cost of adverse selection in several previous studies of the annuity market. When we use the "risky term structure" to perform the annuity valuation exercise, the resulting estimates suggest that adverse selection accounts for a smaller fraction of the differential between the EPDV of payouts and the premium cost for a randomly selected individual in the population.

The findings in table 5.2 suggest that the insurance companies offering annuities are currently charging annuitants less for the administrative, sales, and other charges associated with individual annuity products than previous studies have suggested. This move toward more aggressive pricing may alternatively reflect declining investment risks to insurance companies, rising competition in the annuity market, or the slow adaptation of the assumed mortality tables to improvements in life expectancy. An important issue for further analysis is the source of time-series variation in the EPDV, relative to premium costs, for individual annuities.

Calculations like those in table 5.2 have been interpreted as suggesting that annuities are "expensive" because a sixty-five-year-old buyer with the average mortality in the population gives up at least fifteen cents per dollar of premium in order to buy an annuity. Although it is true that the EPDV of annuity payouts is less than the cost of the annuity, it does not follow that annuities are unattractive to those in the population at large. Results on the utility gains associated with annuitization for representative individuals, with plausible risk tolerance and facing the population mortality risk, suggest that the gains from avoiding uncertainty about length of life are sufficient to warrant purchasing an annuity, even if the EPDV is substantially below the premium amount. Mitchell et al. (1999) report simulation results that support this conclusion. They also suggest that these results are sensitive to several features of the economic environment. In particular, individuals who already have a substantial share of their retirement wealth in an annuitized form, such as social security or a defined-benefit pension plan, will be willing to pay less for an annuity. Married individuals also tend to value annuities less than single individuals. Brown and Poterba (1998) show that this is because of the partial "mortality-risk pooling" that takes place within the household. Finally, there may be a perception among investors of better value from life annuities when interest rates are low.

5.2   Individual Annuities Available to Participants in the TSP

The last section described individual annuity policies that are universally available in the private annuity market. In this section and the next, we describe policies that are available only to participants in two large group retirement-saving plans. The experience with these plans may provide some insight into the potential operation of annuitization options under various government individual accounts saving programs.

The Thrift Savings Plan (TSP) is a 401(k) defined-contribution retirement plan for federal employees. Congress established the TSP in the Federal Employees' Retirement System (FERS) Act of 1986. For federal employees hired after 31 December 1983, the TSP is an integral part of the retirement-income package, which also includes social security and the FERS basic annuity, a standard defined-benefit pension plan. For federal employees hired before 1984 who did not elect to switch to FERS, the TSP is a voluntary supplement to the Civil Service Retirement System (CSRS) annuity, a generous back-loaded defined-benefit plan.

Employees in FERS can contribute up to 10 percent of pay to the TSP. The federal government contributes 1 percent of pay automatically, matches the first 3 percent of pay contributed by the employee dollar for dollar, and matches the next 2 percent at fifty cents on the dollar. Employees in CSRS can contribute up to 5 percent of pay to the TSP but receive no federal government contributions. For all employees, contributions to the TSP are capped at $10,000 per year. There are no nondiscrimination requirements limiting contributions, as occurs in the private sector, although the same dollar limits on contributions apply. There is full and immediate vesting for employee and government matching contributions and earnings, while the service requirement to vest in the automatic government contribution and earnings is generally three years. The service requirement for TSP eligibility is as long as one year.

Contributions can be directed to three investment funds: a short-term government securities (G) fund, a common stock index (S&P500) (C) fund, and a fixed-income index (Lehman Brothers Aggregate) (F) fund. There are plans to add two more investment choices: a small-capitalization stock index fund and an international stock index fund. All investment funds use only a passive indexation strategy. Valuation occurs on a monthly basis; interfund transfers occur at the end of the month. Redirection of future contributions among the various investment funds as well as enrollment can be done only during semiannual open seasons in the winter and summer months. Account-balance statements are sent out semiannually. Loans are allowed from employee contributions and earnings while the participant is in federal service. Limited in-service withdrawals for financial hardship or after reaching age fifty-nine and a half are also allowed.

After a federal employee leaves government service, there are three ways to withdraw assets from the TSP: a life annuity, a lump sum, or a series of monthly payments; these methods may be used in any combination. The lump-sum or monthly payments can be rolled over to another qualified retirement plan, such as an IRA. Like other retirement plans, balances in a TSP account are subject to the federal minimum distribution requirements, mandating distributions after age seventy and a half according to IRS life-expectancy tables. Warshawsky (1998) provides a detailed description and analysis of these requirements.

The Federal Retirement Thrift Investment Board (FRTIB), an independent federal agency, administers the TSP. Governance of the agency is carried out by a five-person, part-time board of presidential appointees and by a full-time executive director selected by the appointees. The board members and the executive director are fiduciaries for the TSP, and they are required to act solely in the interest of participants. Administrative and most investment expenses are paid out of investment earnings and forfeitures of the automatic 1 percent–of–pay contributions, not through any annual congressional appropriation. In 1997, these expenses were 0.09 percent of assets, or nine basis points. This gross expense ratio has declined rapidly from sixty-seven basis points in 1988 as average TSP account size has grown. The FRTIB controls a single record-keeping system, coordinating among 130 different federal agency payroll systems. Administrative personnel throughout the federal government also assist with administration for, and the education of, participants.

The latest available data show that participation in the TSP by FERS employees is 86.1 percent and by CSRS employees about 61 percent. As of October 1998, the TSP had 2.4 million individual accounts, $71.5 billion in investment assets ($28.3 billion in the G fund, $39.2 billion in the C fund, and $4.0 billion in the F fund), and loans totaling more than $2.4 billion outstanding. During 1997, the TSP received $7 billion in contributions and disbursed almost $1.4 billion in benefits. In dollar terms, most payments are disbursed as transfers to IRAs and other qualified plans; the second- and third-largest disbursement categories are lump sums and death benefits. Net investment income, which equals the net change in market value plus investment earnings, was over $8.6 billion.

5.2.1 TSP Life-Annuity-Payment Options

Federal law requires the FRTIB to make available to participants who have left federal service five types of life annuities: a single-life annuity with level payments, a single-life annuity with increasing payments, a joint-life annuity (with spouse) with level payments, a joint-life annuity (with spouse) with increasing payments, and a joint-life annuity (with someone other than a spouse who has an insurable interest in the participant) with level payments. Monthly payouts begin thirty days after a TSP annuity is purchased. Joint-life annuities are available either as 50 percent or as 100 percent survivor annuities. In an increasing-payment annuity, the amount of the monthly payment can change each year on the anniversary date. The amount of the change is based on the change in the consumer price index (CPI-W). Increases cannot exceed 3 percent per year, but monthly payments cannot decrease even if the CPI declines. The fact that the TSP offers a kind of inflation-indexed annuity is of some note. One concern sometimes raised about the private annuity market in the United States has been that most annuities are specified in nominal rather than real terms and that, as such, they expose annuitants to inflation risk. It is noteworthy that partially indexed TSP annuities were offered by a private insurance carrier prior to the introduction of inflation-linked Treasury bonds in the United States.

The FRTIB offers two additional annuity features: cash refund and ten-year certain. Under these features, minimum amounts will be paid to a named beneficiary if the participant (and his or her joint annuitant if applicable) dies before the minimum amounts have been paid out. In particular, under a cash refund, if the participant dies before an amount equal to the balance used to purchase the annuity has been paid out, the difference between the purchase balance and the sum of monthly payments already made will be paid to the beneficiary in a lump sum. Under a ten-year certain annuity, if the participant dies before receiving annuity payments for a ten-year period, payments will continue to the beneficiary for the rest of the ten-year period. This latter feature, however, cannot be combined with a joint-life annuity in the TSP. Of course, utilization of these features reduces the monthly annuity payments that can be made. The

TSP does not offer any variable annuities with payouts linked to the investment performance of an underlying fund or asset class.

5.2.2 The Most Recent Request for a Private Insurance Carrier to Supply TSP Annuities

TSP annuities are purchased from a commercial annuity vendor. They are not guaranteed by the federal government but depend on the annuity issuer's claims-paying ability. These tax-qualified, single-premium-immediate annuities are currently provided through a master annuity contract between the FRTIB and the Metropolitan Life Insurance Company (MetLife), a company chosen by the FRTIB. The competitive bidding process is handled through a request for proposal (RFP) inviting submissions to provide annuity services. The following is a summary of the RFP issued in July 1995 by the FRTIB inviting submissions to provide annuity services. The prior RFP was issued in 1990 and was also awarded to MetLife for three years and a two-year extension. With some exceptions noted below, the 1990 RFP was identical to the 1995 RFP.

The RFP stated that the annuity program had to conform to certain requirements. In particular, the amount of the monthly payment from a life annuity provided by the insurance company (the contractor) per $1,000 of single premium had to be an "interest-adjusted tabular monthly annuity payment for the specified annuity option times the Contractor annuity payment rate." The higher the annuity-payout rate, the more attractive the annuity contracts are from the standpoint of the annuitant. The specified annuity options have been described above. The interest adjustment and tabular monthly annuity-payment methods, described explicitly in the RFP, were based generally on actuarial formulas and will be summarized below. The contractor annuity-payment rate is the single number indicating the relative value of the entire bid; it has to be guaranteed for the term of the contract. In the 1990 RFP, there were two contract rates, one for the first three years of the contract, another for the last two years if the TSP decided to extend the contract. Our calculations suggest that MetLife's winning 1995 bid had a contractor rate of 1.039. This is not a statistic supplied by the FRTIB; it is based on our estimates, which have not been validated by the FRTIB.

The tabular monthly annuity-payment approach was chosen as a mechanism to readily adjust payment levels from newly purchased individual annuities to reflect changes in market interest rates over the course of the contract with the insurance company. This approach tends to reduce the interest-rate risk of the contractor, and it was hoped that it would lead to a more competitive contractor annuity-payment rate. Tabular monthly annuity payments were specified in the RFP on the basis of two assumptions: (1) an interest-rate index and (2) a mortality table. No explicit provision for expenses was allowed. The mortality table selected was the 1983 individual annuity mortality table (1983 IAM) on a unisex basis, assuming 50 percent females and 50 percent males would be using the annuity program. Selection of the 1983 IAM was based on very limited mortality experience with TSP annuities since the start of the TSP in 1987. As of December 1994, the gender distribution for the TSP population was 42 percent female and 58 percent male, although, in older groups, the male share was higher, 63 percent. In the 1990 RFP, the indicated mortality table was the 1971 IAM table based on 80 percent males and 20 percent females. In joint-life situations, the second life was assumed to be 20 percent male and 80 percent female. According to the 1990 RFP, the 1971 IAM was selected because its rates were similar to 90 percent of the mortality experienced between 1983 and 1987 under the CSRS; the 10 percent reduction of CSRS experience factors was to recognize as of 1990 projected future mortality improvement and adverse selection.

The interest-rate index, calculated monthly, is a three-month moving average of the ten-year Treasury note constant maturity series. The monthly calculation of the interest-rate index applies to new annuity purchases only; payments under previously issued annuities are not affected.

The table of monthly annuity payments presented in the RFP was based on the mortality table described above and a 7 percent interest rate. Table 5.3, copied from the RFP, shows the worksheet that describes the interest-adjustment calculations. The interest-adjustment factors were also presented in the RFP in tables for given age ranges and annuity-option combinations. The factors were calculated as a simple linear interest-rate adjustment by taking the ratio of the monthly payment at an 8 percent interest rate to the monthly payment at a 7 percent interest rate and subtracting one; that is, the factors are just a linear interpolation. The adjustment factors are to be multiplied by the difference in the current interest-rate index and 7 percent; this product, in turn, is to be multiplied by the tabular monthly annuity payment to produce the change in the monthly annuity payment, finally resulting in the interest-adjusted monthly annuity payment.

The RFP states that the interest-adjustment factors are highly accurate at market interest rates between 7 and 8 percent. It also noted, however, that accurate adjustment would not be achieved if market rates were to differ greatly from the base 7 percent interest-rate assumption. Therefore, if annuitants were to become disadvantaged, the FRTIB retained the right to recalculate the tabular monthly payments on the basis of a revised interest-rate index assumption reflecting significant long-term changes in market conditions. The November 1998 interest-rate index was 5.25 percent; for a single-life level-payment annuity of $1,000 issued to a participant age sixty-five, the difference between a precisely calculated monthly annuity payment of $7.02 and an interest-adjusted monthly annuity payment of $7.40 was $0.38, to the advantage of the annuitant. This outcome, of course, results in a loss for the insurance company, relative to an exact calculation.

Table 5.3   **Annuity Calculation Worksheet from RFP for Annuities Provided to TSP Participants**

Participant information:	
1. Annuity option	J&S-50%, level, no cash refund
2. Participant age	62
3. Joint annuitant age (if a joint-life annuity)	59
4. Age difference (if a joint-life annuity). Joint annuitant is	3 years younger
5. TSP account balance	$30,000.00
Calculation of monthly annuity payment (before interest adjustment):	
6. Amount available for annuity in thousands of dollars: line 5 ÷ $1,000	$30.00000
7. Monthly annuity factor per $1,000 account balance:	
For single-life annuity, use table J.2.1.a	
For joint-life annuity, use table J.2.1.b	7.64 (see B.3., step 1)
8. Preliminary estimate of monthly annuity payment	$226.20 (see B.3., step 2)
Interest-adjusted monthly annuity payment:	
9. Current interest-rate index	6.625
10. Interest-rate index used in monthly annuity factor tables	7.000
11. Index increase (decrease): line 9 − line 10	(0.375)
12. Interest-adjustment factor:	
For single-life annuity, use table J.2.2.a	
For joint-life annuity, use table J.2.2.b	0.086
13. Adjustment multiplier: line 11 × line 12	(0.032)
14. Increase (decrease) to estimate: line 8 × line 13	($7.24)
Interest-adjusted monthly annuity payment: line 8 + line 14	$218.96 (see B.3., step 3)

Source: RFP-TIB-95-02 (a request for proposal dated 21 July 1995 from the Federal Retirement Thrift Investment Board), p. J-14.

As noted above, the contractor also had to offer an increasing life annuity tied to year-over-year CPI changes (calculated as an average over July, August, and September), capped at 3 percent. The actuarial formula used in the RFP to produce the tabular monthly annuity payment assumes that the annual increases will always be 3 percent; if, however, inflation runs below 3 percent, as in recent quarters, the insurance company issuing these annuities will reap a profit. Furthermore, newly purchased increasing-level annuities are priced to the disadvantage of the TSP annuitant in the current economic environment, in which inflation rates are below 2 percent.

The contract was to run for three years; the contract that we study expired at the end of December 1998. The FRTIB, however, had the option to extend the contract for two more years. Administration and reporting for annuities purchased under the terms of the contract are the responsi-

Table 5.4   **Initial Monthly Payments ($) per $100,000 Accumulation from TSP Annuities Purchased in June 1998**

Age	Single-Life Annuity		Joint-and-Survivor Annuity	
	Level Payment	Increasing Payment	Level Payment	Increasing Payment
55	635	446	568	382
60	688	504	601	422
65	763	581	650	477
70	858	676	709	540
75	996	813	796	628

Note: Increasing-payment annuity is based on the year-over-year change in the CPI, up to 3 percent. The joint-and-survivor annuity rates quoted here are for benefits of 100 percent to a survivor the same age as the annuitant. All annuity rates are unisex. There are no guaranteed periods or cash-refund features chosen.

bility of the insurance company through the termination of the last annuity purchased. There are numerous reporting requirements placed on the contractor, pertaining to the types and amounts of annuities purchased, mortality experience, and significant corporate events of the contractor. If the FRTIB views any corporate events, such as loss of customers or change in agency rating, as particularly harmful, it has the right to terminate the contract at any time or to demand corrective action.

In picking a winning bid, the RFP indicated that technical quality was more important than cost. Technical quality factors included the contractor's rating by Standard and Poor's, Moody's, or Duff and Phelps (required to be AA or higher), ability to do business nationally, a balance sheet indicating financial strength, demonstrated continuing profitability, diversification in lines of business, experience with large master annuity contracts, a sound business plan, and the quality of past performance. Cost factors were evaluated by sole reference to the contractor annuity-payment-rate bid.

5.2.3   Current Annuity-Payout Rates and Utilization Rates

The amount of the monthly payment coming from a TSP life annuity depends on the annuity options chosen, the age of the participant when the annuity is purchased (and the age of the joint annuitant if applicable), the balance in the TSP account used to purchase the annuity, the market interest levels when the annuity is purchased, and the contractor annuity-payment rate. Table 5.4 shows initial monthly payments per $100,000 premium for various issue ages and options for life annuities purchased in June 1998. For example, a level-payment single-life annuity purchased by a sixty-five-year-old will provide $763 monthly per $100,000 premium.

This is 4.2 percent greater than the average payout on a nonqualified annuity offered to men by commercial insurance firms (table 5.1 above) and 6 percent greater than their average payout on qualified annuities. As a point of comparison, a qualified SPIA (single premium individual annuity) issued by MetLife through an agent to a sixty-five-year-old in June 1998 will provide $664 monthly per $100,000 premium. The TSP interest-rate index in June 1998 was 5.625 percent.

Table 5.4 demonstrates that initial monthly payments are an increasing function of the age at which the annuity is issued, that they are higher for single as opposed to joint-and-survivor annuities, and that they are higher for level- as opposed to increasing-payment annuities. For example, for an individual age sixty-five, the level payment is 31 percent higher than the initial payment from an increasing annuity. For those age sixty-five, the level monthly single-life annuity payment is 25 percent higher compared to a level-payment joint-and-survivor annuity.

Almost 12 percent of the TSP participant population is age fifty-five or older. Hence, each year, there should be a considerable number of retiring participants settling their TSP accounts potentially interested in purchasing a life annuity. At the same time, because most of the retiring federal workers are still CSRS as opposed to FERS participants, the TSP system currently represents a relatively unimportant component of the retirement resources of the average retiring worker settling his or her TSP account. The significance of the TSP system for federal workers' retirement incomes will grow over time as the average size of the account balance increases and as FERS participants begin to retire.

Table 5.5 shows the basic type, number, and amount of TSP annuities purchased between the inception of the program and September 1998. Over one thousand annuities worth over $30 million were purchased in 1995, the high point thus far for TSP annuity activity. Since then, annual activity has fallen to about seven hundred purchased. It is possible that the absence from the option menu of a variable annuity whose payout is tied to the performance of the equity market, which boomed in 1996 and 1997, led to reduced interest in TSP annuities. The average size of a TSP annuity purchased has increased significantly, however, in line with the increase in the average size of a TSP account balance as the overall TSP program begins to mature. In 1990, the average annuity purchased was worth only $8,500; by 1998, the average was over $42,000.

Table 5.5 indicates that the majority of annuities purchased contain the joint-and-survivor option, most providing a 100 percent benefit to the survivor. A large minority of annuities purchased, however, are for single lives. FRTIB statistics through March 1995 indicate that most annuities purchased, whether single or joint and survivor, are level payment with no cash refund or ten-year certain features chosen. The increasing-payment annuity was chosen by fewer than 12 percent of annuity purchasers. Fe-

Table 5.5   Basic Type, Number, and Amount of TSP Annuities Purchased, 1988–September 1998

| | Number of Annuities Purchased | | | | |
Year	Single Life	Joint Life—50%	Joint Life—100%	Insurable Interest	Total
1988	3	4	10	0	17
1989	56	33	51	1	141
1990	126	57	103	1	287
1991	248	114	221	2	585
1992	246	111	188	0	545
1993	394	173	226	4	797
1994	366	177	285	7	835
1995	483	220	338	4	1,045
1996	340	137	249	3	729
1997	326	135	240	6	707
1998[a]	241	108	180	7	536

| | Amount of Annuities Purchased ($millions) | | | | |
	Single Life	Joint Life—50%	Joint Life—100%	Insurable Interest	Total
1988	0.015	0.026	0.049	0.000	0.090
1989	0.359	0.240	0.39	0.005	0.914
1990	1.050	0.498	0.892	0.005	2.445
1991	2.664	1.516	2.599	0.018	6.797
1992	3.409	1.847	3.044	0.000	8.300
1993	6.544	3.201	4.322	0.037	14.105
1994	7.080	4.565	6.927	0.117	18.691
1995	12.187	7.392	10.524	0.133	30.236
1996	9.751	5.370	8.815	0.123	24.060
1997	11.475	5.916	9.875	0.209	27.476
1998[a]	9.287	5.749	7.399	0.149	22.585

Source: FRTIB.

[a]Through September.

male participants are more likely than male participants to choose a single-life annuity than a joint-and-survivor annuity.

These statistics provide important information on the operation of the TSP annuitization program. The most important finding is that annuity payouts within the TSP annuity contract are approximately 5 percent greater than those in the private annuity market. This may reflect cost reductions associated with selling a large volume of annuities of a specified type or a weakened competitive position of the annuity provider when negotiating with the federal government. If we use the TSP annuity payouts for a sixty-five-year-old man in our EPDV algorithm, because these payouts are 4.2 percent greater than the average payout for commercial single-premium nonqualified annuity policies at the same time, the EPDV of payouts will also be 4.2 percent greater than the value reported in table 5.2 above. In this case, we conclude that the EPDV is 0.886 (or 1.042 ×

0.850, where 0.850 is the entry in table 5.2, col. 2, row 2) times the premium payment.

5.3 Individual Annuities Offered by TIAA-CREF for Pension-Plan Participants

The Teachers Insurance and Annuity Association (TIAA) is a nonprofit stock life insurance company, organized under the laws of New York State. It was founded on 4 March 1918 by the Carnegie Foundation for the Advancement of Teaching to aid education and research institutions by providing low-cost retirement products and counseling about lifelong financial security to their employees. TIAA is the companion organization of the College Retirement Equities Fund (CREF), the first company in the United States to issue a variable annuity. CREF was established in 1952 by a special act of the New York State Legislature and, since 1988, has been registered with the SEC as an open-end investment company. Together, TIAA and CREF form the principal retirement system for the nation's education and research communities. In addition to funding vehicles for employer-sponsored pension plans, TIAA-CREF also offers a variety of other financial services, including IRAs, individual and group insurance products, mutual funds, trust services, and tuition saving plans.

The basic principles of the TIAA-CREF pension system in higher education, established as a result of a 1917 study by a group of educators and actuaries, still generally hold: (1) institutions provide immediately vested defined-contribution plans sponsored by the employer (obviating the need for insurance agents selling individual annuity policies); (2) plans are funded by contributions from employers and employees adequate to provide acceptable incomes in retirement under reasonable assumptions; and (3) retirement accounts are owned by employees through individual TIAA and CREF retirement-annuity contracts (creating portability as employees, particularly faculty and administrators, move from institution to institution). In this system, TIAA-CREF acts as a kind of multiemployer pension plan, achieving economies of scale and scope in investment management, plan design, and account administration, pooling risks, and acting in the best interests of plan sponsors and participants.

The "classic" TIAA-CREF basic pension plan consists of an immediately vested individual contract arrangement with a 7.5 percent–of–pay contribution from the employer and a 5 percent–of–pay contribution from the employee. Because each TIAA-CREF pension plan is sponsored by a separate institution, however, the contribution rates and other plan rules will differ across institutions. TIAA-CREF assists each institution in the establishment and administration of its pension plans, but the final decision on plan features is made by the sponsoring institution. If an employee wishes to make additional tax-favored contributions, he or she may do so through salary reductions paid to the basic pension plan or to a supple-

Table 5.6   TIAA-CREF Investment Accounts and Asset Classes

Asset Class and Investment Account	Inception Date	Asset Amounts as of 31 October 1998 ($millions)
Guaranteed:		
TIAA traditional annuity (general account)[a]	23 April 1918	99,008
Equity:		
CREF stock	1 July 1952	104,069
CREF social choice[b]	1 March 1990	2,987
CREF global equities	1 May 1992	5,405
CREF growth	29 April 1994	6,108
CREF equity index	29 April 1994	2,889
Fixed income:		
CREF money market	1 April 1988	5,976
CREF bond market	1 March 1990	2,939
CREF inflation-linked bond	1 May 1997	138
Real estate:		
TIAA real estate	2 October 1995	1,082
Total		229,973

[a]Also includes investments held for after-tax (nonpension) fixed annuities and various reserves and liabilities.
[b]The CREF social choice account is a balanced account composed of bonds and, mainly, equities.

mental retirement annuity (SRA) plan sponsored by the institution. Most pension plans established by educational institutions are governed by the requirements of section 403(b) of the tax code.

As of 1998, participants in TIAA-CREF pension plans may allocate their contributions and accumulations among ten different investment accounts, which can be categorized into four asset classes. There is some institutional control at each participating institution with respect to the accounts offered, and some institutions do not offer all the accounts.

Table 5.6 shows these accounts and classes, with their inception dates, and asset amounts as of 31 October 1998. Ameriks, King, and Warshawsky (1997) trace the choices that TIAA-CREF participants have been making in recent years in their allocation of contributions and of accumulations under basic employer-sponsored pension plans. Although each of the investment accounts has unique risk and return characteristics, we will describe only the two largest and oldest accounts—the TIAA traditional annuity and the CREF stock account.

For the traditional annuity—a stable-value account—TIAA guarantees principal and a 3 percent interest rate for accumulations. All major ratings agencies currently give TIAA the highest possible ratings for its claims-paying ability. In addition, there are dividends declared by the TIAA Board of Trustees that remain in effect through the end of the "dividend year" and are added to the guaranteed interest rate. Dividends have been paid every year since 1948. The dividend schedules are somewhat complex, tied to the timing of past contributions and intended to assure equity across groups of participants who contributed to TIAA at varied interest-rate levels. Dividend levels are set at the discretion of the TIAA board and reflect TIAA's investment experience.

To back its guarantees, and to maximize dividends, TIAA invests in publicly traded bonds, direct loans to business and industry, commercial mortgages, and real estate. Many of the loans and mortgages (both domestic and foreign) entail long-term commitments, are relatively illiquid, and hence offer higher returns than publicly traded securities. TIAA's investment returns are consistently among the highest of general accounts in the life insurance industry. Because of the illiquidity of many of its loans, TIAA restricts payouts from the traditional annuity to life annuities or over a ten-year period. (Investment in the traditional annuity through SRAs, however, does not entail these restrictions, although the dividends paid on these accumulations are fifty basis points less than those on accumulations in the basic pension plans. Beginning in 1999, restrictions on converting from a TIAA lifetime-annuity income to an equity-based variable annuity were relaxed, with transfers of up to 20 percent of income in each year permitted.) This restriction on payouts also encompasses the transfer of TIAA traditional annuity accumulations to the other TIAA and CREF investment accounts. All other accounts are variable, marked to the market daily, and generally have no restrictions on transfers or withdrawals. Individual institutions may impose restrictions on withdrawals by participants in their basic pension plans from the TIAA traditional annuity and from the variable accounts.

The CREF stock account is an omnibus growth and income equity account, investing in U.S. and foreign stocks, using a blend of investment styles. The domestic portion of the account, currently over 80 percent of the portfolio, is invested according to an "enhanced" index strategy. The index is the Russell 3000, and the enhancement refers to various quantitative trading techniques intended to take advantage of arbitrage opportunities. The remainder of the portfolio employs active management for domestic and foreign stocks. There are no guarantees of principal or investment return for CREF stock or the other variable accounts. For the variable accounts, valuation occurs on a daily basis; interfund transfers occur at the end of each trading day.

Transfers of accumulated assets and the redirection of future contributions among the various investment accounts can be done at any time through an automated telephone service and via the Internet. Account-balance statements are sent out quarterly; balances are also available daily through phone-service centers and the Internet. An annuity benefit report is sent out annually, projecting for the individual, under reasonable assumptions, future retirement-income flows under certain life annuity options and investment returns. Consultants offer individual and group counseling at regional offices or participating institutions.

Administrative and investment expenses for the TIAA-CREF pension system are paid from investment earnings. At the current level of about thirty to thirty-five basis points, these expenses are among the lowest in the insurance and mutual fund industries. The responsibility for oversight of TIAA-CREF management lies with its boards of trustees. Because TIAA and CREF, the main components of the parent organization, are incorporated under different laws and are regulated by different government agencies, there is one board for TIAA and another for CREF. A board of overseers ensures that TIAA-CREF is meeting its charter purposes; this board also elects trustees to the TIAA Board. CREF participants directly elect CREF trustees, in the same manner as mutual fund shareholders who have votes in proportion to the shares they own. Members of the boards are a diverse group of men and women, representing academic (faculty and administration), business, and philanthropic institutions, with a wide range of expertise and interests, including education, management, government, economics, finance, law, and corporate governance. Most board members are themselves longtime TIAA-CREF participants; only two are TIAA-CREF executives.

Warshawsky and Ameriks (1996) report that pension coverage (at over 95 percent) and participation (at 80 percent) are significantly greater in the higher education sector than in the rest of the full-time labor force (71 percent and 59 percent, respectively). As of 31 October 1998, there were 1,792,942 participants in the accumulation phase, 290,616 participants receiving annuity-income payments in the TIAA-CREF pension system, and 8,711 institutions of all sizes sponsoring TIAA-CREF pension plans.

5.3.1 Life-Annuity-Payment Options

At one time, all TIAA-CREF basic pension plans allowed for distributions only through a life annuity or death benefit (supplemental plans have always been "cashable"). In 1988, this systemwide restriction was removed for basic plans, although a small number of sponsoring institutions chose to retain it. Hence, with the exception of accumulations in the TIAA traditional annuity, for most TIAA-CREF pension plans, when an employee leaves the service of his or her employer, accumulations can be withdrawn as a life annuity, in a lump sum, in a systematic series of payments, or in any combination of lump sum, systematic withdrawals, and life annuities. In addition, for all plans, participants over age seventy and a half can, since 1991, withdraw funds through a minimum-distribution option (MDO), and participants age fifty-five and over can, since 1989, receive payments of current interest credited to TIAA accumulations through an interest-only payment retirement option (IPRO). A retirement-transition benefit is also available from TIAA and CREF, whereby 10 percent of accumulations are available as a lump sum on retirement.

Despite the flexibilities available, most TIAA-CREF participants still choose a life annuity when they retire. TIAA-CREF offers both single- and two-life annuities, with or without guaranteed periods of ten, fifteen, or twenty years. The options available for two-life annuities are two-thirds benefit to survivor, full benefit to survivor, and half benefit to second annuity partner. Payout levels reflect the option chosen. Payments can be made on a monthly, quarterly, semiannual, or annual basis.

Life annuities can be drawn from any of the investment accounts. The TIAA traditional annuity guarantees the interest rate ($2\frac{1}{2}$ percent) and mortality assumptions for payouts through life annuities. These payout guarantees actually begin in the accumulation phase and hence can be in effect for several decades. In addition, the TIAA board declares annual dividends to annuitants.

There are two different life-annuity-payment methods available from TIAA—standard and graded. For both methods, payment is based on assumed mortality, guaranteed interest, and dividends. Under the standard payment method, the initial income level is maintained until there is a change in dividends; year-over-year dividend changes in the payout phase historically have been small. Under the graded payment method, initial income is based on a 4 percent payout. Any remaining dividends are reinvested and used to buy additional future income. This method was first proposed by Biggs (1969) and put in place by TIAA in 1982 to help protect annuitants from inflation. King (1995) calculated hypothetical payments under the graded method for various periods beginning in the 1970s and found that purchasing power was preserved, indeed enhanced, through 1995, although, in the years of high inflation in the late 1970s and early 1980s, purchasing power lagged somewhat. Annuitants who initially choose the graded method can later switch to the standard method, but not vice versa.

Life annuities can also be drawn from any of the variable accounts. Payouts are entirely variable, reflecting the investment performance and expenses of the account and the mortality experience of annuitants using the account. Initial payments are calculated using the accumulation, the income option chosen, an assumed effective interest rate of 4 percent, and mortality assumptions, currently the unisex version of the 1983 IAM table set back two months for each complete year that has elapsed since 31 March 1986 to account for ongoing gains in longevity. After the initial payment, payment amounts change to reflect mainly the performance of the investment portfolio either annually or monthly, at the option of the participant.

Although income from the variable accounts is generally more volatile than that from the TIAA traditional annuity, participants with variable annuities are able to devise a retirement-income portfolio more aligned with their risk tolerances. For the equity accounts, over long time periods, variable annuitants participate in general economic performance, which has been significantly positive in the United States and other countries over most recent historical periods. Annuitants may switch among the variable accounts or to the TIAA traditional annuity on any business day, as often as once per calendar quarter. Income options, annuitant(s), and guaranteed period, however, must be maintained on the switch.

5.3.2 Current Annuity Payout Rates and Annuity Utilization

Table 5.7 shows initial monthly payments per $100,000 accumulation in a basic pension plan for various issue ages and options for life annuities issued by TIAA-CREF on 1 June 1998. For TIAA, the annuity payout reflects current dividend levels assuming that the participant has made contributions from salary, increasing at 5 percent annually, to TIAA since 1 June 1968; various TIAA vintages are represented in this example and produce a blended investment return of 6.9 percent. For CREF, the assumed interest rate is 4 percent. Future payouts on a CREF annuity will reflect investment performance in an underlying variable-investment account, and, if returns exceed 4 percent, payouts will increase.

For a single-life annuity issued to a sixty-five-year-old, TIAA is paying, as of 1 June 1998, an initial monthly payout of $759 per $100,000 accumulation under the standard payment method. This value is higher than the average commercial market payout for men ($732 in nonqualified accounts) and even more dramatically greater than that for women ($662). For a joint-and-survivor annuity issued to a couple, both of whom are sixty-five years old, TIAA is paying $670 monthly per $100,000, higher

Table 5.7   **Initial Monthly Payments ($) per $100,000 Accumulation from TIAA and CREF Annuities Issued in June 1998**

Age	Single-Life Annuity		Joint-and-Survivor Annuity	
	TIAA Standard	CREF	TIAA Standard	CREF
55	665	489	612	435
60	704	534	636	465
65	759	597	670	507
70	838	683	719	566
75	953	807	792	648

Note: Issuance of annuity on 1 June 1998. The joint-and-survivor annuity rates quoted here are for benefits to a survivor the same age as the annuitant. TIAA rates reflect 30 years of participation (1 June 1968–1 June 1998) in TIAA and past salary growth of 5 percent per year; TIAA vintages are recognized. All annuity rates are unisex. There are no guaranteed periods chosen.

than the payout rate for TSP annuities. With a 4 percent assumed interest rate, CREF is initially paying on any of its accounts $597 monthly for the single-life annuity and $507 monthly for the joint-life annuity.

Comparing the TSP (table 5.4 above) and TIAA (table 5.7), we note that TIAA offers superior rates on joint-and-survivor annuities at all ages except the oldest and higher rates on single-life annuities at the younger ages. These generally higher rates result from TIAA's superior investment performance. Comparisons between the TSP and TIAA should be made cautiously as payouts from TIAA may fluctuate somewhat, either downward or, as has occurred in the last several years, upward. Moreover, as noted above, with current market interest rates significantly below the 7 percent assumption of the tabular annuity rates, the TSP offers higher rates than it would if its annuity rates were set precisely like TIAA's. In addition, where mortality is a more important consideration, for example, in single-life annuities issued at older ages, the mandated use of a liberal, that is, old and outdated, mortality table by the TSP will lead to higher annuity-income rates. It is impossible to compare the increasing-payment TSP annuity with a CREF annuity because the assumed interest rate is fixed at 4 percent for CREF while it is (implicitly) constantly changing for the TSP. In June 1998, the (implicit) TSP assumed interest rate for its increasing-payment annuity was 2.625 percent (= 5.625 percent − 3 percent).

About 16,300 TIAA-CREF participants converted some or all of their accumulations into streams of periodic income in 1997. Of these, 11,700 chose a life annuity, 2,200 the MDO, 1,500 the IPRO, and 900 systematic withdrawals. The MDO is particularly popular among participants age seventy and a half and older; nearly three-quarters of this age group chose this form of income stream in 1997. This opting for flexibility represents an expected movement away from life annuities since 1988, when a life annuity was the only distribution form available. Settlements into life annuities are occurring at older ages, and partial settlements into life annuities are becoming more common, as participants choose to keep their options open longer. The graded-benefit payment method for TIAA traditional annuity accumulations has also grown more popular: Almost a quarter of new TIAA annuitants now select this method, compared to 2 percent when it was first introduced in 1982.

King (1996) looked at the choices in 1994 of TIAA-CREF participants among the life-annuity payout options. About three-quarters of male primary annuitants chose the two-life annuity, while about two-thirds of female primary annuitants chose the single-life annuity. About a third of the male and female annuitants choosing the single-life annuity selected no guaranteed period; the rest chose fairly evenly among ten-, fifteen-, and twenty-year guaranteed periods. Nearly all annuitants choosing a two-life annuity selected a guaranteed period. Male annuitants among the two-life annuity group predominantly selected the full-benefit-to-survivor form. Female annuitants in this group also favored the full benefit to survivor but were more likely than men to select the half-benefit-to-second-annuitant form. Among payout sources, the majority of annuity payouts in 1994 came from TIAA, but a sizable minority of payouts were from a CREF variable annuity. More recently, there has been a trend toward payouts from the variable accounts. This may provide some guidance for the design of annuitization systems within other individual account structures. In particular, it suggests a substantial demand for variable as opposed to fixed annuities.

5.4 Conclusions and Future Directions

The results in this paper provide information on the costs of obtaining an individual annuity in three different market environments. The first environment, the current market for single-premium individual annuities, is one in which each annuity buyer has full discretion in choosing among different insurance carriers and no economies of scale occur through participation in a group retirement-saving program. The costs in this environment are higher than those in the other two settings that we consider, namely, the federal government's TSP and the TIAA-CREF retirement system that is available to college and university employees. This is reflected in the higher average annuity payouts offered in these systems, for a given premium, than in the market at large. We show that the annuity payouts available to TSP participants in June 1998 were roughly 4 percent greater than those available (on average) in the private market. It is difficult to make a precise comparison between the annuity payouts of TIAA-CREF, the private market, and the TSP because of differences between nonguaranteed-element, variable, and nonparticipating annuity products. However, the TIAA-CREF payouts appear to be greater than those of the TSP or (on average) the private market.

Our results provide some potential guidance on the costs of annuitization but also raise questions. One concerns the time-series pattern of annuity payouts relative to the premiums for single-premium annuity policies. Comparing the calculations in Friedman and Warshawsky (1990), Mitchell et al. (1999), and the present paper suggests that the EPDV of annuity payouts has been rising, relative to premiums, for the last decade. Explaining this trend is an important issue for further investigation. It may result from declining risk perceived by the insurance companies that offer these products, particularly with respect to interest-rate fluctuations. It could also reflect a failure to take into account ongoing improvements in mortality. For example, consider what would happen if annuity providers were to use information from a given past year (say, 1983, the date of the last major release of annuitant mortality rates by the Society of Actuaries) on the mortality rates of annuitants. If actual mortality rates are declining, then the EPDV of payouts will be rising. While this explanation is consistent with what we observe in the annuity market, we are not aware of any way to distinguish this possibility from alternative explanations.

A second question concerns the design of a menu of annuity options that might be available for potential annuitants. Experience with TIAA-CREF suggests that a substantial number of participants are interested in variable as opposed to fixed annuities. While TSP participants can choose annuities that are partially inflation indexed, relatively few do; the TSP experience, however, does not provide any evidence on whether annuitants would choose real (fully indexed), partially indexed, or nominal annuities if they could make such a decision. Further work should investigate the behavior of individual annuitants in settings in which they can choose among different potential annuity options.

References

Ameriks, John, Francis King, and Mark Warshawsky. 1997. Premium allocations and accumulations in TIAA-CREF—trends in participant choices among asset classes and investment accounts. *TIAA-CREF Research Dialogues,* no. 51 (July).
Bell, Felicitie, A. Wade, and S. Goss. 1992. Life tables for the United States social security area, 1900–2080. Actuarial Study no. 107. Washington, D.C.: Social Security Administration, Office of the Actuary.
A. M. Best. Various issues. *Best's Review: Life and Health.* Oldwick, N.J.
Biggs, John H. 1969. Alternatives in variable annuity benefit design. *Transactions of the Society of Actuaries* 21 (November): 495–528.
Brown, Jeffrey R., and James M. Poterba. 1998. Joint and survivor annuities and the demand for annuities by married couples. NBER Working Paper no. 7199. Cambridge, Mass.: National Bureau of Economic Research.
Friedman, Benjamin, and Mark Warshawsky. 1988. Annuity prices and saving behavior in the United States. In *Pensions in the U.S. economy,* ed. Z. Bodie, J. Shoven, and D. Wise. Chicago: University of Chicago Press.
———. 1990. The cost of annuities: Implications for saving behavior and bequests. *Quarterly Journal of Economics* 105, no. 1 (February): 135–54.
Gramlich, Edward M. 1996. Different approaches for dealing with social security. *Journal of Economic Perspectives* 10 (summer): 55–66.
Johansen, R. 1996. Review of adequacy of 1983 individual annuity mortality table. *Transactions of the Society of Actuaries* 47:101–23.
King, Francis. 1995. The TIAA graded payment method and the CPI. *TIAA-CREF Research Dialogues,* no. 46 (December).
———. 1996. Trends in the selection of TIAA-CREF life-annuity income options, 1978–1994. *TIAA-CREF Research Dialogues,* no. 48 (July).
Mitchell, Olivia, James M. Poterba, Mark Warshawsky, and Jeffrey R. Brown. 1999. New evidence on the money's worth of individual annuities. *American Economic Review* 89 (December): 1299–1318.
Warshawsky, Mark. 1988. Private annuity markets in the United States. *Journal of Risk and Insurance* 55, no. 3 (September): 518–28.

———. 1998. Distributions from retirement plans: Minimum requirements, current options, and future directions. *TIAA-CREF Research Dialogues,* no. 57 (September).

Warshawsky, Mark, and John Ameriks. 1996. Pensions and health benefits for workers in higher education. *TIAA-CREF Research Dialogues,* no. 49 (December).

Comment   David M. Cutler

Jim Poterba and Mark Warshawsky have written a very interesting paper on the cost of annuities in a privatized social security system. Low-cost annuitization is a central benefit of public social security, and many fear that annuity contracts in a privatized system will be too expensive for people to purchase. Poterba and Warshawsky analyze this claim.

Poterba and Warshawsky conclude that the costs of annuitization are quite modest. For a sixty-five-year-old male, the average individual annuity returned 85 percent of the money paid in. Groups annuities, as with the federal government's Thrift Savings Plan (TSP) or TIAA-CREF, return even more. Further, most of the 15 percent loading cost is accounted for by adverse selection—differences between the mortality of annuity purchasers and that of the average person in the population. Only a small amount of the money paid for an annuity—perhaps one-third of the 15 percent load, or 5 percent—represents true administrative expense. Since mandatory annuitization would eliminate the adverse-selection premium, Poterba and Warshawsky argue that incomplete annuitization would not be a significant problem in a privatized social security system.

This paper has many strengths. The questions asked are important. The discussion of the annuitization options in the TSP and TIAA-CREF is valuable.

In my comments, I highlight two features of the Poterba-Warshawsky analysis that trouble me. The first concerns the adjustment for risk in calculating the administrative expenses of annuities. Poterba and Warshawsky take as their base case that individuals discount annuity returns at the tax-free return. This scenario yields the total administrative load of 15 percent. They then present a calculation of administrative expenses if individuals discount annuity returns at the BAA discount rate. The administrative costs are much larger in this case—20–25 percent. The difference between these rates, Poterba and Warshawsky argue, has to do with individual attitudes toward risk. If individuals are risk averse, they argue, the

David M. Cutler is professor of economics at Harvard University and a research associate of the National Bureau of Economic Research.

riskless interest rate is a more appropriate discount rate, and, hence, the lower estimate of administrative expense is appropriate.

I am not convinced by this argument. Annuity companies are providing two services to people. First, they are investing money that individuals give them for future income. Second, they are converting this investment income into an annuity payment. The administrative costs of the second activity (the annuitization of income) should be based on the expected returns that the *annuity company* will earn by investing the money. *Individual* discount rates are not relevant to this problem. Individual discount rates matter for whether the policy offered is worth it but not for how much it costs on an actuarial basis. Put another way, administrative costs are a technological parameter about firms, not a preference parameter about individuals.

I suspect that annuity companies believe that their return will be even greater than the risky scenario that Poterba and Warshawsky consider. The stock market, for example, has consistently outperformed even the return to BAA bonds. If annuity companies expect to earn the stock market return on the funds that they collect, the implicit administrative expense will be even larger. It would be valuable for Poterba and Warshawsky to present administrative-cost calculations using the stock market return as the discount rate.

To determine which rate is correct, one would need to know the expected return of annuity companies. With their contacts in the industry, Poterba and Warshawsky are in an ideal position to answer this question. I hope that this will be the next phase of their research.

One other point about the analysis deserves mention. Poterba and Warshawsky argue that, if annuitization is compelled, the adverse-selection premium will disappear. That statement is true on average, but it is not true for all products and all people. Even if people are compelled to annuitize, they may not be compelled to purchase annuities from the same companies, or companies might not be compelled to sell to everyone. One might imagine that some annuity companies will attract sick people and others healthy people (e.g., companies might attract sick people by offering bereavement services or good advice about oncologists). Adverse selection will thus still be a problem; some will pay more and others less for the same policy. I suspect that this will be a public policy concern.

At the end of the day, I am more skeptical about fair annuities than are Poterba and Warshawsky. I find support for this view in the low level of current annuity purchases. The inability of annuity companies to make much headway in today's market suggests that people perceive the cost of annuities to be greater than Poterba and Warshawsky measure them to be. I suspect that, correctly measured, the administrative costs are much larger than presented here.

Discussion Summary

Before the general discussion, *James Poterba* offered several comments responding to David Cutler's discussion of the paper. Poterba argued that it is a complicated matter to determine the correct discount rate to use in the expected present discounted value (EPDV) calculation. The risk-free rate is appropriate in that the annuity is essentially a riskless contract on the part of the annuitant (except for a very low risk that the insurance company will default). A riskier rate may be appropriate if the intention is to compare the annuity to the investor's next-best alternative in the market. A riskier rate may also be appropriate if the calculation is considered from the supply side: discounting should be done according to the risk-adjusted return that the insurance company can earn on the assets in which it invests. Poterba agreed that using a higher discount rate would imply a higher cost to the insurance company.

Cutler had also taken issue with Poterba and Warshawsky's assertion that adverse selection would be less of a problem in an environment of mandatory annuitization of social security individual accounts. Cutler argued that adverse selection would be eliminated only if every annuitant were required to purchase his or her annuity from the same provider. Otherwise, differentiation among providers would lead to adverse selection. Poterba responded that, although this is true with respect to individual providers, adverse selection would not be an issue in the aggregate, that is, with respect to average costs across the whole population. He also mentioned that variation in mortality rates across income levels may create additional issues. Since lower-income individuals (with smaller accounts) will generally yield higher expected profit to the insurance company than higher-income individuals (with larger accounts), there will be differences between the mortality profile of the average dollar entering the system and the average individual entering the system. *Estelle James* inquired whether any insurance companies charge higher fees for larger accounts given the generally lower mortality rates of higher-income individuals. *Poterba* responded that, in fact, the opposite tended to happen—and he suggested that perhaps this was due to fixed costs of administering accounts.

Martin Feldstein began the general discussion by asking Mark Warshawsky if TIAA-CREF investors' choice of annuity-payout options had exhibited significant self-selection with respect to mortality—for example, the mortality experience of individuals choosing more accelerated payout options tending to be disproportionately high, and vice versa. *Warshawsky* replied that the data were not yet available to answer this question. In response to a follow-up question by Feldstein, Warshawsky noted that the TIAA mortality tables reflect slightly lower mortality than those used by CREF. (Annuity payments from TIAA are generally more accelerated than those from CREF.) *Stephen Zeldes* suggested that the mortality profile of individuals choosing each option should be a major area of research for TIAA-CREF in order to determine the likely costs of adverse selection as they offer more annuity options. *Feldstein* commented that, if the cost were significant, TIAA-CREF would probably have recognized it already.

Andrew Samwick suggested that the Social Security Administration (SSA) would likely be able to handle the annuitization of individual accounts effectively. He noted that the SSA is very efficient at dispersing funds and determining when people have died and adjusting their payouts accordingly, essential skills for acting as a centralized clearinghouse for annuity payments.

Peter Diamond suggested that data from the Poterba and Warshawsky paper could be used to compare government versus private management of individual accounts. Specifically, the Poterba and Warshawsky paper notes that, in June 1998, a single-premium-immediate annuity (SPIA) purchased by a sixty-five-year-old through the federal Thrift Savings Plan (TSP) would have provided $763 monthly per $100,000 premium. The comparable figure for a qualified SPIA issued by Metropolitan Life through an agent was $664. Diamond suggested that, given an assumption regarding average life span after date of annuity purchase, this $99 difference could be converted into a basis-point figure.

Diamond also cautioned that there may be deadweight losses and corruption issues involved with mandatory annuitization if individuals desire to withdraw some of their individual account in a lump sum at retirement and are willing to use kickbacks in order to do so. He noted that there is some evidence of this type of activity occurring in Chile, where annuities are expensive and often include up-front commissions, part of which are alleged to be kicked back to the annuitant. He commented that, although certain regulations discouraging such activity would likely accompany an individual account plan with mandatory annuitization, it may remain an issue.

David Wilcox inquired about the extent of the link between mortality and income level. *James Poterba* replied that the main difference occurred between the bottom income quintile (with *income* referring to social security covered earnings) of the population and everyone else, with sixty-five- to seventy-five-year-old men in the bottom quintile experiencing approximately 60–80 percent higher mortality rates than sixty-five- to seventy-five-year-old men in the top quintile. *Wilcox* also commented that lower-income individuals tend to have sporadic labor force attachment. He suggested that, as a result of this fact, it would be inappropriate to use the social security actuary's framework of comparing a "representative" steady low earner, steady average earner, and steady high earner. Such an analysis would not take into account the effect of sporadic labor force attachment on accumulation in the individual accounts and, thus, the size of accounts being annuitized. Wilcox also noted that the authors' results were relevant to Gary Burtless's (2000) finding that annuity payouts have varied widely over the twentieth century and suggested that the authors could perhaps flesh out this finding a bit more. *Warshawsky* replied that he had performed a similar analysis beginning with the year 1919 and had also found significant variation in payout—which he attributed largely to interest-rate fluctuation. *Poterba* added that it would not be surprising to observe large variations in payouts in the late 1930s and early 1940s as insurance companies who had misforecast interest rates and used outdated mortality tables in the early 1930s adjusted for their enormous annuity losses in part by hiking annuity premiums.

James Smalhout asked the authors why they had chosen to use the SSA's life tables to project mortality rates rather than Census Bureau tables and inquired about the sensitivity of the results to that choice. Smalhout noted that the Census Bureau, for example, had developed its own life tables in part because of dissatisfaction with the SSA tables. *Poterba* replied that, in his and Warshawsky's review of various mortality data sources, they had found the SSA tables to be the most attractive, citing the fact that, since the SSA must closely monitor mortality in the older population in order to avoid paying benefits to deceased individuals, they tend to have much more accurate data than other sources. *Stephen Zeldes* commented that the accuracy of the SSA's historic data did not necessarily imply that their projected data would be similarly accurate. *Poterba* agreed, noting that he and Warshawsky had not attempted directly to compare the quality of forecasting among the various sources of mortality data. In response to Smalhout's second question, Poterba commented that the results are certainly sensitive to the mortality data.

Kent Smetters offered a comment regarding the relevant discount rate for calculating the EPDV of annuity payments. He noted that several states maintain funds that guarantee the solvency of life insurance policies and asked whether similar funds existed for guaranteeing annuities. He suggested that, if these funds were to exist, then annuity providers would take on the risk profile of a limited-liability corporation.

Daniel Feenberg suggested that, as a point of reference for assessing the value of an annuity, one could consider the consumer's decision to purchase an annuity instead of a corporate bond or CD. In purchasing a bond, the consumer would give up the "survival premium" of an annuity (i.e., the longer one lives, the higher the return from the annuity) but would gain the ability to bequeath the remaining principal and interest payments. He suggested that, if the bond had a higher interest rate, it would strictly dominate the annuity as an investment and that, if it did not have a higher interest rate, the value comparison would involve assessing the trade-off between survival premium and ability to bequeath the investment. *James Poterba* commented that, within the framework suggested by Feenberg, annuities come out ahead of government bonds (which would be the relevant instrument of comparison for the Poterba and Warshawsky analysis) but that the comparison with corporate bonds is a closer call. He also noted that annuities may not have been so attractive ten years ago but that the expected present value of annuity payments had clearly risen over time.

On a separate issue, Poterba pointed out that the insurance value of annuities is empirically nontrivial. In the absence of a defined-benefit retirement plan such as social security, a sixty-five-year-old man would typically be willing to give up 20–30 percent of his wealth in order to purchase a guaranteed stream of income for the duration of his life. Poterba noted that the figure would be slightly lower if the individual had a portion of his assets in a social security–type system.

Sylvester Schieber echoed David Wilcox's earlier statement regarding the effect of sporadic workforce attachment, suggesting that the same effect would occur in social security. Specifically, Schieber asserted that the result of sporadic labor force attachment would be to make the average AIME (average indexed monthly earnings) lower than the AIME of the social security actuary's steady average earner. He also noted that the effect on social security benefits would likely be less than the effect on individual account returns owing to social security's progressive benefit formula. Regarding Gary Burtless's finding of substantial volatility in annuity payouts in the twentieth century, Schieber commented that this effect is overstated because Burtless looks only at stock funds (i.e., the underlying funds with which the annuity was purchased had been invested only in stocks throughout the individual's lifetime). Schieber performed a similar analysis based on accounts whose asset mixture was similar to that of a typical 401(k) account and found the volatility in annuity payouts to be significantly less than Burtless's estimate.

Estelle James noted that the high expected present value of annuity payments per dollar of premium seemed to suggest that individuals do not place high value on the insurance aspect of annuities. Assuming that individuals are price takers who have good information regarding their expected lifetime, we might expect the payout-to-premium ratio to be lower if individuals were willing to pay more for a guaranteed stream of income. *Poterba* replied that consumer behavior in the annuity market remains somewhat of a quandary and implied that it is therefore difficult to offer a definitive answer to James's question. He did note that the value of annuities is somewhat diminished for married couples as a result of "mortality pooling"—that is, the ability to allocate assets within the family to hedge against risk to the survivor—and that this effect would lead married individuals to value the insurance aspect of the annuity less than unmarried people.

Reference

Burtless, Gary. 2000. Social security privatization and financial market risk: Lessons from U.S. financial history. Working paper. Washington, D.C.: Brookings Institution, Center on Social and Economic Dynamics.

6

Panel Session
Industry Perspectives

Robert Pozen, Joel M. Dickson, F. Gregory Ahern,
Frederick L. A. Grauer, and Shaun Mathews

Robert Pozen

Thank you for inviting me to this very august group of economists as one of the so-called industry representatives. I thought that it might be useful to look at some of the practical issues from our perspective in two main areas: the investment-management side and the service side.

On the investment-management side, there are basically three main alternatives. You can have centralized fund investing, you can have index funds, or you can have some sort of active management. On the first alternative, I share many of the concerns that Martin Feldstein has articulated earlier in this meeting. I have been involved with the private administration of various defined-benefit plans, and you would be surprised how much pressure is brought to bear on these plans even in the private sphere. The standard response to avoid these pressures is reliance only on index funds, but these also raise concerns.

For the record, I want to say that Fidelity manages over $23 billion in retail index funds. We are the second biggest retail provider of index funds, so we are seriously involved with that aspect of money management. Nevertheless, I am actually quite concerned about a world in which huge numbers of people and huge amounts of money wind up in Standard and Poor's 500 funds. There is a clear free-rider problem on active research posed by index funds. They do not do any research on stocks or companies, so they have no idea about whether the prices of stocks in the index are appropriate. Index funds basically rely on active managers to set ap-

Robert Pozen is president of Fidelity Management and Research Co.

propriate prices for index stocks: they are simply parasites living off active research.

This absence of securities research—the core characteristic of index funds—raises fundamental questions about their effect on the capital allocation function of the stock market. If more and more index money is invested without looking at the stocks or the companies, then capital may not go to those companies that are the best users of that capital. Moreover, the popularity of the Standard and Poor's 500 index tends to disfavor smaller and mid-size companies. For example, will there be a disparity in ability to raise capital between the 490th and the 510th company on the Standard and Poor's list? It is easy to argue that we should simply shift to broader indexes, such as the Wilshire 5000. However, these broader indexes have attracted relatively little investor interest or support.

When I consider the alternative of active management, I am attracted by the structure of the proposal from Fred Goldberg and Michael Graetz. Their proposal contemplates a default option for those who do not want to choose an active manager plus a "contract-out" procedure for those who want to use a private money manager. I support a strong default option because it may be difficult to educate all citizens about the range of fund options.

In thinking about how to design a low-cost, highly structured default option for those taxpayers who do not want to make investment choices, I would suggest that we look to what we call *lifestyle funds*. Lifestyle funds are ones where the mix of stocks and bonds changes automatically as the investor cohort ages. For example, when investors are twenty-five, the lifestyle fund has 80 percent stocks and 20 percent bonds; then, as they get to forty-five, the mix shifts to 40 percent bonds and 60 percent stocks; and, as they get toward retirement, the mix shifts to a majority of bonds. Such lifestyle funds are much simpler than even the government thrift plan, which offers participants several options to choose from.

I think that you need a strong default option because many members of Congress seem quite concerned about whether all citizens will know enough to make intelligent investment choices. With the lifestyle funds, we can meet these concerns—if a citizen does nothing, then he or she will be given an appropriate mix of stocks and bonds, which will be changed automatically over time.

As for the contract-out procedure for those who want to choose a private money manager, I would suggest that we use as a model the Department of Labor's safe harbor under section 404(c) of the Employee Retirement Income Security Act (ERISA). This safe harbor relieves the employer of liability for specific investments chosen by participants if certain conditions are met. Most important, a qualified investment manager must offer participants at least three different investment options. One must be a money market fund or stable-value account such as a bank deposit or insurance account with guaranteed return. A second must be some type of high-quality bond fund. And the third must be some sort of diversified stock fund. Having three options is just the minimum; there can be more investment alternatives. Moreover, the safe harbor requires participants to receive educational materials about how to choose among these investment alternatives.

I would be concerned about a contract-out procedure that would be thrown open to any vendor regardless of qualification and would allow a vendor to offer only one investment option (such as individual Venezuelan stocks). It is this type of high-risk investment that is likely to produce political repercussions. By contrast, when you explain the 404(c) model to most people in Washington, they think that it is reasonable. It has the advantage of being used successfully in the context of defined-contribution plans.

Now, on the service side, I like the idea of having the IRS do as much as possible and using the present system for collecting social security contributions. However, I think that there still are a lot of questions about how often private money managers would receive contract-out monies and how they would actually get these monies. In my view, allowing a participant to choose only one private manager and transferring the money only once per year are probably the two most important features in terms of cost drivers. Costs would be too high if a financial institution received $12 a week, divided among four different mutual funds. A weekly contribution of $12 would equal $624 per year, which is close to 2 percent of the average social security contribution per year.

I think that many people are underestimating the cost of marketing, enrollment, and education for the contract-out procedure. On the other hand, if we have a system constructed with a default option, I am not at all worried if people wind up paying fees to investment managers that are higher than those currently charged by the federal thrift plan. Some investors may want a broad range of investment options plus other extras and may very well be willing to pay more for these. I am not bothered by this possibility as long as we have a strong default option and good disclosure by private money managers competing for contract-out business.

Then we get to the cost of administrative servicing. Many fund sponsors provide a very high level of customer support—for example, twenty-four-hour phone service, consolidated reports, and Internet tools. Problem resolution itself is an expensive service. Again, I am not worried if we have a strong default option and good disclosure from a number of qualified financial institutions. If someone does not demand a lot of service and wants to pay very low fees, he or she can stay with the default option. If someone wants more services, then he or she can consider the cost-benefit trade-off offered by various private money managers.

Finally, on implementing any new system for individual accounts under social security, I think that it is a good idea to have something like a three-year transition for several reasons. One is that it will take time for the government to build the new system and make all the proper connections to the old system. A transition period allows time to educate people about the available choices in the new system. A transition period also allows time for accounts to build up to a reasonable size. Given the number of young people who have part-time and summer jobs, you can have very small account sizes. I think that it might be useful to have a rule requiring a minimum account size of $2,000 or $5,000 before someone could contract out. Otherwise, it would be possible to have people invest $29 in a fund, which would not be economical.

Joel M. Dickson

A broad consensus has developed regarding the need to reform the U.S. social security system. As part of this national debate, numerous proposals have been advanced that would provide participants with the ability to direct some of their social security investments through individual accounts. Unfortunately, to date, little attention has been given to the administrative costs of running these new accounts. This conference will likely provide an important platform as administrative-cost considerations begin to be integrated with the design proposals.

The costs of any particular proposal will vary depending on its characteristics. However, existing retirement-savings-plan options—namely, 401(k)s and IRAs—can provide some guidance on the costs of and trade-offs in servicing social security accounts. Record keeping for 401(k) plans is a very transaction-intensive business where two different groups must be serviced: the plan sponsor and the participants. There are multiple pay periods and multiple sources of funds (e.g., employee pretax contributions, employee after-tax contributions, employer matching contributions) that must be tracked separately. There is also a lot of flexibility in plan design, making each plan unique in terms of investment choice, plan provisions, and required services. In short, a typical 401(k) plan's costs are quite expensive. However, financial services firms have one important tool at their disposal: voluntary selection. Firms can decide whether they want to provide services for a given provider, thereby targeting those plans whose asset-based revenue can pay for its servicing costs. In a universal social security plan, providers would likely lose this ability to select their client base.

Although there is no such thing as a typical 401(k) plan, some parameters can be placed around the major cost areas. Overall, servicing a 401(k) plan probably costs on the order of $100 per participant year, depending on the plan's complexity and the range of services offered. A reasonable

Joel M. Dickson is a principal at the Vanguard Group, Inc.

estimate of the servicing costs—that is, the systems, staff, and array of services needed to interact with both the employer and the employee— may represent about 50 percent of that total cost. Another significant portion of the costs can be accounted for by transaction processing (e.g., plan contributions, exchanges, withdrawals, loans) and ongoing research and development of new services needed to attract and retain clients. All other plan expenses, including participant education, statement mailings, and miscellaneous other expenses, may account for just about 20 percent of the total cost. These costs simply represent the ongoing costs of servicing the accounts. One-time start-up costs would also need to be accounted for in any overall pricing model, and these marketing and plan conversion costs can be considerable.

Providing services to an IRA is generally less complex and, hence, less costly than providing them to a 401(k) plan. With an IRA, a financial services provider is interacting with only one client—the account owner. This relationship is less transaction intensive, with fewer reporting requirements than exist under the ERISA-based 401(k) structure. In addition, providers retain some ability to select their client base through the institution of minimum account balances, account-maintenance fees for small accounts, and targeted marketing to "profitable" shareholders. Overall, ongoing servicing costs probably run about $30 per year. In addition, first-year costs associated with attracting a new account might represent an additional $40 in order to cover phone calls, account setup, and literature fulfillment.

The wide range of ongoing administrative costs within existing IRA and 401(k) models provides the ability to identify areas of cost savings. In particular, four general questions need to be addressed in evaluating the potential administrative costs of any individual account proposal: Who does the record keeping, who are the clients being serviced, how often are the accounts valued, and what are the types and frequency of allowable transactions by participants?

Centralized or decentralized record keeping is probably the most important issue to address. If it is determined that individual financial services companies should provide record-keeping services, the reporting-requirements transaction activity will likely be more complex than with current IRAs. This would be especially true if firms would have to interact with both the employer and the employee. However, these accounts would probably be less complex than a 401(k) plan because it would be a more standardized program. With decentralized record keeping, administrative costs will naturally be higher because thousands of different marketing, education, and advertising programs will have to be developed and tailored to that particular institution. Service enhancements and the constant competition to retain and attract clients will also lead to generally higher costs.

While the actual costs would depend on the ultimate individual account structure, a reasonable assumption for a bare-bones model might be an ongoing cost of $50 per participant year with decentralized record keeping. Given this figure, what are the business implications for providing these accounts? Consider an individual earning $30,000 in social security income (which is above the mean social security income level) with 2 percent contributed to an individual account, and assume that the first-year cost of establishing the account is $40. A low-cost provider charging expenses of thirty basis points (0.3 percent) would generate first-year revenue of about $1.80 (0.3 percent × 2 percent × $30,000) but would incur costs of roughly $90.

Under the commonly proposed 2 percent individual account model, the break-even period for this example would be nearly twenty-five years, assuming an 8 percent nominal return and a 5 percent real return. On a stand-alone basis, this is not a particularly attractive business proposition, especially if firms would not be able to choose their client base. In short, asset-based revenue would not cover operating costs unless other fees— like low balance fees—could be used. Even if firms generated 1 percent in asset-based fees, the break-even period would still be on the order of a decade. Two general conclusions can be drawn from this example. First, a number of providers might choose not to offer individual accounts if only 2 percentage points of payroll taxes were used to fund the accounts because of the substantial start-up costs. In addition, the firms for which the accounts would be the most attractive are those that can generate significant asset-based revenue over a relatively short time horizon—that is, higher-cost providers that, all else equal, would provide lower returns to the system's participants.

Costs could be lowered dramatically by adopting centralized record keeping, although this approach may also decrease investment flexibility and service development. In particular, with a single record-keeping system, significant economies of scale and scope are available. For example, there would be a need for only one coordinated education program and one set of marketing initiatives. In addition, error reconciliation is much simpler, and no conflicts would result from trying to move accounts between different financial services providers.

One way in which to reduce client-servicing costs would be to develop a way of getting either the employer or the employee out of the picture. Because the individual accounts would likely be owned and controlled by the employee, it might make sense to eliminate any employer involvement that is required in servicing the individual account. One approach might be to direct the individual account investment through an individual's tax forms; that is, use the IRS as a conduit for account contributions. In this way, the account is based on social security wages, which are already detailed on individual W-2 forms, requiring no further employer involvement. Even an individual account proposal with decentralized record keeping could lower costs by using the tax-filing process to allocate contributions. However, the combination of centralized record keeping and minimal involvement by employers would dramatically lower overall costs.

One often-overlooked consideration is the valuation period of the account, which can significantly alter administrative-cost calculations. There are two general industry models: daily valuation and periodic valuation. With periodic valuation (e.g., monthly or quarterly), there is an overall trust account that represents the employer-sponsored plan and is reconciled on a regular basis. Participants own shares in the trust. This is a fairly straightforward approach because all that is required is to reconcile the trust's investments and then allocate this pool of money to participants on the basis of their ownership shares in the trust.

Daily valuation works in the reverse direction. That is, the reconciliation process begins by auditing each participant's account on a daily basis. These individual accounts must then be aggregated and reconciled at the trust level. This is a much more complex and expensive process than periodic valuation. As a ballpark estimate, monthly or quarterly valuation (and associated transaction activity) would probably reduce administrative costs by one-quarter to one-third relative to daily valuation. However, this approach would make more sense with centralized record keeping and limited investment choice because much of the cost savings would be eliminated by using existing mutual funds—which are daily valued and subject to many different dividend-distribution schedules—in a periodic valuation system.

The final area of potential cost savings would be in limiting transaction activity. Factors that would lower administrative costs would be limits on exchanges and contributions, no ability to make withdrawals before retirement or to take loans, and limited investment options. As with many of the other factors discussed, limited investment options probably work better within a centralized record-keeping framework. However, even without centralized record keeping, there are ways in which to limit transactions, such as limiting investment to a series of so-called lifestyle funds, as others have suggested.

In summary, financial services firms have considerable experience managing individual accounts and understand many of the cost considerations needed to evaluate alternative proposals for social security reform. Although the key decision might well be whether to employ centralized or decentralized record keeping for the accounts, there are many other factors that would significantly affect overall administrative costs. In particular, the number of relationships needed to ensure the accuracy of the account information, the valuation frequency of the accounts, and the degree of flexibility offered in terms of available services and transaction capability would all affect the costs associated with providing and servicing a social security system with individual accounts.

F. Gregory Ahern

I would preface my comments by saying that the paper that was presented earlier today by Goldberg and Graetz is one that tracks some of the remarks that I was going to make, so, in the interest of not being repetitive, I will offer only a few brief comments.

First, the real challenge when you look at individual social security accounts is the fact that you are talking about a market that would ultimately be five times bigger than the 401(k) market is today. It would involve 140 million individual accounts. At State Street, we have been actively involved with the issue of social security reform for a couple of years now. We have operated under a set of principles regarding what we think is relevant not only from a political standpoint—because you have to build political support—but also from the national policy standpoint. The first of these is that you have to protect current retirees and the soon to be retired from benefit cuts. Any new program has to be phased in very gradually.

Second, there are two big questions regarding individual accounts: Can they be made to work for low-income workers, and can you organize them in such a way as to address the time lag between contributions and the crediting of individual accounts? We think that there are acceptable answers to both these questions. Many of the ideas that look attractive to us at State Street have been touched on in the papers presented at this conference. We think that a realistic program of individual accounts with some right of ownership requires a low-cost structure. We also agree with the notion that the program will require a safety-net element (perhaps with a defined-benefit first-tier part) and keep survivor and disability benefits intact as well.

Third, we agree that you have to work off the existing tax and data codes already available: the IRS/Treasury, Social Security Administration (SSA), or some combination of both. You need to use a centralized record keeper in order to make this work. And, more important, you need to keep it simple, particularly in the early years, whether you call it an *incubation account* or a *cash-balance account*. The only realistic way in which to get individual accounts off the ground is to be able to provide something that people can afford, at least in the initial years. An evolutionary model, which has been discussed here today, would involve a cash-balance approach with unitized investment and ownership rights that really would have to be tracked back in the reconciliation process. That is, the money would remain in the cash-balance account until the payroll-tax receipts had been allocated to individual contributors. And, when that has been completed (which, in an ideal world, would be a year to eighteen months

F. Gregory Ahern is director of external affairs for State Street Corporation.

but realistically might take even longer), the money could go into either an individual investment account with a lifestyle approach, modeled in a way that is similar to what Bob Pozen was describing, or into a default option offering three basic funds. If you use the lifestyle model, then asset allocation would depend only on the age of the contributor.

I think that the accounts need to reach a certain level either in terms of assets or in terms of age before you can allow people to roll out into a program with many vendors and a high level of service. Before doing this, the account system must be allowed to build up assets to a point at which costs as a fraction of assets are reasonable. If the basis-points approach for allocating costs is used, you want to be able to cross-subsidize smaller accounts without imposing exorbitant fees on larger accounts. You also want to begin to add the bells-and-whistles service features that have become common in the 401(k) business today. All these features require a large asset base over which to spread costs. As the system matures, it could become similar to the 401(k) world with which we are all familiar today.

What do I mean by *starting simply?* I am talking about one statement per year, no loans, as well as perhaps a single annual contribution, distribution only on death or retirement, and some reasonable way to manage call volume. At least in our experience, call volume is the single biggest driver in terms of costs after the education component. For example, if you established 140 million accounts tomorrow, a very conservative estimate is that you would have to handle 150–175 million inquiries per year. Even if you are able to use Internet technology or some other automated system, that is still a staggering volume of calls and inquiries with which to deal. In terms of education, I assume that we will rely on the government and the media to provide the bulk of the service, particularly in the beginning. The need for education and its cost can be mitigated to some degree by having the incubation-account approach, which really is automatic, as well as a simple default option.

I feel that allocating costs according to account assets (the basis-points approach) is the only way to go. In terms of total costs, you are looking at a minimum of $25–$30 per account, and that number could range up to $75–$100; charging fees on the basis of total costs is just not going to work with this kind of system. With the basis-points approach, you get the cross-subsidization effect, which has got political elements to recognize, but I think that it is probably the fairest way to go. And, as you know, from a seller's standpoint, all participants get the same returns as long as they are in either the level 1 unitized account or a level 2 individual account.

To summarize, individual accounts can be made to work; you need to begin simply, and you need to use an evolutionary approach. If you align investment choice and service features with the growth in balances, you can make a really good case for evolving to the 401(k) model three to five years down the road.

Frederick L. A. Grauer

The U.S. social security system may be reformed in the near future. One change proposed is that participants in the system direct the investment of their social security account. Administrative costs of self-directed investing, such as accounting, safekeeping, reporting, phone servicing, managing, and transacting, affect the design of the system itself. Under a budget constraint, the greater are these administrative costs, the fewer investment choices would be available. Since administrative costs may have substantial fixed costs and thus exhibit economies of scale, the optimal set of investment choices may be small.

The discussions at the conference envision a social security system that is either defined benefit (DB), like the current system, or defined contribution (DC), or a hybrid. Almost by definition, the investments behind a DB plan cannot be self-directed. Participant-directed investing is a feature of a DC system. A conventional DC system, under which benefits equal contributions plus (or minus) the participant's investment success (or failure), cannot assure funding of a predefined benefit. If social security were converted entirely to a DC system, there would be no assured social safety net.

If a hybrid is contemplated where a social safety net is provided in the form of a defined benefit and, in addition, a DC plan is also provided, the DB portion must be invested according to a policy designed to ensure funding of those benefits.[1] The DC portion may be invested according to each participant's policy. Of course, the need to reform the social security system arises in part because the investment policy currently followed does not ensure funding of the defined benefit. Conversion to a DC system will not solve this problem. A social safety net and self-directed investing are incompatible.

The administrative costs of investment choice are relevant if social security is to move in whole or in part to a DC system.

Two comments are offered. First, the administrative costs of investment choice will be different depending on whether one is building a system from scratch or modifying an existing system. The analyses offered at the conference have carefully examined the administrative-cost functions of large private-sector servicers of DC employee retirement plans. The conclusions are of the form, If the social security system adopts the private-

Frederick L. A. Grauer is the former chairman of Barclays Global Investors.

1. There is, of course, some debate as to whether a society can self-insure and deliver a defined benefit for certain.

sector administrative model, then the administrative costs of the system should approximate those of large private providers, which have been estimated to be in the range of 75–150 basis points of assets administered.

The implicit assumption is that adoption of the private model involves either the replication (duplication) of an existing system or the allocation of all historical costs of the existing system if the existing system is used, including the costs of building it in the first place and the marketing costs of asset gathering. What has not been examined is the incremental cost of modifying existing systems to provide a social security subaccount.

It is common practice for private providers to customize their systems to meet their customers' needs. Costs of modifying existing systems will depend on the nature of the modifications. The modifications could be made quite standard across different systems if the SSA specified standard investment choices and standard interfaces to itself, the IRS, and payroll servicers. Simple and uniform standards would reduce the costs of modification substantially. The true incremental administrative cost of a social security subaccount would be a fraction of the cost of building an existing system from scratch. As an added benefit, the integration of the social security account into participants' retirement reports can only enhance the quality of their retirement planning. At the conference, I suggested that the average incremental administrative cost at full funding of adding a social security account to existing DC or IRA systems could be as low as 5 basis points. This may be low, but surely 75–150 basis points for a redundant system is high.

A problem exists with the modification approach—lack of universal coverage. Approximately 50 percent of working Americans are currently covered by DC plans and/or IRAs. Significant growth in coverage remains as DC-plan formations extend into the public sector and to companies with fewer than fifty employees. Over the next five years, covered American workers should exceed 60 percent.

Several low-cost approaches to expanding coverage must be considered. The simplest approach for those not covered by a DC plan or an IRA would be to maintain existing DB coverage under social security—no change, no harm. Another approach would involve the creation of a national DC-investment-pooled account without participant direction that would have a more aggressive investment policy than social security currently; that is, it would include stocks in its policy mix. Still another approach would contemplate a DC account or an IRA equivalent to the so-called lifeline account used in the regulated utility industry to assure minimum service access for those not able to afford regular service. Such an approach should involve incentives for DC-plan sponsors to extend coverage to nonemployees or financial institutions to create lifeline IRAs.

The administrative costs of privatizing investment choice should be substantially reduced through modification rather than replication of existing private delivery systems. Cost-effective alternative approaches probably exist to address shortfalls in universal coverage. To hold modification (vs. replication) hostage to uniform universal coverage is tantamount to forced cross-subsidization.

The second comment focuses on investment choice itself. If the existence of administrative costs implies limited investment choice, what are the best, limited choices to offer social security participants? This kind of question inevitably elicits heated debate. The existence of administrative costs forces the issue, however.

The last fifty years of academic research has witnessed significant growth in investment wisdom. Markowitz (1952) demonstrated the power of cross-sectional diversification to control risk and improve the reward-to-risk ratio on investments. Samuelson (1965) showed how intertemporal diversification reduced risk and why buy-and-hold investing dominates market timing. Sharpe (1991) emphasized that the costs of investing were the key determinant of the average active investor underperforming the market—an argument in favor of index funds. Brinson, Hood, and Beebower (1986) showed that the asset-allocation decision—the choice of what mixture of stocks, bonds, and cash to hold in a portfolio—"explained" more than 90 percent of realized pension portfolio risk and return. In other words, asset-class selection is more important than security selection for long-term portfolio performance.

This wisdom suggests the desirable scope of investment choice within social security—a set of low-cost, buy-and-hold, diversified stock, bond, and cash portfolios. What we cannot afford is high turnover, actively managed funds. Index funds would be appropriate; sector funds and funds that place big bets on a handful of stocks would not be allowed.

These types of investment choices greatly simplify the question of what are the best investment options for the DC portion of social security. Investment choices limited to indexed stocks and bonds with infrequent trading intervals (yearly, perhaps) would dramatically lower administrative costs and significantly increase the prospects for investment performance over the long run.

In summary, the incremental cost of modifying existing DC or IRA administrative systems to support a simple social security subaccount must be analyzed before committing to the replication of existing administrative systems. Alternative approaches to the coverage of those not covered under existing DC or IRA plans must be evaluated in order to determine whether the cost-effective expansion of social security DC coverage is possible. Cross-subsidization should be avoided. Finally, both administrative costs and investment performance are improved if we heed the investment wisdom of our time: diversify within and across markets, invest for the long term, and mind costs.

Shaun Mathews

I prepared some formal remarks for today, but I will not use all of them because much of the substance has already been discussed in earlier sessions. Aetna has been analyzing these issues over the last twelve months primarily from the public policy side with a major consideration being a "customer perspective."

I should probably tell you a little about Aetna because, as I listened to the group talk about other countries' plans today, I realize that Aetna provides retirement plans in all these countries. We are in Chile, Argentina, Mexico, Canada, New Zealand, and Australia (to name a few), and, in the United States, we provide retirement plans for all the markets and tax codes. We do 401(k) business and are a very large player in the small to mid-size end of the business. We provide retirement plans for primary and secondary education and a lot of university systems and do a lot of work with governments and municipalities as well as some individual investment products: annuities, IRAs, and mutual funds. We sell products in two structures: in a mutual fund structure, like all the folks around the table, but also in an annuity/insurance wrapper for both retirement accumulation and payout.

We do a lot of things; we have a lot of different customers and many different constituencies we have to think about. Our president, Tom McInerney, has been very involved in the National Savers' Summit. Working with a few of you, he has spent a lot of time on CSIS (the Center for Strategic and International Studies), and we can keep coming back to a fundamental question: Isn't this all about a national retirement policy? And we keep wanting to take the discussion back to the "three legs of the stool": employer system, private savings, and social security.

When we start to look at issues like private accounts, we always ask this question: What problem are we trying to solve? And it is very hard sometimes to have, in my opinion, a good debate around the private accounts without knowing what problem you are trying to solve. For example: Is this about program solvency? Or is this about transferring cost and risk to the private sector? Is it about expanded access? I have heard a few people today talk about piggybacking the employer system. Are we attempting to move retirement plans down to the smaller end of the market? Or is it some combination of all those things? An informed discussion ultimately involves making decisions around some of these questions.

When we talk to plan sponsors, as a few of you have suggested today, there are a lot of concerns, particularly in the 401(k) market. It is not

Shaun Mathews is senior vice president of Product and Brand Management at Aetna Financial Services, Inc.
This contribution is used with permission from Aetna Retirement Services, Inc.

just about social security or getting involved in one more administrative responsibility as an employer. It is also about ERISA concerns; it is about fiduciary liability. In my mind, given the capacity of payroll and record-keeping systems today, this liability question is as important to address as is the question of administration. How might this connect to the current regulatory system in the 401(k) market? I think that there is a lot of noise around administration because it is easier to understand. But, if you are the fiduciary or the trustee of a plan, you worry about this. That is what a lot of our employers say to us. At the same time, a lot of our plan participants tell us that they are concerned about the solvency of the social security system. From a participant perspective, how do you restore some of the confidence in the system?

And, last but not least, we do lots and lots of work with financial advisers who also are very interested in this issue. Whenever they talk to their customers about financial planning and savings for retirement, social security is an integral part of these discussions and plays an important role in establishing a plan.

So there are lots of different issues from a constituency perspective. We talked about the three model alternatives: working off the current tax system; individual directed accounts; and the employee-based system. In my mind, each of these has strengths and weaknesses that must be debated in the context of what problems we are trying to solve. I believe that it is important to look at the strengths and weaknesses in the context of how we service our customers today. At Aetna, we break down the services that we provide into six components: money collection, plan administration, participant record keeping, investment management, participant education, and participant services. We have already discussed today how much or how little of that you can choose to provide and how that affects the cost of providing service. Again, each of the options for implementing private accounts has different effects on these service components.

Without looking at every nuance, let us look at a couple of examples. We talked earlier today about the option of "piggybacking" private accounts onto existing defined-contribution plans. All the companies here today already provide a great deal of participant education in support of the retirement plans that they provide to sponsors. In this regard, if private accounts were enacted, assuming that transitional and fiduciary concerns have been addressed, there is a possibility of leveraging operating structures already in place for defined-contribution plans. This issue of education in the context of private accounts is very important as we find 70–80 percent of our individual customers want information to help in planning for retirement and making the appropriate risk-adjusted investment choices. One cannot overlook this need for help in establishing a system of private accounts because of the potential risk of suboptimizing the long-term social objectives.

Another consideration: recognizing all the complexity and cost of administering small accounts, I have been struck by the discussion of making "once-a-year" deposits into individual accounts. Being a proponent of dollar cost averaging, I would suggest that you look at market returns over the last thirty years and consider what happens when you are out of the market the best thirty days over the last thirty years—a huge difference in returns.

The next thing that I would mention is that I think that the idea of using lifestyle accounts for individual accounts is interesting. One of the options that the Clinton administration has just put forth is a "negative election" option for 401(k) plans. Under negative election, the employer can decide that all employees will participate in the 401(k) plan unless they expressly opt out. Some of our sponsors have actually used negative election in their plans and have used our asset-allocation funds for these deposits. Also note that asset-allocation funds cost more than indexing as it involves making certain sector-rebalancing decisions on a regular basis. But, as someone said earlier today, 80–90 percent of returns come from asset-allocation decisions.

In closing, I believe that the amount of choice that you give people in terms of controlling their private accounts and/or making investment decisions has a lot to do with who bears the risk at the back-end or payout phase of the retirement account. If the account is going to continue to be linked to a concept of providing a minimum level of income (e.g., an annuity), this "safety-net" concept must be linked with the choices provided in establishing and managing private accounts. Otherwise, there is a risk that future balances will not reach the levels anticipated and/or necessary to meet the minimum income needs in retirement.

References

Brinson, Gary L., Randolph Hood, and Gil Beebower. 1986. Determinants of portfolio performance. *Financial Analysts Journal* 42:39–44.
Markowitz, Harry. 1952. Portfolio selection. *Journal of Finance* 7:77–81.
Samuelson, Paul. 1965. Proof that properly anticipated prices fluctuate randomly. *Industrial Management Review* 6:41–49.
Sharpe, William F. 1991. The arithmetic of active management. *Financial Analysts Journal* 47:7–9.

Discussion Summary

Peter Diamond began by emphasizing a point made by Shaun Mathews of Aetna—that 40 percent of investors are self-directed and that 60 percent of investors want or need investment advice. He next offered a correction of a point in Joel Dickson's presentation. Dickson had performed a calculation of the expected costs to a financial institution of managing the individual account of a representative individual in which he assigned the individual an annual income of $27,000—identified as the median income of workers covered by social security. Diamond pointed out that the $27,000 was a *mean,* not a *median,* figure and that the relevant number for the purposes of Dickson's calculation was actually mean *covered* earnings, which is $23,000. *Dickson* remarked that this change would support his point even more strongly. *Diamond* then suggested that the administrative cost figures from Dickson's presentation ($50 per participant year and $40 for initial setup) could be reconciled with Diamond's own $150 per participant year figure. His argument proceeded in several steps:

First, he noted that Dickson's costs included only record keeping, communication, and advertising and did not include fund management. Diamond suggested that fund management would add $10 per participant year. *Dickson* and *Estelle James* argued that this may not be the case, observing that $10 extra in costs may not translate into $10 extra in fees.

Second, *Diamond* observed that charges for adjustments necessitated by divorce were not included in Dickson's calculations but that they should be. He argued that, in any mandatory national individual account system, divorce-adjustment rules would likely be built into the charges and would not be up to the discretion of the fund manager. *Dickson* countered that this would likely be a small effect. He argued that, under a national, standardized system of mandatory individual accounts, provisions for divorce would be simple to administer. He noted that divorce is complicated for 401(k)s largely owing to the heterogeneity of 401(k) accounts. Any domestic-relations order that has to be qualified for a 401(k) under ERISA has to be qualified under the specific plan to which it is to be applied. Dickson argued that this would not be an issue under a national, standardized plan.

Finally, *Diamond* ventured that Vanguard has lower costs than the average investment-management firm and that therefore we should view Dickson's cost estimates as below the likely average cost of administering individual accounts. He suggested that, if the ratio of industry average charges to Vanguard's charges is multiplied by the $60 per participant year figure, it would likely bring the figure up to roughly $100—still below his estimate of $150 but much closer than Dickson's original $50 figure. *Dickson* countered that there is a difference between costs and charges and that, although Vanguard's charges were lower than average, their costs are likely not significantly different from average. *Diamond* recognized the distinction and argued that his adjustment to Dickson's figures to bring them up to industry average was still valid for charges.

Martin Feldstein raised two questions regarding Robert Pozen's discussion of a two-tiered system of individual accounts with a default option and a more expensive plan for those who choose to opt out of the default option. Feldstein wondered (1) what would be the nature of the mechanism for collecting the extra fees from individuals in the "opt-out plan" and (2) whether people in the opt-out plan would enjoy a government guarantee/safety net on their returns (as individuals in a default plan are likely to enjoy under a politically feasible privatization proposal)? On the first point, *Pozen* noted that a centralized collection mechanism already exists. Discussion of the second point centered around what type of government guarantee/safety net, if any, should and/or would accompany the individual accounts. Pozen noted that his conception of the individual accounts did not include a government guarantee of returns at all, whether in the default option or in the opt-out plan. Further, he envisioned that individuals choosing the opt-out plan would receive a lower defined benefit (i.e., a pay-as-you-go benefit) than they would had they stayed in the default plan. *Feldstein* argued that, on the basis of the current discussions in Washington, it was possible that politically feasible reform options would have to include some form of government guarantee, perhaps a guarantee of a certain level of "all-in" social security benefits—that is, on the combined defined-benefit and defined-contribution amount. *Estelle James* argued that guaranteeing individuals who opt out would introduce a significant moral hazard problem. *Feldstein* countered that, nonetheless, a good deal of the politics involved in making individual accounts acceptable revolves around being able to guarantee that individuals will do at least as well under the reformed system as they would have under the status quo. *Pozen* opined that, if this is the political reality, the system will work only if the guarantee is applied *only* to the default package and if the default package is made very conservative. Individuals who opt out would forfeit their guarantee, and they must take that into account when deciding to opt out.

Robert Pozen argued that, in order to make the two-tiered approach (i.e., a default option and an opt-out plan, as specified above) most effective, it would be critical not to bundle the default accounts with 401(k)s. Keeping the low-cost, standardized default option separate from the opt-out plan, he suggested, would make a government guarantee (on the default tier only) more feasible. In addition, the availability of a low-cost default option would likely reduce the perceived need for regulation of fees and costs in the opt-out plan. That is, given that individuals have the option of staying in a very low-cost, guaranteed default plan, they should not be prohibited from going outside the plan and spending more money on a less restricted account. *Martin Feldstein* noted that the counter-argument to this position is that clever advertising will lure innocent people to give up their guarantee and move into an opt-out plan with high fees; the individuals will invest badly and end up with only the pay-as-you-go piece at retirement, which is only a fraction of what they otherwise would have received. Consequently, the argument goes, the opt-out plans ought to be subject to regulation regarding allowable types of investment. *Pozen* pointed out that this type of regulation is already embodied in the "404(c)" model, which mandates that the account manager provide at least three highly diversified investment options (a money market fund, a bond fund, and a stock fund), provide investor education, and meet various other requirements in order to be a "qualified provider." *Feldstein* wondered whether it might not be possible to extend the government guarantee to the opt-out plan if it were to operate under a 404(c)-type model. But *Pozen* argued that there would still be enough choice and risk to cause a serious moral hazard problem. *John Shoven* concurred, noting that, even under the 404(c) model, a government guarantee would essentially subsidize equity investment. *Kent Smetters* suggested that applying different tax rates to the different accounts could offset this effective subsidy. *Estelle James* and *Shoven* replied that this would be quite complicated.

Estelle James commented that the concern that a large percentage of the individual accounts would be extremely small during the initial period after reform may not be a serious problem, given that it would take several years for the necessary supporting systems (e.g., information systems) to be developed as well. She estimated that the development and implementation of information systems would take at least three to five years. During this time, accounts would be growing, and individuals could begin to think about and learn about different investment options. She also questioned Fred Grauer regarding the assumptions underlying his presentation and his claim that administrative costs for individual accounts could be as low as five basis points per account. Specifically, she questioned the compatibility of his assumptions that (1) many costs could be kept low by "piggybacking" (i.e., utilizing the infrastructure of existing defined-contribution and IRA systems for communications, record keeping, and disbursement of funds) and (2) custodial and managerial costs would be extremely low (based on the experience of the federal TSP). James suggested that the second assumption relies on maintaining a very small number of large pools while the first assumption implies many pools (associated with employers), some of which are small. *Grauer* agreed, noting that he envisioned approximately three types of funds (stock, bond, and cash) that every defined-contribution plan would offer. But *James* argued that there would be additional internal administration and communication costs that Grauer had not figured in, with respect to setting up and maintaining this new system.

James Poterba posed two questions to the panel regarding costs in the 401(k) market. First, he asked whether total costs to 401(k) participants had been rising recently, citing anecdotal and journalistic evidence that suggested such a trend. Poterba noted that the cost figures being discussed at the conference seemed lower than the figures he had heard from various sources. Second, he asked whether there was a substantial difference in the *average* cost to participants in 401(k)s versus the costs of the *marginal* people currently coming into the system as it expands to a universal structure. He conjectured that some of the small firms that have recently come into the 401(k) market resembled less sophisticated, lower-income investors who would be brought into the system if it were to expand under a system of social security individual accounts.

Regarding the second question, *Robert Pozen* noted that financial institutions are currently offering to smaller firms a highly standardized and simple 401(k) option that is the type of cost model that he would suggest using for less sophisticated investors under a system of individual accounts. Pozen also noted, however, that detailed data do not yet exist on the trading-behavior or customer-service needs of these smaller firms relative to the total 401(k) population. Regarding the first question, Pozen pointed out that a significant driver of increased cost in 401(k)s has been increased demand for services and greater flexibility on the part of employers. He suggested that this escalation in demand for greater services has been quite substantial and that, in particular, large employers exert significant bargaining pressure to increase their level of services. *Estelle James* wondered why the firms do not bargain for lower fees. *Pozen* replied that they do bargain for lower fees but that benefits executives are especially concerned with delivering expanded services to their constituents. *Martin Feldstein* pointed out the implicit principal-agent issue in this dynamic—the benefits manager gets credit for delivering greater service but perhaps is not penalized for a slight increase in fees. *Joel Dickson* noted that mutual fund managers are prohibited by law from offering different fees to different customers but agreed that administrative fees for 401(k) management can differ and that, once fees are driven down to virtually zero, negotiations necessarily turn to other issues, such as services. *Shaun Mathews* commented that, in the small business market (fewer than one hundred lives), in which Aetna does most of its retirement business, retirement-plan costs are extremely small relative to the costs of other benefits programs, such as health care plans. Therefore, a slightly higher fee is not likely to seem an onerous burden in return for a higher level of service. He noted that, on average, Aetna offers these clients plans with a choice of six to twelve funds, of which the average participant chooses three or four, and 80 percent of participants call for customer service once per year or less. According to Mathews, Aetna's cost for administering such a plan is seventy to one hundred basis points, including distribution costs and taking into account the fact that some of the funds are active management (i.e., not index) funds.

Robert Pozen suggested that perhaps we should be concerned about the volume of funds that would be funneled into index funds under a social security system with individual accounts. He noted that, currently, companies added to the Standard and Poor's 500 get an immediate premium as a result of the high volume of investment already being diverted into index funds. *Martin Feldstein* suggested that, eventually, active investors would arbitrage this premium away. *Pozen* cautioned that we do not know the level of investment in index funds at which this trend begins to be a problem. *Joel Dickson* countered that Vanguard currently estimated net cash flow to index funds to be negative as a result of defined-benefit plans taking money out, despite the large inflow from defined-contribution plans.

Contributors

F. Gregory Ahern
State Street Corporation
225 Franklin Street
Boston, MA 02110

David M. Cutler
Department of Economics
Harvard University
Cambridge, MA 02138

Peter Diamond
Department of Economics, E52-344
Massachusetts Institute of Technology
50 Memorial Drive
Cambridge, MA 02139

Joel M. Dickson
The Vanguard Group
P.O. Box 2600
Valley Forge, PA 19482

Martin Feldstein
National Bureau of Economic
    Research
1050 Massachusetts Avenue
Cambridge, MA 02138

Gary Ferrier
Department of Economics,
    BADM 418
University of Arkansas
Fayetteville, AR 72701

Fred T. Goldberg Jr., Esq.
Skadden, Arps, Slate, Meagher, and
    Flom, LLP
1440 New York Avenue, NW
Washington, DC 20005

Michael J. Graetz
Yale Law School
Box 208215
Yale University
New Haven, CT 06520

Gloria M. Grandolini
The World Bank
1818 H Street, NW
Washington, DC 20433

Frederick L. A. Grauer
52 Atherton Avenue
Atherton, CA 94027

Estelle James
The World Bank
1818 H Street, NW
Washington, DC 20433

Shaun Mathews
Aetna Financial Services
Mail Code TN-41
151 Farmington Avenue
Hartford, CT 06156

Olivia S. Mitchell
Department of Insurance & Risk
   Management
University of Pennsylvania
The Wharton School
3641 Locust Walk, 307 CPC
Philadelphia, PA 19104

James M. Poterba
Department of Economics, E52-350
Massachusetts Institute of Technology
50 Memorial Drive
Cambridge, MA 02142

Robert Pozen
Fidelity Management and Research
   Company
82 Devonshire Street, MS E35D
Boston, MA 02109

Sylvester J. Schieber
Watson Wyatt Worldwide
6707 Democracy Blvd., Suite 800
Bethesda, MD 20817

John B. Shoven
National Bureau of Economic
   Research
30 Alta Road
Stanford, CA 94305

James Smalhout
5835 Osceola Court
Bethesda, MD 20816

Peter Spiegler
24 Norris Street, #4
Cambridge, MA 02140

Dimitri Vittas
The World Bank
1818 H Street
Washington, DC 20433

Mark J. Warshawsky
TIAA-CREF Institute
730 Third Avenue, 24th Floor
New York, NY 10017

David A. Wise
National Bureau of Economic
   Research
1050 Massachusetts Avenue
Cambridge, MA 02138

Author Index

Subject Index

Administration: centralized for personal security accounts ("PSA Central"), 58–67; of proposed social security–related individual accounts, 166–67; of SSA-sponsored individual accounts, 13–20; structure for individual accounts, 55, 57–67; of Thrift Savings Plan, 183–84. *See also* Asset management

"Administration Costs," 50

Administrative costs: annuity products, 178; of centralized fund without individual accounts, 86; government-organized individual accounts, 5, 137–49, 162–68; hypothetical percentage of assets and dollars per account, 81–85; of investment choice, 216–18; model of components of, 80–81; predicted decline in, 168; privately organized individual accounts, 5, 137–39, 149–57, 162–68; of proposed individual accounts for retirement, 211–13; record keeping and communications (R&C), 78, 80–81, 120–25; in retail, centralized, and constrained-choice markets, 4–5, 127–30. *See also* Asset management; *and specific programs*

Adverse selection: conditions for reduction in annuity market, 6, 179–81, 201; in insurance company annuity purchases, 179–81; with mandatory annuitization, 202–3; in private insurance markets, 70–71; in voluntary purchase behavior, 174

AFPs (*administradoras de fondos de pensiones*), Chile: administrative costs and fees, 50, 79, 86–93; role in Chilean pension savings account system, 32–33, 42

Annuities: actuarially fair, 181; available to federal Thrift Savings Plan participants, 6, 182–91; British inflation-indexed, 70; choices of, 204–5; conversion of disability benefits to, 70–71; under defined-benefit plans, 173; 401(k) voluntary life annuity payout, 173–74; government-organized individual accounts, 5, 146–49; inflation-indexed in proposed U.S. system, 3; mortality rate probabilities, 178–81; offered on group basis, 147–48; offered through insurance companies, 176; options for SSA-sponsored or private market individual accounts, 26–29; private market or mandated, 148–49; single premium individual annuity, 189; Thrift Savings Plan inflation-indexed, 184; TIAA-CREF, 6, 191–99

Annuity payments: comparison of Thrift Savings Plan and insurance company annuity, 203; expected present discounted value, 6, 178–82, 198–99, 205; of insurance company annuities,